REA

D1536738

READING ARAB WOMEN'S
AUTOBIOGRAPHIES

Nawar Al-Hassan Golley

READING ARAB WOMEN'S AUTOBIOGRAPHIES

Shahrazad Tells Her Story

UNIVERSITY OF TEXAS PRESS, AUSTIN

Requests for permission to reproduce material from
this work should be sent to Permissions, University of
Texas Press, P.O. Box 7819, Austin, TX 78713-7819.

⊗ The paper used in this book meets the minimum
requirements of ANSI/NISO Z39.48-1992 (R1997) (Per-
manence of Paper).

Library of Congress Cataloging-in-Publication Data

Golley, Nawar Al-Hassan, 1961–
    Reading Arab women's autobiographies : Shahrazad
tells her story / Nawar Al-Hassan Golley. — 1st ed.
        p.   cm.
    Includes bibliographical references and index.
    ISBN 0-292-70544-1 (cl.: alk. paper) —
    ISBN 0-292-70545-X (pbk.: alk. paper)
        1. Women—Arab   countries—Biography.   2. Au-
tobiography—Women   authors.   3. Feminists—Arab
countries—Biography.   4. Feminists—Egypt—Biography.   I. Title.

CT3748   .G65   2003
920.72′089′927—dc21
                                2003010933

To my idols, Mother and Father,
to my darlings,
Jinan Petra and Cezanne-Jawad,
to my sisters and brothers,
to the memory of
my grandfather and aunt,
to the one I love the most,
I dedicate this book,
with love

ACKNOWLEDGMENTS

This book would have been impossible without the constant support of my family. I am especially grateful to them for looking after my children while I was working on the last stages of it. My friend Dr. Pauline Homsi Vinson has been very generous with her time in commenting and making valuable suggestions. I owe her a debt of gratitude. Thanks are also due to my professors, Dr. Elizabeth Boa and Dave Murray of the University of Nottingham, who supervised my Ph.D. dissertation, the original manuscript of this book. I thank the great poet Adonis for inspiring me and Dr. Nawal el-Saadawi for her generosity in responding to my questions. Special thanks to my friend Dr. Ahmad al-Issa, at the American University of Sharjah, for believing in me. I am grateful to Frances Fawkes for her suggestions and for proofreading the manuscript. I must also thank my friend Dr. Kate McKafferty for her encouragement. The librarians at both the University of Nottingham and the American University of Sharjah were very helpful. My thanks to them all. Last but not least, I thank the University of Texas Press, in particular Jim Burr, the humanities editor, for publishing this book.

The idea for this book began as an attempt to investigate the common belief among many, both in the academic world and outside it, that women write differently and about different things than men. This investigation led to examining such questions as: Why is it taken for granted that a woman writes in a different way, and about different things, than a man? When writing about the self, is it true that a woman writes about "private" and domestic matters while a man is more interested in "public" and political issues? What is "private" and what is "public" after all? Is it adequate to define a text in terms of the sex of the writer in the first place and then to generalize about what and how a woman or a man writes? Do women express themselves in the same way across cultures?

To this end, I am exploring the representation of female subjectivity and the construction of identity in a selection of autobiographical writings by Arab women. I believe that many recent theories have something to offer to the interpretation of texts. In addition, it is difficult and incomplete to rely on one theory alone due to the complexity of the question of identity and the even more complex situation of Arab identity. This is why I draw on a wide range of theories from Marxism, colonial discourse, anthropology, and psychoanalysis to deconstruction. I do not prioritize theories which emphasize only colonial issues, for example, in their analysis of representation and identity. Neither do I use crude Marxism, which reduces all questions to the class struggle, or crude feminism, which looks only at patriarchy. Factors addressed by all of these theories are essential to the constitution of identity, but so are many other factors such as national consciousness, religious belief, family, ways of upbringing, and educational background.

The aim of this book is twofold. First, it examines examples of Arab women's autobiographical writings in the light of various fields of modern western critical theory, in particular feminism and narrative theory. Second, it interrogates such theories against the chosen texts in order to see how adequate or appropriate these models are to analyze texts from other cultures. In this regard, my study may be described as applied theory, for it does not add to theory as such, but I hope that the interplay of theory and texts will be mutually illuminating.

I am using aspects of feminist narrative theories in order, first, to examine the ideological positions from which the writers/tellers of their stories write—to see whether writing these texts is part of a struggle against oppression; and, second, to explore other questions, such as: Are these women writing from within any kind of tradition, whether local or influenced by writing from other parts of the world? To what extent are they writing about themselves? Why do they feel it essential to write about themselves? What difference is there between writing explicit autobiography, semifictional narrative, and fiction?

Autobiographical writings of any form have the tendency to publicize the "private." I want to make it clear that I use these two terms, the "private" and the "public," cautiously; for they also have different meanings in different cultural contexts and for different classes within the same culture. In a bourgeois and western context, it has been a feminist concern to break the private/public dichotomy; for women traditionally have been restricted to the "private" world, while men have always enjoyed access to both spheres. The "private" and the "public" were (and still are) supporting for men, whereas for women they were (and perhaps still are to a large extent) two opposing spheres. Neither in practice nor in theory were women expected to violate the sacred world of men, the "public." Writing about the "private" used to be considered one of the weak aspects of women's writings. But now, and in feminist terms, representing the domestic can be a political act in itself; for the goal is to change the situation imposed upon women. In its critique of the family and of the division of social life into "private" and "public," feminism also puts the private in the public sphere. We shall see how Arab women may use the "harem" and the *hijab* (the veil), two concepts associated with the private world of women, to enter the public sphere without supposedly incurring the risks to be found therein.

One of the issues here involves cultural representations, especially the prevailing image in the west that women in Arab countries probably suffer more oppression than women anywhere else in the world. I, for one, should know that not all Syrian women are downtrodden. I have never suffered sexual discrimination within my own family; but I have seen bad forms of sexual discrimination in my society. Indeed, women's oppression takes different shapes from one society to another; it operates in a complex way in every society. Hence, the term "patriarchy" should not be used indiscriminately and without definition, for it is often taken to refer to a universal and transhistorical category of male dominance which leaves little hope for change. In this book I use the term from time to time to refer both to modes of thinking which tend to promote the subordination of women and to social practices which are oppressive. We should bear in mind, however, that women's oppression cannot be simply measured and compared between cultures or countries, as if all women in a certain culture or country lived under the same conditions regardless of class, education, religious affiliation, or other social factors.

Since the publication of Edward Said's *Orientalism* (1978), it has become very easy to label as "Orientalist" every attempt to represent an "other" even when this representation tries to challenge some existing stereotypes from within. My book may also be labeled in this way. Nonetheless, I tend to believe that, no matter what side of the "border" one is on, questions of representation are always problematic. To some, there is no escape from Orientalism when one speaks of others. However, as long as one offers a persistent critique of what one is up to, as I frequently do, representing the other should not become trapped in homogenization: constructing the "other" simply as an object of knowledge. Still, if anyone is capable of seeing the "real others," it is someone from within rather than from without, someone sympathetic rather than antagonistic, critical rather than romanticizing. I try to look at a culture of which I am part without reducing it to a homogeneous body. I try to show that what is seen as unified from the outside may be very different within.

Like many today, I am uneasy using terms such as "west" and "east," "western" and "nonwestern" or "eastern," "developed" and "undeveloped" or "Third World." Although I sometimes do use them for mere convenience, I do not think it is adequate to separate the world rigidly into these oppositional categories. Colonial discourses tend to divide world culture into a monolithic "western" culture which is contrasted with an equally monolithic "nonwestern" culture or cultures, such as the "Arab world," which is seen in homogeneous, collective terms. I use terms such as "west" and "Arab world" strategically and without capitalization because I do not consider them to be referring to homogeneous entities.

The question of authenticity is another issue that needs to be challenged here. Different cultures have been influencing each other for centuries. In our age of mass communication, it seems inadequate to talk about any culture as if it were completely pure and indigenous, except in a very few examples. In this book, I try to raise problems of selfhood when it comes to both the person who knows and the person who is known. In other words, I represent myself as a problematic self and not as an authentic Arab woman offering the "real" or correct alternative to the representation that has been offered before by western selves. I note the difficulty of defining personal and cultural identity in the matrix of Arab societies. I also show how problematic my own position has been in looking at the texts produced by women's identities as complex as my own.

This is not to say that lines cannot be drawn—there are still elements of cultural specificity wherever we go. For feminism to be universally useful, it has to take into account cultural differences and cross-racial, regional, social, and economic boundaries. I myself am cross-cultural; so is my book. As an Arab who has been educated in both Arab and western institutions, I am using western critical theory to look at texts by and about women from Arab countries from a double stance. Many of these women, like myself, are under the influence of at least two different cultures. Their texts should be seen in this light.

This multicultural context makes me challenge the usefulness of another problematic division: between the "literary" and the "nonliterary." The "literary" cannot be the main issue in relation to texts written or recited by illiterate or uneducated women and textualized, in differing ways and to different degrees, for English consumption. Hence I believe it is as important to raise questions of readership and audience as questions of authorship. Indeed, language is an instrument of power; but one is also overpowered by one's readers, wherever they come from. Throughout this book, questions about who the texts are written for, how they are received, and the nature of their conditions of publication, distribution, and translation have higher priority than aesthetic questions.[1] In addition, like Janet Wolff, I believe that literary or artistic creation does not differ from any other form of creative action; and for this reason, art and literature "have to be seen as historical, situated and produced, and not as descending as divine inspiration to people of innate genius."[2]

Indeed, notions of "good" writing undergo transformation in any culture. In my analysis, I draw on theories that assign historical significance to women's daily experience as a cultural activity. Hence, I am interested in the role that writing plays in women's social consciousness and in encouraging a feminist voice that will end the silencing of women.

To explore the textual constitution of identity through modes of autobiography where the parameters are "Arab" and "women," I have divided the book into three parts. Part One works out the politico-theoretical positions and the frame within which I am reading the texts in hand. In Chapter 1, I situate my study in relation to the arguments of colonial discourse, because such discourse is very useful for what it has to say about subjectivity and the reception of female autobiographical narratives. In Chapter 2, to demonstrate the interaction of class, race, and gender in the constitution of self-image, I consider the main arguments offered by feminism and Marxism in the light of the Arab situation. In Chapter 3, I look at Huda Shaarawi's *Harem Years: The Memoirs of an Egyptian Feminist,* to which the issues raised in Chapters 1 and 2 are relevant. Part Two considers questions of identity and subjectivity within a study of autobiography and cultural and sexual difference.

In Part Three, I examine the texts themselves in the light of the theories studied in Parts One and Two. First, I look at three texts based on interviews with women, mostly those who cannot write for themselves: *Khul-Khaal: Five Egyptian Women Tell Their Stories,* edited by Nayra Atiya; *Doing Daily Battle: Interviews with Moroccan Women,* edited by Fatima Mernissi; and *Both Right and Left Handed: Arab Women Talk about Their Lives,* edited by Bouthaina Shaaban. Second, I look at a text based on Fadwa Tuqan's autobiography, *Mountainous Journey, Difficult Journey.* Third, I analyze three texts by Nawal el-Saadawi: *Memoirs of a Woman Doctor, Memoirs from the Women's Prison,* and *My Travels around the World.*

Throughout I consider to what extent the texts I am studying still bear the traces of story-telling under oppression and how far this consciousness of oppression leads to expressions of selfhood similar to those which emerged in western feminism. Like Shahrazad, the heroine of *A Thousand and One Nights,* a metaphor of both oppression and liberation through the act of story-telling, these women and their narratives need to be seen in sociopolitical contexts.

My concern in this book is to find out how literary theory, colonial discourse, and feminism can help in looking at Arab women's expressions of the self. Although there has been an increasing interest in women's narratives of self generally in western literary and critical theory, there is an almost complete lack of any theorization of Arab women's autobiographical texts specifically. I hope that this book will make a contribution toward filling this gap.

READING ARAB WOMEN'S
AUTOBIOGRAPHIES

PART ONE POLITICAL THEORY

Colonial Discourse, Feminist Theory, and Arab Feminism

CHAPTER ONE

Why Colonial Discourse?

Orientalism, Edward W. Said's (1978) critique of western attitudes toward the east, has instigated a great deal of criticism and feedback, forming a major body of writings termed "colonial discourse," which has proved to be one of the most productive and fruitful recent areas of study.[1] Said was by no means the first to engage in colonial discourse analysis. Soon after the end of World War II, some third-world writers published their critiques of colonialism (actual occupation) and/or neo-colonialism (economic and political exploitation). Anouar Abdel-Malek (1963) saw the downfall of Orientalism in its own essentializing history.[2] Frantz Fanon constructed texts exposing the structure of colonialist ideology through which he aimed to liberate the consciousness of the colonized. However, *Orientalism* marked the beginning of serious attention to the discourse of colonialism on the part of western literary theorists and critics.[3]

This book is an attempt to apply and test the relevance of western theory by examining texts written by Arab women. This chapter briefly outlines the theoretical framework that has informed my study, discussing only those issues that are directly relevant.

Feminism and Colonial Discourse

Said's critique of colonialism is still valid, for although we might be living in a "post-colonial" age, the imperialist project, as Gayatri Chakravorty Spivak notes, is "displaced and dispersed into more modern forms."[4] Some, such as Masao Miyoshi, go so far as to argue that "colonialism is even more active now in the form of transnational corporatism."[5] However, I would like to make it clear from the outset that, like many today, I believe that feminism has a lot to offer to the critique of colonial discourse. The two practices should complement and not oppose or be reduced to each other. The critique of colonial discourse is less effective when it does not consider gender-related issues. Some colonial discourse analysts do not investigate the ways in which gender features in the discourse of the "Orient," although Said raises the question of the relationship between the feminization of the "Orient" and

"Orientalism."[6] He refers to such theoretical absence in his own discourse in the following passage:

> Why the Orient seems still to suggest not only fecundity but sexual promise (and threat), untiring sensuality, unlimited desire, deep generative energies, is something on which one could speculate: it is not the province of my analysis here, alas, despite its frequently noted appearance.[7]

After Said, many theorists (such as Spivak, Chandra Mohanty, and Homi Bhabha) have developed new arguments which combine race, ethnic, gender, and class analysis, among other issues.[8]

Colonial Feminism?

Western feminist theories have themselves been subject to critique,[9] and some forms have been accused of being colonial. The critique of colonialism becomes especially valid, according to Spivak, when the "emergent perspective of feminist criticism reproduces the axioms of imperialism."[10] Western feminists, in other words, have created a theory which establishes the female subject in Europe and North America as the feminist norm. Such a subject, which is highly individualistic, cannot be used as a model for feminists in nonwestern countries, according to Spivak. If female access to individualism marks the first historical moment of feminism, as argued by Elizabeth Fox-Genovese, then feminism has not even been born yet in most nonwestern countries.[11] For example, in the case of early Arab feminists at least, we shall see how the sense of individualism, when visible, does not control their sense of identity.

Feminist theory is colonial when it studies "Third World Woman" as a monolithic subject regardless of class, ethnic, or racial location, according to Chandra Mohanty:

> An analysis of "sexual difference" in the form of a cross-culturally singular, monolithic notion of patriarchy or male dominance leads to the construction of a . . . reductive and homogeneous notion of . . . "third-world difference" — that stable, ahistorical something that apparently oppresses most if not all the women in these countries.[12]

Mohanty argues that western feminism constructs "third-world women" as a category of analysis, as a "homogeneous 'powerless' group often located as implicit victims of particular cultural and socio-economic systems"; Arab women are frequently depicted as victims of male violence, of the Arab familial system, of the economic development process, and of the colonial process or as victims of the economic basis of the Islamic code.[13]

Marnia Lazreg argues that modern western academic feminism has indeed challenged the biases, in both theory and practice, in conventional social sciences. It rejects the traditional reduction of women to one dimension of their lives such as reproduction and housework and conceptualizes women's status in society as historically evolving. However, according to Lazreg, when it comes to studying women of nonwestern societies, western feminists have committed the very mistakes for which they have criticized others—in particular, generalizations. For example, Lazreg points out that even when the studies are restricted to a seemingly less generalized category, such as women in Algeria, the studies were "subsumed under the less-than-neutral label of 'Islamic women' or 'Arab women' or 'Middle Eastern women.'"[14] These same scholars would not dare to subsume "French or English women" under the all-encompassing label of "European women" or "Caucasian women."[15] In this sense, western feminism reflects the dynamics of global politics: racism.

Recently, Charles Hirschkind and Saba Mahmood have criticized the overwhelming attack of the 1999 Feminist Majority's campaign against the Taliban's "brutal treatment of Afghan women."[16] The Feminist Majority was able to rally support even from "skeptics who are normally leery of western feminists' paternalistic desire to 'save Third World women'" because the

> restrictions that the Taliban had imposed on women in Afghanistan seemed atrocious by any standards: They forbade women from all positions of employment, eliminated schools for girls and university education for women in cities, outlawed women from leaving their homes unless accompanied by a close male relative, and forced women to wear the *burqa* (a head to toe covering with a mesh opening to see through). Women were reportedly beaten and flogged for violating Taliban edicts.[17]

However, the authors show that such representation is "highly selective and limited" in that it only applies to a "tiny minority of urban dwellers" and fails to acknowledge the sense of security that the Taliban brought to Afghan women.[18] This representation can be seen as colonialist because it fails to "connect the predicament of women in Afghanistan with the massive military and economic support that the US provided, as part of its Cold War strategy, to the most extreme of Afghan religious militant groups."[19] Indeed, colonial discourse analysis is extremely relevant to the crude and unapologetic colonialist American project in Afghanistan today.

One of the aims of my study is to challenge some colonialist assumptions about Arab women. By reading texts by different women, I want to show the wide variety of conditions under which Arab women lead their lives. Before this reading, though, I would like to look at the question of culture itself.

Culture?

The following passage from Said may serve as a threshold:

> How does one represent other cultures? What is another culture? Is the notion of a distinct culture (or race, or religion, or civilization) a useful one, or does it always get involved either in self-congratulation (when one discusses one's own) or hostility and aggression (when one discusses the "other")? Do cultural, religious, and racial differences matter more than socio-economic categories, or politicohistorical ones? How do ideas acquire authority, "normality," and even the status of "natural" truth?[20]

Basically, formulating such questions is in itself as problematic as answering them. To define another culture, one presumes that there is a consensus on how to define a culture. This is clearly not the case. The term can mean different things in various societies, to different groups of people in the same society, and at different points in history, to mention some areas where culture oscillates from one definition to another. What is the west, and what is western culture? What is the Arab world, as part of the east, and what is Arabic culture?

As I have noted, the terms "east" and "west" are political and imply a racist point from which other places are either east or west. Geographically speaking, because the earth is round, it should not be possible to have west and east as places rather than directions. For this to occur, a center is needed. Where is the center? How did these terms become possible, and who was the first to use them?

It has never been more difficult to define the notion of a culture than at the present time.[21] Peoples, societies, and cultures have integrated, mixed, and interchanged more than in any previous period in history. The more they do so, the more difficult and problematic the notion of a separate or distinct culture becomes. In order to avoid generalizations, which always lead to complications and usually to wrong conclusions, my argument here is confined to the example of western and Arabic cultures.

"Arab World"?

Defining "Arabic culture" is complicated, for the word "Arab" is itself ambiguous: what it signifies has shifted over the centuries.[22] Racially and ethnically, it is difficult to speak of an "Arab world" in terms of any biological similarities. A debatable theory argues that the people who inhabit the so-called Arab world today all relate to the Arabs of the Arabian Peninsula. However, even these "Arabs" do not appear to share any biological similarities. Since the fourteenth century, the Hijaz alone has been "one of the most racially mixed communities on earth."[23] Every physical type can be represented in contemporary Arab communities. Today's Arab can be brown, black, pale, blond, tall, or short. Politically speaking, the term "Arab world" covers a complex area where one finds vast differences in politics and ideologies. Yet underlying similarities are evident in cultural and social formations of Arab societies, despite apparent differences in proclaimed political programs (from monarchical to republican "multiparty" to "revolutionary" single-party systems).

Today the use of the term "Arab world" is loose and metaphoric. Being an Arab now, as Fatima Mernissi stresses, "is a political, not a racial claim";[24] she is referring to the political aspirations of some Arab people to achieve unity. Nowadays the term can be manipulated for whatever end is desired. Some authors use the term "Arab" even when they are studying a specific area or one Arab country. For example, Nawal el-Saadawi subtitled her book on Egyptian women "Women in the Arab World."[25] However, the term "Arab" is used in western contexts collectively and in a homogenizing fashion. While most "Arabs" would rather refer to themselves as Syrians, Egyptians, Jordanians, Lebanese, Omanis, and so forth, they are all referred to as Arabs by westerners. In fact people in the west use the term in a demeaning manner—it becomes part of their colonial terminology. Ironically, the truth of the matter is that the immediate boundaries between any two Arab countries are the result of the western imperialist policy of "divide and rule."

Having said all that, two fundamental factors could make the term "Arab world" meaningful: religion and language.[26] First, any reference to the Arabs necessarily includes the 1,400-year-old world religion Islam, for the overwhelming majority are Muslims. There are minorities with different religions, however; even Muslim Arabs do not constitute one racial or ethnic group. Islam does not distinguish between nations or races. Hence over the years it has helped to formulate a more or less fictitious "Arab" character whose origin has been forgotten. Second, all Arabs speak Arabic. It is Islam again that helped spread the Arabic language, the language of the Holy Quran, throughout the countries that constitute the Arab world today. If we have to define the "Arabs," language is probably the best criterion, for there are many Muslims in the world who are not Arabs and do not speak Arabic.

Here again we have to exempt certain Arab communities that also speak Arabic but would define themselves according to some criteria other than language. The Arabic-speaking world includes the Arabian Peninsula, Iraq, Syria, Jordan, Egypt, the Sudan, Libya, Tunisia, Algeria, and Morocco, but even this division is not definitive. There are areas whose Arabism can be debatable, such as the southern region of the Sudan; Somalia, which is a borderline case; and Morocco, Tunisia, and Algeria, with their strong Berber populations.[27] Neither are the descendants of the pharaohs in Egypt too happy to be called Arabs.[28] In addition, it is only written Arabic that is shared in Arabic-speaking countries, as many different dialects are spoken. Nevertheless, Arabic language and literature have created some kind of cultural unity among Arab countries.

To sum up, the Arab world is already a multicultural place, before and without considering the influence of the west. When western influence is considered, the Arab world appears more culturally plural than ever. The relationship between the west and the Arab world goes back at least to the time of the Greek and Roman civilizations and even earlier. For both the Greeks and the Romans conquered the area to the north of the Arabian Peninsula, which already had established civilizations. Hellenistic culture (the basis of western civilization), through the medium of Christianity and other earlier cultures, influenced Islam, which later became the dominant culture in the area.[29] Neither should the effect of Islam on the rejuvenation of western culture be denied. According to Joel Carmichael:

> Just as primitive Islam found no difficulty in absorbing so much of Christian thought just because Muhammad in his basic ideas had already been formed by Christianity as well as by Judaism, so it was possible for Western Europe to digest so much Muslim thought just because it had roots in Christian soil. In the last analysis, both systems were rooted in the Middle East and in the intellectual universe of the Middle East.[30]

Carmichael argues that, from the seventh to the thirteenth century, western Europe suffered a profound cultural decline resulting from Teutonic incursions into the former Roman Empire. In the Middle East, however, Islam—because of its flexibility and adaptability—was able to build a whole new empire based on the existing cultural frameworks and social structures.

From the thirteenth and fourteenth centuries on, Islam, the heir of different civilizations, took the upper hand over western Europe.[31] In time, this complex and heterogeneous religion was absorbed into the religious life of Christendom. It also became intertwined with the roots of the Renaissance, "which freed the Western world from the ecclesiastical fetters of antiquity and ultimately eroded the traditional view of the world."[32] Gradually, the west developed new ways of life based on the separation of church and state and acquired a new superiority over the Islamic east. The Arab world, as part of the Islamic east, which eventually fell under the grip of modern western empires, is still undergoing a process of self-transformation as it modernizes, a change in which western influences play a complicated part.

This brief survey of the evolution of the Arabic and western cultures, based on the evolution of Christianity and Islam, is not meant to be blind to the individual differences of dogmas between the two religions. Neither is it intended to be homogenizing and generalizing or trapped in the classical east/west dichotomy. On the contrary, it is meant to show that any study of western and (Islamic) Arabic cultures which does not consider both together is bound to be incomplete, colonial, misleading, or irrelevant—or even all these together. As Carmichael concludes, "despite the exotic encrustations that Islam has taken on, from the Western point of view, the cultural roots are somehow closely intertwined and in many ways identical."[33]

Multiculturalism

As we have seen, the modern evolution of the Arab world cannot be considered in isolation from its relation to the evolution of the west. The west today is no more homogeneous than the Arab world, so it might be more appropriate to talk about multiculturalism than about single cultures. We surely live in a new kind of social space, as Roger Rouse argues:

> We live in a . . . world of crisscrossed economies, intersecting systems of meaning, and fragmented identities. Suddenly, the comforting modern imagery of nation-states and national languages, of coherent communities and consistent subjectivities, of dominant centres and distant margins no longer seems adequate.[34]

This multicultural world is economically, scientifically, technologically, intellectually, and politically by and large dominated by western values and standards. It is also no exaggeration to say that western domination has been confronted, resisted, and criticized from within the west itself.[35] I am not suggesting that the west is without fault or that colonial discourse analysis is redundant because western culture is self-critical anyway. Colonial discourse analysis is valid up to a point. The west has undoubtedly economically exploited and politically dominated the rest of the world, and world politics is a power game which governs identity politics. However, ancestral purity is an illusion. It is more useful to think of culture as "porous, dynamic and interactive, rather than the fixed property of particular ethnic groups."[36]

Ideally and generally, multiculturalism aspires to revise traditional and established definitions of cultural norms and identities and to replace them with new definitions which are more appropriate to the heterogeneous type of societies in which we live both within and across nations. It challenges the "west versus the rest" debate. According to multiculturalism, there is no use in looking for a single identity or political interest, like ethnicity, sexuality, or nationality, for social subjects are sites of a variety of differences. The multiculturalist looks for difference in unity or rather unity in difference; unity of identity comes from "a whole variety of heterogeneous, possibly antagonistic, maybe magnificently diverse, identities and circumstances."[37] As a social movement, multiculturalism challenges established norms linking "together identity struggles with a common rhetoric of difference and resistance."[38]

Problems with the Multiculturalist Project

What are the theoretical pitfalls in this approach? In its eagerness to bridge cultural differences, multiculturalism might lose the critical capacity for exploring cultural relations. It might become a mere clustering of race, gender, and class together without critical attention to the way in which these intricate issues interact. There is also the danger of overgeneralizing to the point of eliding the differences. This may lead to a tendency "in cultural studies to assume that cross-cultural comparisons are universalizing and imperialist in their covert cultural and institutional horizons."[39] It is true, then, that multiculturalism has sometimes to content itself with translation, in postulating cultural universality, and that translation might not always be possible, symmetric, or transitive.

Multiculturalism also denies autonomy to the arts. As long as the arts are not transformed "into a species of political propaganda and virtue mongering," as Roger Kimball fears,[40] there should nonetheless be no harm if questions of basic injustice come before aesthetic ones. However, the question of priority arises when different discourses are mingled. As my study draws on feminism, Marxism, and a critique of Orientalism, which discourse should be foregrounded? This issue has been worrying many in interdisciplinary fields.

According to John McBratney, such privileging is inevitable. He admits that, although he realizes that "issues about women are intimately connected with issues of colonialism,"[41] he will remain more interested in colonial issues first. To solve the problem of privileging which is always implied in prioritizing, he suggests that a

> constructive interdisciplinary practice would encourage related studies, particularly those which are fledgling and marginalized, to speak to each in their emphatically different accents without talking past each other or shouting each other down. Although strain will continue to exist among the converging languages of race, class, generation, and gender, we should not allow these tensions to weaken the incipient community . . . of scholars and critics interested in these studies. Ideally, we would both project our individual voices and act as a sounding-board for others.[42]

My reading of texts prioritizes the issues that are most urgent in each text, without trying to privilege them.

Hybridity and Cultural Specificity/Relational Sense of Identity

I want to defend fluid and changing identities which mix and mingle and are historically mobile. As we all occupy a world of global communications, trade, and migrations of peoples, it is politically disastrous and personally alienating to argue for a culturally closed identity or "authentic" self. I see myself as occupying a complex position and as such do not wish to divide myself into an "authentic" Arab self and an internally colonized "other," for I do not see myself as one. It is more constructive to break, without doing away with, the classic dichotomy of self/other or us/them—which is premised on corollary demarcations between high/low, public/private, and history/memory, as argued by Peter Stallybrass and Allon White[43]—and consider "I" and "other" or "us" and "them" mutually imbricated. Thus one of my points of departure in this book is Mohanty's call for the urgent need to rethink the latent tendency in contemporary cultural analysis to reinscribe an ideology of radical alterity.[44]

However, unless one understands the relationship between various modes of being different in the world, difference becomes essentialized. Antihumanist feminism, through essentializing difference, has "resulted in the erasure of 'other' women."[45] The individuality of "other," meaning nonwestern, women is erased when they are studied within the categories of religion, race, or color. A "Muslim woman," for example, becomes an abstraction as a "woman of color"; she is not a concrete individual, as Marnia Lazreg argues.[46] This is where the antihumanist feminist project fails, when it does not treat "other" women in the same way it does western women. For "other" women's

> lives like "ours" are structured by economic, political, and cultural factors . . . these women, like "us," are engaged in the process of adjusting, often shaping, at times resisting and even transforming their environment . . . they have their own individuality; they are for "themselves" instead of being "for us."[47]

Any different treatment of "other" women, any appropriation of their individuality to fit the generalizing categories of "our" analyses, is an assault on their integrity and on their identity.[48] Hence a certain form of humanism has to be affirmed, according to which all women and men of different cultures are entitled to express their humanity in their own varying cultural modes. Differences between people do not mean they are any less human than others. Difference should not be seen as mere division.

This is the crux of my study. Spivak's "strategic use of a positive essentialism" enables me to utilize the term "Arab women" (as in my title), which on the surface refers to an ethnic identity.[49] This is a strategy to reveal the internal differences and contradictions, while at the same time claiming some kind of shared identity. The notion of difference that I use is a positive one, a notion also used by Trinh T. Minh-ha. In her various works, Minh-ha criticizes western knowledge and politics and offers a multicultural revision of knowledge in her attempt to find alternative politics which can not only ideologize reality but transform it.[50] In one of her articles, "Not You/Like You: Post-Colonial Women and the Interlocking Questions of Identity and Difference," she explores the relationship between identity and difference in the constitution of subjectivity. Minh-ha argues that the ideology of dominance, by the dominant sex or the dominant culture, has long governed western notions of identity, a notion which "relies on the concept of the essential, authentic core that remains hidden to one's consciousness and that requires the elimination of all that is considered foreign or not true to the self, that is to say, non-I, other."[51] Here Minh-ha offers a new concept of identity, a new model which allows for the negotiation of similarities and differences. She does not believe that "a clear dividing line can be made between I and not-I, he and she; between depth and surface, or vertical and horizontal identity; between us here and them over there."[52] In other words, Minh-ha takes difference out of "the boundary of that which distinguishes one identity from another."[53]

According to this notion of difference, "self" and "other," "us" and "them," are not separate entities. Otherness exists within every "I," or vice versa, as Minh-ha argues. Hence, subjectivity consists not only in "talking about oneself, be this talking indulgent or critical,"[54] but also in talking about others. This is a definition most appropriate to my reading of texts. Thus, I do not wish to completely break the dichotomies of "self" and "other," "us" and "them," premised by colonial and sexist discourses, for I would like to keep some sense of the "self" as distinct, though not necessarily different from others. It is like Trinh T. Minh-ha's interlocking model of sameness and difference for the study of identity. Difference, for Minh-ha, "is not opposed to sameness, nor synonymous with separateness," for there are differences and similarities within this concept of difference. In this sense, difference can be used as a tool of "creativity to question multiple forms of repression and dominance" and not as a tool of "segregation, to exert power on the basis of racial and sexual essences."[55] According to this model, for example, instead of either defending or attacking the veil (a discussion that appears in the texts examined here), the act of veiling is interpreted in different ways depending on the context in which it is carried out.

Conclusion

I have tried in this chapter to acknowledge some of the recent arguments in the fields of colonial discourse and cultural studies that are relevant to any research which deals with texts that are translated and marketed in the west. Colonial discourse critique is essential as far as it is intertwined with feminist critique and as far as it considers other important issues such as class, family background, education, and religion, all of which govern the way people perceive and identify themselves. I have also argued that despite all political and other existing divisions, the world is a multicultural village, and people should be free to utilize whatever is useful to them wherever it comes from. As I noted earlier, I do not believe in the way the world is divided today: west versus east. In the same manner, I do not believe that the theories I am using are purely western.

I would like to see the texts that I am examining as part of the "writing back" discourse and, in this sense, as part of the alternative to "Orientalism." The stories in these texts about Arab women's identities are different from the ones already written by westerners about Arab women. I would also argue that the women are writing back in a double way: they are writing back to the west and, probably more importantly, are writing back to Arab "patriarchy."

They are fighting the image through which both the west and Arab male chauvinists have depicted them. Instead of arguing that colonialism has ended and that postcolonialism governs us today,[56] I would argue that we actually live in both eras, colonialism and postcolonialism together. The present U.S. intervention in many countries, especially in South America; the bombing of Libya, Iraq, and Afghanistan; and other examples of American atrocities are acts of sheer imperialism. There is some kind of analogy between "colonialism" and "patriarchy": they are both complex, and they both coexist with opposition. Huda Shaarawi's memoirs *Harem Years: The Memoirs of an Egyptian Feminist* (considered in detail as a case study for Chapters 1 and 2) is a good example to show how both colonial and postcolonial discourses, on the one hand, and "patriarchy" and women's rights issues, on the other hand, are at play in one text.[57]

CHAPTER TWO

Feminism, Nationalism, and Colonialism in the Arab World

Section I

Plurality, multiplicity, and multiculturalism characterize our world today. Neo-colonialism is part of this reality, although it functions in complex ways. It has become more difficult simply to divide the world today into separate entities: colonial and colonized. It is not easy to decide who is colonized or liberated, nor to define the process by which domination takes place. Still, colonial discourse remains highly relevant when it comes to issues of marketing, editing, and reception of texts. These issues are considered in relation to every text I study. For example, in the case of the anthologies of interviews with women, in which the questions are determined by the editor, one can legitimately ask whether this is a colonial situation.[1] However, colonial discourse can disempower the subject if one stays trapped in discourse in the Foucauldian sense.

Writing is a means of empowerment. In this regard, I argue here that all the texts that I am studying are "writing back" texts, each in its particular way. By this I mean that these texts offer different discourses about Arab women's lives than those already written about them by westerners and by Arab males. These texts might not be able to change the world individually. Collectively and together with other similar texts, however, they can contribute to changing the political climate. The Arab world has been undergoing constant, and sometimes radical, changes for the last 150 years. Change in the situation of Arab women and the way they perceive and identify themselves is reflected in the texts that I analyze in Part Three.[2]

In this chapter, I discuss the issues that have shaped the identities and lives of modern Arab women, notably feminism, nationalism, and colonialism. These three discourses have been argued to be interconnected in the Arab world, as in many other developing countries. As a case study for the theoretical issues raised, in Chapter 3 I examine Huda Shaarawi's *Harem Years: The Memoirs of an Egyptian Feminist.*

ORIENTALIST VIEWS AND COUNTER-DISCOURSE

As in the case of many developing countries, the pace and extent of change in the Arab world grew with the intervention of western imperialism. National consciousness was a reaction to western colonialism, which started early in the eighteenth century. Since then, national liberation movements not only have changed the political map of the Arab world but have changed the socioeconomic structure of the whole region. It goes without saying that this change has also included the situation of Arab women.[3] In the Arab world, feminist consciousness has developed hand in hand with national consciousness since the early nineteenth century.[4] Some have even gone further to argue that because feminist and national consciousness emerged at the same time and as a reaction to western imperialism, feminism is an illegal immigrant and an alien import to the Arab world and, as such, is not relevant to the people and their culture. This has been mainly argued by Arab traditionalists and political conservatives and those who oppose the emancipation of women,[5] who consider feminism irrelevant to Arab culture. As Kumari Jaywardena sums it up, they believe that feminism is

> a product of "decadent" Western capitalism . . . it is the ideology of women of the local bourgeoisie, and that it either alienates women from their culture, religion and family responsibilities on the one hand, or from the revolutionary struggle for national liberation and Socialism on the other.[6]

This kind of argumentation is only to be expected, but it is no ground for rejecting and opposing Arab feminism. I want to argue that the rise of the women's movement in the Arab world has indeed been affected by women's movements from other parts of the world, but that does not make it alien to Arab culture as such.

Neither has Arab feminism had a positive reception in the west. The textured image of exoticism which has been woven in the west over the centuries still dominates the way in which the Arab world is perceived. Orientalist discourses have influenced the way that Arab feminism, in particular, has been received and understood in the west. According to such discourses, the movement for women's liberation is, again, not indigenous to Arab countries. When such movements are recognized, they are described as mere imitations of similar movements in Europe and the United States.[7] It is even argued that western feminists have described Arab women's lives as being so different from theirs that they cannot possibly develop any kind of feminism.

Even when Arab women speak for themselves, Elly Bulkin argues, they are accused of being "pawns of Arab men."[8]

It is true that for most westerners, even today, the phrase "Arab woman"

conjures up heavily veiled, secluded women, whose lives consist of little more than their homes, their children, and the other females in the "harem" or immediate kinship circle.[9]

One of the aims of this book is to refute the argument against the relevance of feminism to Arab culture. Without giving any rosy pictures, I argue that feminism is not alien to Arab culture. I want to challenge both the colonialist representation and what I call the counter-representation of Arab women and to show that basically Arab women's need for positive change in their lives is neither more nor less than the need of women for positive change anywhere else in the world. When one considers the vast differences in Arab women's lives from the Atlantic to Iraq and throughout the different social, economic, educational, religious, sexual, and other determining factors, the aura of exoticism that surrounds the term "Arab women" may dissolve, giving place to a more realistic and practical way not just of representing women but also of changing their lives. Some religious practices can be determining factors in women's oppression; but they are not the only ones. In this chapter, I do not engage in debates on women under Islam as such.[10] I do, however, discuss certain important issues which have always been the subject of attacks on and misunderstandings of both Islam and the position of Arab women.

ISLAMIC REACTIONS AND RELIGIOUS CONTROVERSIES

Islam has always been the pot within which the subject of Arab women has been cooked. The west has a generalized view that Arab women are Muslims and that Islam, viewed as a monolithic religion, oppresses women. The reaction to this view has also centered on Islam, this time defending its treatment of women.

As a result, the position of women in the Islamic Arab world has always been misconstrued in the west. Each side of the debate has selected and stressed certain facts and incidents in the history of Islam but ignored other facts and incidents that do not help its argument. The counter-discourse, which produces rosy images of women under Islam, is as problematic as the western colonialist discourse.

The puzzling double image of woman as being both "witch" or prostitute and angel or virgin found in other religions, as well as in Islam, cannot be explained or resolved purely within any religious context, certainly not within Islam. For religion cannot and should not be seen independently from the socioeconomic and political context within which it unfolds. Like any other human activity and product, it is subject to change, at least in its function. As Lazreg argues, in order to understand how religion affects women's lives, one must "address the ways in which religious symbols are manipulated by both men and women in everyday life as well as in institutional settings."[11] Hence gender relations can only be analyzed in terms of religion when the latter is conceptualized within the relevant socioeconomic and political background.

The debates about the veil and the "harem" are two issues which illuminate many of the problems of interpretation and the ideological battle line. It is ironic that whereas early-twentieth-century feminists, such as Shaarawi, fought to discard the veil, we hear today of heated debates between Muslim communities and the governments in western countries on whether Muslim schoolgirls should be allowed to wear the veil! A term such as "the veil," which might sound purely religious, can be a powerful political term to denote resistance on behalf of the women who choose to wear it, as we shall see.

THE VEIL AND THE "HAREM": SECLUSION AND POWER?

The veil and the "harem" have always been associated with Arab women and especially with their oppression. It is a fact that various forms of the veil are still being worn by many Muslim women around the world and that there are some Arab or Muslim women who still live in some form of seclusion or "harems." However, first, not all Muslim women wear a veil and are segregated from men; and second, it was not Islam which first introduced the idea of either the veil or the harem.

WESTERN REPRESENTATIONS

The word "harem" (in Arabic *hareem*) can be used to mean simply women. *Hareem* is derived from the word *haraam*, meaning "sacred," "forbidden," "inviolable," and "holy."[12] Hence the section of the house where women and children dwell is figuratively referred to as the "harem." Even today, however, for a westerner the mere utterance of the word conjures up a whole set of exotic and erotic images because of a long history of representing the harem through the eyes of the colonizer. In colonialist fiction, ethnographic writings, and Orientalist paintings, the harem has always been used as a means of

[e]voking every possible venue of erotic fantasy. Abduction, exhibition-ism, voyeurism (between eunuch and captives), bestiality (as when mon-keys intervene in lieu of the sultan), sapphism, onanism, masochism (fe-male bondage), and visions of the "dark side" of femininity itself, constituted a mosaic of "aberrant" sexual preferences to be grouped un-der the rubric "harem."[13]

The harem has also often been described as a closed space within which females are imprisoned. In Pierre Loti's *Les trois dames de la Kasbah,* for example,

the "harem" is ensconced within walls and labyrinthine streets of the casbah, a colonnade protects the courtyard, the courtyard frames a house itself encased in a complex network of iron bars and grills. The only apertures consist of tiny peepholes, "little openings disguised in the thickness of the walls." The women imprisoned within are "plunged in darkness," their eyes "drowned" and their minds fogged over in a cloud of kif.[14]

Because the image of the harem as known to the west has been greatly af-fected by ethnographic writing about the Middle East, most of which has been done by, it is only fair to say that their depiction of the harem can-not be authentic—as alien men, they could not have had any access to any true harem or female quarter.[15] Nevertheless, it is only fair to mention that some western women travelers, especially those who had firsthand experience through visiting some harems, tried to give a more realistic representation of them, hence casting doubt on the assumption that they oppress women. For example, Lady Mary Wortley Montagu was somewhat sympathetic in her de-piction of the harems she visited when she accompanied her husband to Tur-key in 1716. She admired the freedom and the friendships that the women enjoyed within the female quarter itself.[16] In 1944 the Frenchwoman Lucie Delarue-Mardus saw no difference between the females' quarters in Arabic households and European ones:

To begin with, let us make ourselves clear once and for all on the subject of the harem, which since eternity has hypnotized the West. The harem is neither the decor of an operetta nor the mysterious realm of all plea-sures. Harim, in Arabic, means that which is sacred. Let us translate: the feminine elements of the house . . . Thus, without knowing it, the Rou-mis [Europeans] all have harems.[17]

THE VEIL: PRE-ISLAMIC

There are three theories about the origin of the veil: that it was introduced together with the harem by the Ottomans at some stage during the Ottoman Empire; that it came from Persia; or that it is as old as the first century A.D. Several critics have argued, however, that the practices of veiling and sex segregation were already in practice before Islam. According to Fatima Mernissi, for example, the veil was already known to earlier civilizations and was only introduced to Muslim women in the fifth year of Islam. Until then, the Prophet, as Mernissi presents him, was a gentleman who never refused visitors: he lived in a household which was never closed to the public. Eventually, however, he got fed up with boorish people who paid him long visits without notice and who also addressed his wives. Hence the concept of segregation became necessary. Mernissi offers a specialized and detailed study of how the veil and seclusion of women developed in Islam. According to her, the veil—with its connotation of seclusion—is

> a key concept in Muslim civilisation, just as sin is in a Christian context, or credit is in American capitalist society. Reducing or assimilating this concept to a scrap of cloth that men have imposed on women to veil them when they go into the street is truly to impoverish this term, not to say to drain it of its meaning, especially when one knows that the hijab, according to the Koranic verse and al-Tabari's explanation, "descended" from Heaven to separate the space between two men.[18]

The veil, in Arabic *hijab,* which linguistically means anything that hides, separates, and makes something forbidden, was introduced to Islam but went through different stages of meanings, which Mernissi explains. The first refers to a curtain that separates the Prophet from other men, and the last means the veil that covers women's bodies and faces.[19] The first women to be advised to wear a veil were the women in the family of the Prophet, in order to distinguish them from other women; for in those days women, especially slaves, were sexually harassed and abused by men in the streets. Eventually, most Muslim women, whatever their class, were required to wear the veil.

Mervat Hatem argues that sexual segregation was practiced in pre-Islamic Egypt and that it was difficult to maintain or enforce in older and more mobile tribal settings. Due to the nomadic nature of their lives, women needed freedom of movement and interaction with men. However, in "ancient Judaic, Greek, and Byzantine societies, segregation was the common mode of organizing sexuality in societies undergoing the process of sedentarization."[20]

The main source for Islamic teachings and practices is the Holy Quran, a highly literary text with a sophisticated language which is open to various interpretations; two opposing views can be supported by the same verse.[21] Thus, there are also disputes as to whether the veil and the segregation of women are essential requirements of the Islamic faith itself. According to Nawal el-Saadawi, there is no reference in the Holy Quran itself to the imposition of the veil. There is only the precept that women should dress modestly and should not wear makeup and ornaments, "which are a source of seduction and temptation to men."[22]

In Arab and Islamic countries which are not governed by strictly religious governments today, only practicing Muslim women wear the veil, which can take different shapes. Some women wear the veil strictly—a long, dark buttoned dress, a scarf and light cover for the face, and gloves. Others wear western clothes (like a knee-high or just below the knee skirt or dress with stockings, which could be very sheer, or even tight trousers) but cover their hair or part of it with a scarf. Some might wear makeup. There are also other variations in the way in which women wear the veil. In strict Islamic countries such as Iran, Saudi Arabia, and others, the veil is sanctioned, and women who do not wear it are penalized. In countries such as Algeria and Egypt where recent Muslim fundamentalism prevails, mobilized women wear the veil as a sign of commitment. During the Iranian Revolution of 1977–1979, for instance, Iranian women wore the veil as a sign of defiance against the shah's regime and as a sign of devotion to an Islamic identity.[23] Thus, both wearing the veil and discarding it in different situations should be seen as symbolizing political struggle and women's political agency.

A HISTORICAL VIEW: THE POWER OF SECLUSION

The veil and the harem are better understood within social and economic contexts. Even before Islam, in Assyrian society, for example, the veil served to mark the upper classes and also to differentiate between women who were considered "respectable" and those who were perceived as publicly available, according to Gerda Lerner.[24] In medieval Islam and until the first decades of the twentieth century, the veil continued to be worn mainly by urban upper- and middle-class women. Rural and lower-class women wore the veil, but not in any strict fashion. In the same way, the seclusion and segregation of women differed dramatically according to their respective class positions. Keeping a harem or a female quarter requires architectural space and financial means; hence the size of the harem expressed a man's class and power.[25]

As the veil took different shapes throughout history, the harem also changed in all eras and areas. Even when women lived in actual harems or female quarters, however, they were never completely secluded from public life. Most modern studies of women in the Middle East show that traditional western anthropological and ethnographic writings have tended to apply their western social and economic standards to Middle Eastern societies. For example, the public/private dichotomy, inherent in western socioeconomic philosophy, has always been the basis for ethnographic studies. Most ethnographers have implied that the Middle Eastern human universe is divided into two segregated social worlds: the private world of women and their domestic duties and the public world of men and their political activities.[26] Such an observation is only true at first sight—the reality is not as simple.

Cynthia Nelson writes that among nomads there is no equivalent Arabic term for the concept of a "public" arena and that the tent and the camp are not synonyms for public and private.[27] Although I do not want to take this discussion any further, I wish to argue—contrary to what has been believed—that Arab women's sphere, even when it takes the shape of the harem, has an influence on the public sphere of politics. Nelson, for example, finds evidence for the important role that Middle Eastern women play in public life in the very ethnographic data which suggest that such societies are characterized by segregation of the sexes. Looking at such data from a woman's point of view, and reevaluating the notion of power from the standpoint of "reciprocity of influence," she contends that

> women do approach public affairs but they do so from private positions. In public, women are separated from men, and men mix widely in the public circle of the market. The women, on the other hand, mix in a large number of smaller groups, more exclusive than the society of men and consisting largely of closer and more distant kin, affines, and other women who are friends of the women of the family . . . [Middle Eastern] families are one of the basic groupings in its economic and political, as well as its moral aspects . . . Women, in general, are a necessary part of the network of communication that provides information for their menfolk, and at the head of the social hierarchy are some women who form a focus for the smaller groupings of women and a bridge between their concerns and the public concerns of men.[28]

Rosemary Sayigh also argues that both Orientalists and western feminists have used the basic tool of social scientists: dividing the social sphere into "public" and "private." As she points out, however, field studies since the

1970s, carried out mainly by Arab women, show the multiplicity of roles that women actually play in Arab societies.[29] Such studies show that Arab women's conventional roles, previously supposed to be merely domestic and hence private, contain a much stronger element of the social, economic, and political. In Arab countries—where the family, the basic social unit, performs obvious political, economic, and cultural functions—there is no sense in drawing a hard line between the "public" and the "private" sphere. Women affect public life through the family structure, but this differs according to their relative class.

However, even within their harems, women have extradomestic roles to play.[30] On a basic level, women (through marriage, for example) play an important role in creating societal bonds. In Arab societies, it is women who are readier to help other families in trouble and who often store community histories, genealogies, and popular culture. In pastoral communities, marriage alliances can "provide vital access to grazing, water, loans, wasta: resources crucial to group survival in difficult times."[31] The roles that Arab women play might seem to have only social dimensions, but they can also greatly affect male politics. Interfamily women's quarrels, for example, may "diminish intrafamily male solidarity, 'flatten' lineages, and encourage factionalism. They may precipitate tensions between males, or raise issues."[32]

Arab women's involvement in politics at large, especially in modern times, is not confined to the preceding examples. The various political roles that Arab women have played (and are playing) in national liberation struggles should at least eliminate any claim that they are completely secluded, passive, and domesticated beings, as the "harem" is conceptualized in western Orientalist terms. There are many studies of Arab women's capacity for political struggle, including Fanon's pioneer book on Algeria, *Studies in a Dying Colonialism*. Women have been integral to the nationalist struggles in all Arab countries, including Syria, Egypt, the Sudan, Yemen, and Palestine.[33]

MODERN APPROACHES TO
DISCARDING OR WEARING THE VEIL

As noted earlier, the wearing of the veil can signal a political position. Here I wish to consider the significance, in different historical contexts, of discarding or wearing the veil. Since the early days of Islam, Arab women have expressed their opposition to issues that they felt were oppressive to them, such as veiling. It is not my intention to list all the women known for discarding the veil; they are just too numerous. However, one example serves to prove that even as early as the first years of Islam women had the courage to oppose the system. One of the most famous early Muslim women, known for their acts of rebellion against what they thought was diversion from the real teachings of the Prophet, was the Prophet's own great-granddaughter, Sukayna (born in A.D. 671). Sukayna, who was renowned for her beauty and wit and her interest in politics and poetry, discarded the veil, parading her beauty to stress women's position in Arab tradition. She is said to have had married five or six times and to have never pledged *ta'a* (obedience, a key principle of Islamic marriage) to any of her husbands.[34] Early in the twentieth century, Huda Shaarawi (1879–1947), whose memoirs are examined in the next chapter, is another example of many more recent women who have discarded the veil. I want to return to the contemporary argument about discarding the veil at the end of this discussion.

In the light of modern western feminist theories, especially radical ones, some Arab feminists have revised their critical position on the harem and the veil. Instead of looking at the harem as an enclosed space within which women are locked up and domesticated, Leila Ahmed sees it as a source of women's strength and mobilization. She argues that if, according to Doris Lessing, "men and women are so profoundly different, so alien to each other, so fundamentally incompatible that they probably originated on different planets and would probably have been happier had things stayed that way,"[35] then Saudi Arabian society is probably the only ideal place on earth to verify Lessing's notion about men's and women's natures. According to Ahmed, segregation in Saudi Arabian society is based on the notion (like Lessing's) of alienness and incompatibility of the sexes and has nothing to do with their alleged adherence to Islam or Allah. This condition of total opposition, materialized in the visual symbolism of black dress for women and white for men, necessitates the need for separate worlds.

However, contrary to the general belief that it was men who imposed segregation upon women, it was women who desired it, according to Ahmed. One of the variants of the term "harem" is *haraam,* meaning "forbidden," which suggests to Ahmed that "it was women who were doing the forbidding, *excluding* men from their society, and that it was therefore women who developed the model of strict segregation in the first place."[36] Within the harem, women are free to engage in certain activities; they "share living time and living space, exchange experience and information, and critically analyze — often through jokes, stories, or plays — the world of men."[37] In segregated societies, activities are performed by men and for men; in contrast, within the harem, activities are performed by women and for women. Still popular in the Arab countries are "the woman saint, the woman soothsayer, the witch, the seances held for women by women to exorcise or empower (practices for which women were destroyed in the West)."[38] On this basis, Ahmed argues that women in segregated societies are not necessarily more oppressed than women in sexually integrated societies.

The veil also has recently been considered a means of empowerment, rather than oppression, especially when worn as a personal choice. In her article "Post-Colonial Feminism and the Veil: Thinking the Difference," Lama Abu Odeh argues, as a feminist who personally rejects the veil, that it must be recognized that the veil has an empowering effect on Arab women.[39] Looking at urban lower- and middle-class professional women such as schoolteachers, civil servants, secretaries, nurses, university students, and bank employees in their twenties and early thirties who were unveiled in the 1970s, Abu Odeh investigates why these women adopted the veil in the 1980s.

Arab women's relationship to their bodies during the 1970s reflects the complexity of the sociopolitical situation of Arab societies at that time. Women's bodies were the battlefield for the "post-colonial" cultural struggle between new "capitalist" forces and old "traditionalist" ones, according to Abu Odeh. She argues that, because "capitalism" has not really won the day in Arab societies, it has to cohabit with precapitalist social formations. Women's bodies, which have been "traditionally" constructed as "trustees of family (sexual) honour," have also had to reflect new "capitalist" constructions of the female body as sexualized and objectified. The reflection of such double constructions cohabiting the female body has been highly conflictual. The "capitalist" forces pressure women to be sexual and seductive, while "traditionalist" forces compel them to be asexual, conservative, and prudish. "Capitalist" constructions are supported by the "attraction of the market (consumption of Western commodities)," and "traditionalist" ones are supported by "threat of violence (the woman is severely sanctioned, frequently by death, if she risks the family sexual honour)."[40] As a reaction to such conflicts, many of these women adopted the veil.

The veil is worn by some professional women as a means of protection in the streets and in the workplace, according to Abu Odeh. She argues that women in Arab societies are frequently exposed to sexual and verbal harassment. A veiled woman is less liable to be harassed and, even if she is, has stronger grounds than her unveiled sister to fight back. While an unveiled woman might swear or walk away quietly, a veiled woman's sense of self-righteousness gives her ground for answering someone harassing her: "[H]ave you no fear of Allah treating his believers in such a shameless fashion?"[41] Unveiled women are supposed to feel powerless in the face of harassment, according to Abu Odeh. Playing the devil's advocate, she tries to argue for the disempowering effects of the veil; but she finds that, unless she engages in intellectual elitism by accusing veiled women of false consciousness and not knowing their own good, she can establish no such instances.[42] When the veil is adopted as a defensive means on the streets and on the way to work, this is not necessarily considered an antifeminist position. However, the problem arises when the veil carries the logic of spatial and functional segregation of the sexes to the workplace itself. In this sense, wearing the veil, though it might be empowering, is ambivalent and also self-deconstructing. The fundamental ideology of the veil is to keep women at home. Its effectiveness as a tool to protect women on the streets and at work should thus be questioned.

VEILED OR UNVEILED: THAT IS NOT THE ISSUE

The conflict experienced by Arab women today, as argued by Abu Odeh, reflects the predicament of modern Arab feminism. The call for women's freedom, for example, is instantly challenged by men who might very well believe in equality between the sexes, arguing that, in the light of the oppressive regimes that prevail in most Arab countries, women cannot be free because men are not free either. Equality between the sexes can also be appropriated to mean that men should be women's superiors because they are more qualified. In other words, feminist discourse is weakened in a society where sexual freedom is not a priority and where the number of professional women has yet to match the number of professional men in all fields. Besides, for an Arab, feminism is often associated with western societies, which in turn are often presented as socially sick and suffering from "rape, pornography and family disintegration." Instead of looking at feminism as a political response to such social phenomena, it is frequently seen as the cause.[43] Taking into consideration the rising hostility against the west and many western values in modern Muslim societies, an Arab feminist can be accused of preaching rape, pornography, and family disintegration. In such circumstances, Arab feminists could do better if they sought the support of and solidarity with other women who might—due to the fact that they are veiled—see them initially as nonfeminists. This of course opens a whole debate on the coherence of fem-

inism, which I do not wish to engage in here. I would like to go back in time
to look at the first decades during which Arab feminism grew.

Section II

EARLY ARAB FEMINISM: A HISTORICAL SURVEY

> Feminism is not autonomous, but bound to the signifying network of
> the national context which produces it.[44]

It has been argued that the earliest calls for the emancipation of Arab women
were voiced at the turn of the nineteenth century, which marks the beginning
of the Arab renaissance. Opponents of women's emancipation contend that
feminism is alien to Arab culture and that it was imported during the western intervention in the Middle East by the French and later the British.[45] As
a cultural phenomenon, feminism is viewed as the result of westernization:
the adoption and adaptation of western ideals, values, and ways of life in Arabic culture. Such an approach ignores the extent to which ideological shifts
are reflective of indigenous social change. However, if considered in the context of the class conflict and social changes at the time, Arab feminism can be
seen as indigenous.

Arab feminism was not imported from the west. It was an inevitable result
of the changes that took place in the area, which encompassed all aspects of
life. Arab feminism was born out of the struggle between the dying traditional, religious, feudal Ottoman way of life and the rising modern, secular,
capitalist European ways of life. The story of Arab feminism can be outlined
in the following fashion. First, the call for women's rights was part of the general movement to reform Islamic practices and hence the whole social order
of Islamic societies. Second, the first calls for women's emancipation were
voiced by educated men and women of the national bourgeoisie, who were
later joined by men and women of the petit-bourgeoisie, struggling for liberation and democratic rights. Third, Arab feminism was born within and
continues to suffer from the predicament caused by the double struggle: internally against the old religious, social, and economic order and externally
against European colonization. While challenging European domination,
the reformists still admired modern European ideals. In other words, asserting a new national identity meant necessarily drawing on the very model they
were resisting: the Europeans.

What are the general conditions that shaped the events which led to the rise of feminism at the turn of the nineteenth century? The situation was very complex, but it can be simplified for my purpose as follows. Except for parts of Arabia, the Sudan, and Morocco, all the Arabic-speaking countries were under Ottoman rule from the beginning of the sixteenth to the end of the eighteenth century. Although the Ottoman Empire was a multireligious state, recognizing both Christians and Jews, it is considered the last great expression of the universality of the world of Islam. The administrative and military elites were largely drawn from converts to Islam coming from the Balkans and the Caucasus (Mamluks).

By the latter part of the eighteenth century, and with pressure from the west and north, the Ottomans lost most of their European territories. Gradually the central government in Istanbul loosened its grip over its territories, and the local Arab governments increased their autonomy, only to fall under European control later.[46] The further the province was from Istanbul, the more independent it grew.[47] That explains why, for example, the influence of the Ottomans was stronger in Syria than in Egypt. This is also relevant to the fact that Egypt was until the mid-twentieth century the center of modern Arabic cultural life. For this reason, and also because most of the writers I am dealing with come from Egypt, my argument here is limited to Egypt's socioeconomic and cultural-political life during the period that preceded the rise of feminism; but this is not to suggest that Arab feminism only started in Egypt at that time. In fact, many of Egypt's notable cultural figures of the period came from other countries, such as Syria, Lebanon, Palestine, and Iraq.

One of the most productive ways to examine the rise of new issues concerning women is to examine the class structure of Egypt at the time. By the beginning of the nineteenth century, Egypt, under Muhammad Ali (1805–1848), had become a semiautonomous state, the first of the Arab countries to be rescued from the Ottoman grip.[48] The Egyptian revenues from cotton and grain were readily exported to Europe through the Suez Canal. This commercial demand was to have its impact in accumulating capital in the hands of the rising urban merchant class in Egypt. European countries were already dividing the world among themselves; in 1882 the British claimed Egypt as theirs (the French having left Egypt in 1801 after the failure of Napoleon Bonaparte's expedition in 1798).

Muhammad Ali's new system encouraged the modernization of the country's educational, cultural, and administrative structures and included the introduction of private property. Thus, the land was no longer the state's. Making the most of their presence in a growing city, the new class of landholders became heavily involved in commerce and banking, forming the new "agrarian capitalist" classes. Their relationship with the colonial British was apparently very close; the British were keen to maintain a good relationship with them, allowing them to pay lower taxes than the rest of the people. In their social lifestyles, this class gradually replaced Turko-Circassian manners and customs with European ones, thus encouraging closer integration with the growing number of European settlers. Another rising class was the new petit-bourgeoisie, rural notables who had lost their land and moved to the city to join the new service sector. This class soon split into two categories. On the one hand, there were the old shopkeepers, artisans, bazaar merchants, and ulamas (religious leaders), who had a defiant attitude toward European culture, which they regarded as a threat to their own. On the other hand, a new class of westernized professionals and clerks arose, who saw in European systems a better outlook for Egyptian society, which they thought had been ruined by Ottoman rule. Unlike the upper classes, however, who were more likely to have benefited from the effect of western industrial capitalism on Egypt, the petty bourgeois of both divisions were more nationalistic, and it was among them that the heroes of the twentieth-century Egyptian revolution were to be born.

Such a transformation in Egypt's social structure had its impact upon women. Under the new capitalist system, with the growing size of the working urban population (which resulted in greater competition), many women lost their jobs. Women were forced to go back to the home, the only sphere where they enjoyed some kind of authority and a restricted form of management. Keeping women at home was also a practical expression of stressing Islamic or Arabic or even Egyptian identity against the threat of the expanding influence of European culture. The upper classes could afford private education for their women, which was carried out in foreign languages. Although it cost them a lot of money, upper-class men, who were usually in the company of the royal family and the privileged Europeans, wanted their women to appear equal to their royal and European counterparts. The lower-middle and working classes could not afford private education for their women, but these women enjoyed a less secluded life simply because their unpaid help was needed by their husbands, who were small merchants, shopkeepers, or even laborers. The private property law is said to have caused legal conflicts over inheritances and was often used to the detriment of women of all classes. Thus, new economic and social conflicts can be argued to have played a major role in bringing about the feminist revolts in nineteenth-century Egypt.

No wonder, then, that the women who revolted against their situation, at first verbally, were the women who were most secluded from public life and were more likely to be eloquent and equipped for such a struggle—namely, upper-class educated women, such as Huda Shaarawi, whose memoirs are discussed in the following chapter.

European colonization has had a mixed effect on Arab countries, especially Egypt. Some, especially the rich and educated, felt that European culture and advanced industrial technology could be used to revive and reform Arabic societies, which were left corrupt and "backward" by the "declining" Ottomans.[49] On the whole, for these reformers, "backwardness" was the real enemy rather than "foreignness" or the presence of the Europeans.[50] Others, especially religious leaders, thought that Arab societies should be very careful in adopting European ideals and systems, lest they run the risk of losing their cultural Islamic identity. The reformers had their feelings toward the Europeans shattered, especially when Britain did not keep its promises to the Egyptians and officially invaded the country. The educated, while still admiring European culture and lifestyles, felt unhappy with the aggressive and colonial behavior of Britain. They had to show their nationalistic and patriotic feelings in times of threat, thus in some cases supporting the call to adhere to an Islamic identity.

Nineteenth-century reformers were, understandably, moderate when it came to women's issues. The right to education was the main issue raised by both male and female reformers. Among the male reformers who raised the issue of women's right to education were Ahmed Fares el-Shidyak, who published "One Leg Crossed over the Other" in 1855; Rifaa Rafi el-Tahtawi (1801–1871); and Shaikh Mohammad Abdou (1849–1905).[51] Their argument was imbued with their defense of the basic teachings of Islam, which were considered to have become distorted and misunderstood.

Gradually, the argument for women's rights grew out of the religious context. Qasim Amin (1865–1908), who can be considered the Egyptian equivalent of the English John Stuart Mill, was more radical in that he called for more than just education for women. Amin believed that the nation could not be advanced without improving the position of women. He "advocated the right to work for women as well as legal reforms to improve their status."[52] His later books such as *Al-Mara al-Jadida* (The New Woman) upset orthodox Muslims because his argument was based less on religion and more on the doctrine of natural rights and the concept of progress. Nationalists did not like Amin either, for they felt that his views were weakening the main issue, which for them was the liberation of the country from the British.[53] Jamil al-Zahawi, an Iraqi poet settled in Egypt, is said to have been imprisoned in 1911 for advocating unveiling.[54] However, it is argued that early reformists only advocated women's rights as part and parcel of the general reform project, the "national regeneration project articulated in the language of moral redemption."[55] By representing early Islam as the ideal, especially as far as its treatment of women was concerned, the feminist project "harkened back to more distant and presumably more authentic origins,"[56] instead of breaking away from the past.

Huda Shaarawi, whose memoirs provide an example of early Arab feminism embedded in nationalism, is by no means the first Arab woman to fight for women's rights. Before her, there were many women from Syria, Lebanon, and Egypt, such as Zainab Fawwaz (1850–1914), Warda al-Yazigi (1838–1924), and Aisha al-Taimuriya (1840–1902).[57] The site for struggle for those early women was mainly literature, both poetry and prose; later they founded literary salons, women's clubs, and women's journals, which showed a fairly sophisticated awareness of women's subordination and separation from public life in their respective social and economic backgrounds. In their poems, stories, essays, articles, and discussions, these women—privileged in terms of education due to their upper- and middle-class backgrounds—not only discussed literary issues and competed with male literary figures at the time; they also expressed their unhappiness with the situation of most women and started fighting, although politely and unmilitantly in the beginning, for basic rights for women, such as access to education and amendments to the marriage and divorce laws to secure women's livelihoods. They also raised the issues of veiling and segregation, which they had been led to believe were essentially Islamic but had since discovered (after studying Islamic texts) were not. In this way they contributed to the general debate on reform.

However, turn-of-the-century Arab feminism was politically militant as well in that it was connected to the nationalist movement, which intensified during the first few decades of the century. Women of all classes contributed to changing the political situation in Egypt. Through demonstrations, strikes, and assassinations, Egyptian women supported the Wafdists who in 1922 achieved partial independence from the British, which was completed after World War II. Sir Valentine Chirol wrote in the *London Times:*

> In the stormy days of 1919, (the women) descended in large bodies into the streets, those of the more respectable classes still in veil and shrouded

in their loose black coats, whilst the courtesans from the lowest quarters of the city, who had also caught the contagion (of political unrest) disported themselves unveiled and arrayed in less discreet garments. In every turbulent demonstration women were well to the front. They marched in procession—some on foot, some in carriages shouting "independence" and "down with the English" and waving national banners.[58]

In other Arab countries, women have also played an essential part in the nationalist and liberation movements.[59]

The fact that women's issues were first raised by upper- and middle-class women, or aristocratic and bourgeois women, is no accident; there are a number of factors that helped these women to find a way to make their views heard, if not respected. Education is one of the most important. Although the first school for girls in Egypt was opened in 1832, upper-class women received a private education, due to their strict seclusion from other classes in society, for there was a feeling that schools were not for "respectable" women. Private education has always been available for women of privileged backgrounds in Arabic history. Even before Islam, women in the families of the chiefs of Arabian tribes were always educated, for they had the leisure time to spend reading and memorizing poetry, still highly valued in Arab societies today, and also studying the sciences available at the time. Even within a system that concentrated power and wealth in a few hands (i.e., in a structural patriarchy), some women nonetheless could find certain ways to express their intellectual capacities.

Upper-class women benefited from education and increased contact with European women (through the growing influx of westerners). They also benefited from modern transportation (imported carriages, the new railway, and the Mediterranean steamer services), which allowed them to socialize more; to go to the Opera House; and to travel to the country, the seaside, or even Europe. Meeting different types of people, knowing other cultures, and (sometimes) attending women's conferences must have encouraged some of them to raise the issue of women's liberation publicly. Some middle-class women benefited from the new educational and technological system as well. New careers were opened for them, such as schoolteaching and journalism.

In the second half of the century, Arab women continued their struggle to achieve more rights. Ironically, the pace and success of women's liberation movements are not based on how old the movements are. For example, although Egyptian women are supposed to have been the first among Arab women to fight for abolishing polygamy and to change the laws of marriage and divorce, other Arab countries (such as Tunisia, Syria, and Iraq) have been more successful than Egypt in introducing measures to render polygamy and unilateral divorce more difficult.[60] It is even more ironic that, although turn-of-the-century feminists have certainly paved the way for later feminists, women have had to fight certain battles all over again. The rise of what is called Muslim Fundamentalism, led by the Muslim Brethren, has resulted in the call for reveiling and for women to return to the home to look after their families, claiming that this is a holy duty. In some Arab countries, women have felt betrayed. In Algeria, for example, where women played a great role in achieving independence, they were hoping to attain more rights as women than they have actually won. This happened in most countries which had to fight for national liberation. What has been even harder for women to accept is that, after independence is achieved, "men often prefer to return to 'normal'; they take up the old role pattern and the double standard again goes into operation," something which reveals "a painful contrast between principles of freedom and equality and the docile acceptance of traditional female submission."[61]

One could argue that national identity becomes more of an issue when one's country is politically and militarily colonized. However, this is not a rule. The texts that I am examining show various ways of national identification and senses of belonging in different historical periods. Indeed, a great deal of analysis has been generated on the issue of how national identity can sometimes become an oppressive issue for women and a medium of control in the hands of men.[62] Arab women themselves have different perceptions of the meaning of the struggle and the way to achieve what they consider to be their rights. The texts I discuss here illustrate the diversity of the struggle and the variety of consciousness. Fadwa Tuqan's text, for example, shows that for some women at least, and even at the height of the struggle in Palestine, national liberation was not the main issue.

Before moving on, I would like to comment on the terms "feminism" and "feminist" in the Arabic context. Although I use these terms throughout this book, there are no directly equivalent Arabic terms. The nearest Arabic term for "feminist" is *nisai,* but this also means "womanly."[63] Nevertheless, the lack of this terminology should not deter us from talking about "feminism" in Arab-speaking countries or from calling some people "feminists." A person or a text is "feminist" when s/he or it raises feminist issues. In other words, "feminism," which refers to the "awareness of women's oppression and exploitation within the family, at work and in society and conscious action by women and men to change this situation,"[64] is in the content. This is exactly what we find in the Arabic texts that I have chosen to call "feminist."

CHAPTER THREE

Huda Shaarawi's *Harem Years:*
The Memoirs of an Egyptian Feminist

A Double Text

In this chapter, I look at a text by Huda Shaarawi (1879–1947) entitled *Harem Years: The Memoirs of an Egyptian Feminist.*[1] Huda Shaarawi must have been known throughout the urban upper and middle classes of her day for her leading role in establishing the first Egyptian women's union and for her participation in the nationalist uprising against the British. Nowadays she is known to those interested in the history of the Arab women's movement primarily through her memoirs. *Harem Years* is the only English-language book associated with her name. Shaarawi's memoirs are a good example of early Arab feminism, which is embedded in the nineteenth-century reform movement and in the early-twentieth-century nationalist movement. The tensions and conflicts recounted by Shaarawi in her memoirs are typical of the lives of many women of her generation, class, and background. *Harem Years,* as it is presented by Margot Badran, is also a good example of how nonwestern women and their writing have recently been introduced to the west and of the issues raised by this process.

Harem Years can be looked at as a double or a two-in-one text: the first is Huda Shaarawi's memoirs (dictated in Arabic to her secretary, Abd al-Hamid Fahmi Mursi, in the 1940s); and the second is Margot Badran's English-language text (published in 1986), although the book is overtly presented as by Shaarawi. It is quite important to keep this in mind when reading the book, because the memoirs and *Harem Years* are meant for two different sets of readers. Shaarawi's memoirs were originally written—and, according to Shaarawi's cousin, meant to be published—for an Arabic-speaking public. *Harem Years* is obviously addressed to the English-speaking world: it is translated, edited, and introduced in such a way as to make the book as attractive to an English reader as possible. The book thus raises a whole set of ideological assumptions connected with modern feminism. My analysis examines the implications of such issues as the conditions of production and publication for a feminist reading, for whom the text is meant, and the lack of shared knowledge between different cultures. But before dealing with such editorial and technical concerns, I want first to deal with another set of issues related more to Shaarawi's memoirs as an autobiographical act by a woman—and to do so without rigidly separating *Harem Years* from the memoirs.

The Memoirs

My reading of Shaarawi's memoirs centers on three main closely related issues. First, Shaarawi's feminism is strikingly embedded in her sense of nationalism. Second, she is constantly identifying herself socially, through a family structure and within the Ottoman upper class. Third, through the act of writing her memoirs, Shaarawi nevertheless appears to present a constructed self, fully aware of its distinctiveness. In my attempt to define autobiographical writing as a political/textual site of subject formation, Shaarawi's memoirs may be viewed as a tool for the development of her political consciousness—jointly in terms of family position, class, and gender—and as a means of self-construction and self-evaluation, in light of these questions.

Shaarawi's Nationalist and Reformist Feminism

As previously argued, most women's liberation movements in the developing countries are closely associated with the rise of nationalism; that is, the struggle for women's rights is a main part of the general political struggle against both colonial and local forms of oppression.[2] This is an especially appropriate way to approach the memoirs of Huda Shaarawi, a turn-of-the-century Egyptian advocate of women's rights who lived at a crucial time in Egyptian and Arab history. Shaarawi was by no means the first Arab or the first Egyptian woman to fight for women's rights. Nor was she a literary figure, unlike most of the early Arab generations of women's rights advocates. Her memoirs, however, are considered one of the earliest (if not the earliest) nonfictional autobiographical works by an Arab woman to be published in modern Arab literary history. Although written in the early 1940s, Shaarawi's memoirs were published posthumously in 1981 as *al-Raida al-Arabia al-Haditha* (The Modern Arab Pioneer) by Dar al-Hilal in Cairo. We do not know whether other Arab women published their autobiographies before Shaarawi, but we do know that most of the Arab women writers of the nineteenth and twentieth centuries used autobiographical elements in their fictional works; an early example is Zainab Fawwaz's novel *Husn al-Awaqib aw Ghadat al-Zahra* (The Happy Ending, 1985).[3] We also know that in 1923 Shaarawi founded the Egyptian Feminist Union, which some translate as the Egyptian

Women's Union or the Egyptian Women's Federation, as Nawal el-Saadawi translates it. Within this organization Shaarawi wrote articles about national concerns as well as about women's liberation that were published in the union's journal, *L'Égyptienne.*

As was typical of her generation of women who publicly fought for women's rights in one way or another, Shaarawi came from an upper-class family.[4] Being the daughter of an indigenous upper-class "absentee landholder," she was exposed to firsthand contact with Europeans from childhood. Like other "ladies" of her time, Shaarawi was educated mainly in French, but she also learned Turkish, which used to be the everyday language of the aristocracy before French took over. There is evidence that she knew English too, because later in her life, when she got involved in the public nationalist movement at the end of World War I, she sent letters of protest to the British high commissioner and his wife on behalf of the "women of Egypt, mothers, sisters and wives of those who have been the victims of British greed and exploitation."[5] Arabic, the language of the Egyptian masses, was not needed by an upper-class "lady"; but Shaarawi, as an educated Muslim, had to learn the Holy Quran, which she did by heart. The language of the Holy Quran inspired her as a little girl to know more about the language so that she could read other Arabic books, of which her father kept large quantities. In order to do so, of course, she had to know Arabic grammar; but she was told that because she was not going to "become a judge" (*HY*, 40), she did not need to learn it. In other words, Shaarawi was literally prevented from learning Arabic when she was a child and also later on when she separated from her husband and wanted to resume her studies. Threats only made her more fond of the language she could never master.

Shaarawi could have written her memoirs in the language she knew best, but she chose to record them in Arabic, the national language, even though she had to dictate them to her secretary. This can be interpreted as an act of high national awareness, whereby only Arabic could express her identity as an Arab or an Egyptian. It perhaps also suggests that she wished to communicate with women beyond the limits of the upper classes, that is, with women who would know only Arabic. Recording her memoirs in Arabic can be seen as at once a feminist and a nationalist act. Of necessity, the political dimensions of this act are obscured when we read an English translation (but they are also obscured by a lack of historical knowledge, because not all Arab readers would necessarily know that she could not write in Arabic).

Linked to her sense of nationalism is Shaarawi's attempt in her memoirs to defend her deceased father's reputation, as he was accused of helping the British to invade Egypt in 1882. The editor of *Harem Years* claims that this section in Shaarawi's memoirs did not "form part of the central narrative of her own reminiscences" (*HY*, 3). Yet it is quite clear that refuting the charges against her beloved father is of extreme importance for Shaarawi; and perhaps it is not going too far to think that defending her father's reputation is one of the main reasons why she recorded her memoirs at all. One wonders how the memoirs would have looked without the intervention of the editor. Even with the editor's shaping of the memoirs, the section "My Father" is still the biggest of the sections on her family.[6] Indeed, the charges brought against her father are of significance in terms of Shaarawi's sense of nationalism, and her relationship with her father is another issue that is of considerable interest for a feminist approach to her work.

Shaarawi's Relational Sense of Identity

Shaarawi's nationalism is an extension of her political collective consciousness; it is a public expression of her need to define herself in relation to a group: the Egyptian people, men and women. Although recording one's own memoirs is obviously a highly individualistic act, some women use this personal act only to uncover a self defined collectively (as discussed below). Shaarawi must have had some sense of individuality, a sense inherent in all autobiographical acts—otherwise she could not have recorded her memoirs at all. She may well have felt that she had achieved something that made her atypical of other women yet also able to speak as a woman for other women, bearing in mind that she was decorated by the Egyptian state for her involvement in fighting for the national cause and supporting women's rights.

FAMILIAL BACKGROUND AND SOCIAL CIRCLES

Shaarawi's sense of individuality is limited by her feeling, though it might be unconscious, that she could not have become what she was had it not been for her familial background and the socioeconomic circumstances in which she was raised. For she starts her memoirs with a section on her parents' backgrounds. Shaarawi recalls what she knows about her mother's Circassian relatives and her father's Egyptian origin before she says anything about herself. Thus she acknowledges the importance of telling her readers that it is the background which comes before the self. Even when Shaarawi goes on to talk about her childhood, she starts with her "Two Mothers" and brother first. All through her memoirs, she constantly refers to the people who influenced her deeply, such as her French teacher, Mme. Richard, and Said Agha. Shaarawi mentions many people who had a considerable impact on her personality, including Bashir Agha, nicknamed "father of mankind"; Shaikh Ibrahim, her Quran teacher; Shaikh Ali al-Laithi, "who lavished affection" on Shaarawi and her brother; Zubair Pasha; and many others whom she remembers, either as a little girl or as an adult woman. She gives hardly any negative or highly critical accounts of anybody—even the aspects she does not like about some people she describes with great politeness.

More noticeable still in Shaarawi's memoirs are the many other women (such as May Ziadah and Malak Hifni Nasif) as well as pioneers who contributed to the women's movement (such as Labiba Hashim, Saiza Nabrawi, Princess Ain al-Hayat, and Princess Nazli Hanim) whom she acknowledges as gifted literary figures. Acknowledgment of such women is an indication of Shaarawi's sense of following others and of being a member of a larger group within which her feminist consciousness has been developed. She even includes short life-histories of two women who became her close friends: the Frenchwoman Eugénie Le Brun (Mme. Rushdi) and Atiyya Saqqaf, a relative of her mother. Shaarawi's admiration for the former and sympathy for the latter must have been so great that she includes their life-histories within hers as if her own resonated with theirs. The inclusion of first-person narratives, even if they are indirectly quoted, within her own memoirs is a feminist act. For in them, Shaarawi is allowing a space for other women whose voices emerge side by side with her own. Moreover, it is clear that the kind of self that she tries to represent is a self that is defined in relation to all the people that she has known throughout her life since childhood.

MATERNAL SEXISM AND ROOTS OF AWARENESS

Although Shaarawi also had a stepmother, to her distress and agony it was her biological mother who was the person whose sexual discrimination depressed her most. In her nightmares and fantasies, Shaarawi imagined that she was not the daughter of her mother, that her "real mother was a slave girl who had died, and the truth was being withheld from her" (*HY*, 34). According to the memoirs, her mother was actually married to her father (*HY*, 1–2); but in the edited English version, she is said to have been a concubine.[7] If Shaarawi's mother was a concubine (not surprisingly at all, for it was very common for upper-class Egyptian men to have concubines and wives, who were mostly Turko-Circassian slaves in those days, like Shaarawi's mother), then her preference for her only son over her daughter can be partly explained in economic terms. Although discrimination between boys and girls is not exclusive to upper-class families, it is intensified by the question of inheritance. Daughters in Islam do inherit from their fathers, but they inherit half of what their brothers do. This conflict over money, either nonexistent or very marginal in poorer families, can and does result in different types of emotional strife between brothers and sisters, brothers and brothers, sons and mothers, and daughters and mothers. Shaarawi's mother must have been aware that her wealthy existence depended on her son, since, not being married to the pasha by law, she would not inherit. Her son, who would inherit, could have been taken away by his uncles, his legal guardians, had his mother not proven that she was a good mother and thus qualified to look after him.

According to the memoirs, Shaarawi's mother was the main source of her misery, because she focused her attention on her son, Shaarawi's brother. When Shaarawi asked why, her mother said that it was the weakness and bad health of the brother that made people, including herself apparently, give him more attention than his sister (*HY*, 36). The answers of the "two mothers" did not satisfy young Shaarawi for more than a minute. She would always be sensitive to such discrimination; she even wished to be ill (and very seriously), but it was the brother's condition which worried the mother and other members of the extended family, not Shaarawi's. The only thing Shaarawi could do was to retreat into solitude, seeking affection in nature from animals, birds, and plants in the surrounding garden.[8]

Hence, Shaarawi's sensitivity to issues of gender and sexual inequality, or what is called today feminist consciousness, developed in childhood. As a little girl, she was troubled and depressed because people around her favored her brother over her. In a society where respect in a family is dictated by the hierarchy of age, the young Shaarawi, who was older than her brother, thought that she should have been the one attracting more attention and care. After she realized that a hierarchy of sex superseded the hierarchy of age, she "began to prefer death to [her] miserable lot" (*HY*, 37). When she asked for an explanation for such apparent discrimination in the way her brother was treated and the way she was, her affectionate "big mother," Umm Kabira, told her that her brother was being given more attention and care than her because he was the only boy in the family and that one day "the support of the family will fall upon him. When you marry you will leave the house and honor your husband's name but he will perpetuate the name of his father and take over his name" (*HY*, 36).

The male child is in some sense the model child in a patriarchal society; he continues the lineage. Posterity is only assured through a son. Moreover, in many Arab countries, fathers and mothers are addressed using the name of their eldest son. Abou Ahmed and Umm Ahmed, for example, are the father and mother of Ahmed, their eldest son. Shaarawi loved her brother because he would continue to honor her beloved father, but she still did not like the idea of people preferring him to her. She was caught between her sense of responsibility in showing respect for her family's name—the family which she had great love for and which her brother was going to perpetuate—and her sense of alienation from this same family, whose discrimination against her as female caused her a lot of pain. Throughout her life, Shaarawi continued to experience such cultural duality, manifested in various ways: her attitude toward her mother, her husband, and her sister and later toward the British.

THE SISTER/BROTHER RELATIONSHIP

Despite jealousy, Shaarawi loved her brother very much and continued to love him even after his death. In fact, she records in her memoirs:

> When my brother departed my interest in life departed with him. We had shared great intimacy. He had been the joy of my life and a source of communication and consideration. With his passing I felt I had lost a link between myself and the world. If it were not for my children I would not have lived a single moment after my brother's death. (*HY,* 110–111)

The brother-sister relationship is one result of the contradictions inherent in "patriarchal" families. Being strictly prevented not only from having any kind of sexual relations before marriage but even from having any type of friendship with other women, young women—naturally seeking friendship or just communication and affection—may have very intimate relationships with an understanding brother, a loving father, a sympathetic sister, an affectionate mother, or any other person within the family to whom they form a great attachment. In Shaarawi's case, which is typical of an upper-class "patriarchal" family at the turn of the century, when she reached the age at which she was considered to be an adult (which was probably ten or so), she was told to limit her friendship to girls and not to have anything to do with boys anymore. Shaarawi had her brother, whom she trusted; thus there was great space for her trust and love to grow, as they lived in the same household. A reader acquainted with Freudian psychoanalysis could easily read Shaarawi's relationship with her brother in sexual terms. As a person who was raised in a society where familial relationships are usually very close and very passionate, I think that close relationships in families could unconsciously develop cross-sexual feelings, usually denied, of course, because they are forbidden by society. However, I do not want to develop a Freudian reading of my texts.[9]

THE DAUGHTER/FATHER RELATIONSHIP

In close "patriarchal" families, fathers also can become a kind of ideal that daughters love and look up to (and they probably look for lovers resembling their fathers, as the cliché suggests). Shaarawi loved her father dearly; and although he died when she was only five, she claims to remember his kindness, justice, and affection. Throughout her memoirs, Shaarawi's father is conjured up many times, especially when she is in distress. The image of the father that she constructs is of a fair, pious, and affectionate man who, had he been alive, would have supported her decision to study what she wanted and opposed her early arranged marriage (*HY*, 35).

Shaarawi's brother and father are represented as two men who did not, or would not have, discriminated against her because she was female. Her continuous act of associating herself with the male figures and her apparent attempt to dissociate herself from the female ones—intensified by her recurring childhood fantasies that she was not the daughter of her mother (*HY*, 34)— can be explained according to some feminists, such as Julia Kristeva, as an act of raising herself to "the symbolic stature of her father."[10] Following this line of critical discourse, one could further say that Shaarawi's identification with the father/brother image has been conditioned by repressing the mother or the female in her, becoming in the process a "phallic woman" or an "artificial or man-made product turned in the cultural and linguistic machinery of androcentric discourse."[11] By showing loyalty to male-defined culture and its ideology of selfhood, Shaarawi is supposed, according to such criticism, to have gained cultural recognition by embodying such male-defined ideals. I suggest that in doing so she perpetuates the political, social, and textual disempowerment of mothers and daughters.

Although Shaarawi cannot be found completely innocent of this critical charge, she nevertheless cannot be said to be promoting the very essentialist ideology that renders women's story a story of silence, powerlessness, or self-effacement. My argument is that in androcentric societies most, if not all, girls grow up with an image of an ideal male figure toward which they aspire, thinking, quite justifiably, that they will gain respect through such identification. This is a stage that many women go through. When women develop feminist consciousness, however, they usually pass beyond this stage of self-negation. The realization that the limits set on women and the value placed on men are socially produced and not an essential feature of womanhood or manhood helps women appreciate and value their identity as women and understand other women better. In Shaarawi's case, feminist maturity materialized in different ways. As I argue below, her attitude toward her mother develops into understanding and sympathy. Her later contribution to the women's union is major evidence as well. But Shaarawi also has special admiration (no less than the admiration she has for her father) for a female figure in the family: her stepmother.

THE RELATIONSHIP WITH HER STEPMOTHER

The female character that Shaarawi recalls as her only source of consolation is her "Big Mother," the invalid old widow of her father, with whom she shared many things. She loved this woman dearly because of the great affinity of their tastes in many things and because her stepmother was the only one who "talked frankly with [Shaarawi] on a number of matters" (*HY,* 34), making her trust and confide in her. (Here Shaarawi is being discreet and probably polite because she does not reveal what sort of subjects she discussed "frankly" with her "Big Mother"; it could be sex, for example, for if it was religion or politics she could have said so.)

Shaarawi's close relationship with her stepmother at first sight seems remarkable. Jealousy is usually reported to overwhelm relationships among women involved in polygamous marriages, although not in all cases.[12] Shaarawi does not mention in her memoirs whether her own mother got on well with the first wife of the pasha, Umm Kabira (an indication of politeness as well, as she probably thought it was not proper for her to interfere in such issues). She makes it very clear, however, that she herself got on extremely well with her stepmother, in fact better than with her own biological mother. This is unusual, for within a polygamous family—whether the wives live together in one large household or whether they live in separate houses—jealousy and conflict usually affect the children as well. (A stepmother is usually thought of as a source of evil; she is sometimes a synonym for a witch, in life and especially in folktales. Nevertheless, there are examples where stepmothers are reported to be very good to their husband's children.[13] It could be perhaps that the stereotypes of the wicked stepmother which appear in fairy tales reflect less actual stepmothers than the double role which the mother, whether a biological mother or a stepmother, plays in early childhood as the main source of affection but also the main source of discipline. Thus, the motif of the good true mother and the wicked false mother reflects the tension in the mother/child relationship.)

According to the memoirs, Umm Kabira is more affectionate to Shaarawi than her own mother is. She is an old woman who lost her only son and her husband and later became an invalid. Shaarawi talks about her with great affection and sympathy. She loved her more than she did her own mother because her stepmother answered her questions with love and understanding. Umm Kabira, in fact, represented a living image of Shaarawi's construction of her dead father. Unlike her Turko-Circassian biological mother, but like the pasha, Umm Kabira is affectionate and just and is, after all, an Egyptian Arab. Shaarawi's association and continuing attempt to identify herself with her Arab stepmother can be read as an attempt to define herself nationally and culturally as an Arab.

THE ABSENCE OF A SISTER/SISTER RELATIONSHIP

Of all Shaarawi's relationships with people she identifies herself with, one relationship is left obscure: her relationship with her sister. I would like to refer here to the useful concept of the "silences" of a text, offered by Pierre Macherey and developed by Terry Eagleton.[14] According to this concept, the critic's task is to give birth to what is hidden inside a text, not what is already said but what is "not said"; it is to make eloquent the most muted aspects of a text. The critic must "show the text as it cannot know itself, to manifest those conditions of its making (inscribed in its very letters) about which it is necessarily silent."[15] What is "not said" in a text, then, according to Eagleton, is an absence; for Macherey, a text is a combination of what is "spoken" and what is "unspoken" or what is visible and what is "hidden." The critic has to seek to articulate or utter the "unspoken" or the "hidden."[16]

The almost invisible sister is an example of the kind of absences in Shaarawi's memoirs that one reads for. Shaarawi's sister, who must be the daughter of Umm Kabira, is only mentioned at the end of her memoirs. We do not even know whether this sister was raised in the same household or whether she was brought up in the village with her relatives. Shaarawi did not show great sadness when she was told that her sister had died; instead she was worried about leaving behind her own ill son if she went to the funeral. Yet when she realized that it was her brother who had died, she was completely out of her mind with grief. If it was not for her children, as she records, she could never have recovered from the shock of losing her brother. The extreme concern for her brother contrasts with her relative indifference to the sister.

The main point to notice is the conflict in Shaarawi's feelings between the sense of injustice at the preference for her brother and her love for her brother and tendency to assimilate him to her dead father. This conflict indicates the extent and the limits of Shaarawi's feminist consciousness. Its limits are very evident, for example, in the passage where she thinks that her sister is gravely ill but is far more shattered on discovering that it is her brother who has died. This indicates how Shaarawi's feelings accord with the "patriarchal" family and the value ascribed to males over females: she herself shows for her sister just the kind of lower esteem which so hurt her. Thus, we see that Shaarawi's constructed self is not completely liberated, for she herself was not conscious of her own discriminating attitude that she inherited from her very background.

FILIAL AND MARITAL PIETY

In spite of her discrimination, Shaarawi was never bitter toward her mother. She still had respect and love for her. Although Shaarawi was curious to know about her mother's origin, she respected her privacy; she describes her as "a very private person," whom she "never once dared ask" about her background; instead she asked her uncle. Shaarawi showed love to her mother; when she heard of her death, she was deeply saddened. The growth of Shaarawi's love for her mother perhaps has an element of feminist maturity; it shows her feelings of solidarity with and sympathy for this woman whom she felt to be oppressive toward her as a child but whose position she came to understand better as an adult. However, Shaarawi's gentle words regarding her mother and her idealization of her father can be explained in other terms too. Although she does not talk much of Islam in her memoirs, she was brought up in a very Islamic way and was very proud of memorizing the holy book of Islam. One of the main teachings of Islam and indeed one of the ways leading to heaven is through obedience, love, respect, and looking after one's parents. True Muslims are not supposed to criticize their parents, in private or in public, no matter what they say or how they behave, as long as they worship the one and only God that Islam believes in. One could say, then, that Shaarawi's gentle attitude toward her parents is an extension of her religious belief.

Shaarawi's attitude to her husband is similar to her attitude to her mother. Before marrying him, she never really liked her cousin, who was her legal guardian. She describes him as being not gentle but "abrupt and curt," a man whom she feared and who was sexist in the way he treated her and her brother. When he married Shaarawi, he was already married, with children of her own age. Shaarawi's marriage to her cousin was arranged by the family, not only to extend it but also to keep the wealth confined to it. She recorded in her memoirs that she tried resisting this marriage by the means available to her as a little girl: tears. As expected of an upper-class daughter, however, she had to behave as a good girl and tell her mother to decide what was suited for her. But Shaarawi was not only ruled by her religious obligation to obey her parents; she also felt that she had the right to do what she wanted—within, of course, the boundaries of the family institution. Shaarawi's first feminist act was manifested in her separation from her husband, which was legal because he had signed a paper before their marriage promising to sever all relations with any woman except Shaarawi, a promise he failed to fulfill. To Shaarawi's advantage, her husband could not have made her come back to him by force, as would have been the case had he not signed that paper.

Shaarawi spent the seven years apart from her husband reading and studying, as she had always wanted to do; she was still a married woman, who had more respect in society than a divorcee and had a say, although limited, as far as her own life was concerned. It was also during these years that Shaarawi started to have access to public gatherings, still within the women's sphere, for she joined Mme. Rushdi's Saturday salon, where women discussed many issues. She also made strong friendships with women during this time. Even after returning to her husband and having his children, Shaarawi still never mentions that she ever loved him. At the same time, nowhere in her memoirs does she record anything bad about her husband. She herself writes that she only gave him companionship because he started showing her kindness—and after all he was a relative of her dear father. It is interesting to note that Shaarawi talks about her closeness to her husband especially after the national events of 1919. She says that her involvement in the Egyptian national movement brought her husband and herself closer to each other. Indeed, participation in national political and economic life has been argued to have the effect of altering women's understanding of their own lives.

An Individualistic Sense of Self?

Thus, we see that the kind of self that Shaarawi represents in her memoirs is caught between her sense of individuation and her sense of relatedness, and indeed unrelatedness, to others. The self recorded in the part about her childhood is more introspective and personal than that represented in later stages of her life. As a child, Shaarawi is constructed as distinct and special within the family; she is extremely sensitive to discrimination and hungry for learning. The absence of friends in her record of childhood intensifies her singularity and concentrates the light on herself. The self Shaarawi constructs to represent herself as an adult is less conscious of its uniqueness. The seven years of separation from her husband give Shaarawi communal experience; for during this period of her life she starts to have contact with people outside her immediate family. Her friendships with women become numerous. Shaarawi must realize through her friendships that many women share her feelings of injustice and that she is not the only wronged woman in Cairo. After her childhood years, Shaarawi does not desire death anymore, except when her brother dies; even then it is more despair than the desire for death that she feels, whereas as a child she always thought of death whenever she felt she was discriminated against. The older Shaarawi grows, the stronger she becomes and the clearer is her need for a collective identification. In other words, her sense of self is not static by any means; it is a developing process of change and of improvement, for that matter. Shaarawi develops the urge and the need to work together with other women in order to bring about change in their situations.

Although Shaarawi's tone of voice changes throughout the pages, the overall style of her memoirs can be described as consistent. It is not confessional at all. This relates to the propriety of her style too, as I have noted on many occasions.[17] Indeed, the representation of her relational identity can also be seen as part of Shaarawi's general genteel style, which could be part of a convention of the literary style in those days. In her memoirs, there is nothing that the members of the Egyptian aristocracy would have considered improper. Shaarawi's genteel style of writing reflects herself in real life and also her practical feminist demands, as we think of them today. She was brought up according to a strict set of morals which she adhered to throughout her life. One of the aims of the women's union, of which she was president, was "encouraging virtue and combatting immorality," as the constitution of the union puts it.[18] Even her approach to the British invasion of Egypt was based on moral criteria. In one of her letters to the British high commissioner in Cairo, Shaarawi expresses her disappointment and anger in the most polite and gentle style. She says, for example:

> We hope, your Excellency, that our petition from Egyptian women will gain your acceptance and approval so that you will then return to the support of the principles of liberty and peace.[19]

Reminding the wife of the high commissioner of their summer conversation when she told Shaarawi that Britain had no intention of invading Egypt or any other country and that Britain's participation in World War I was mainly to defend the oppressed nations, Shaarawi writes in her letter:

> In these sorrowful times that my country is passing . . . would you tell me whether this is still your opinion today? What do you think, Madam, . . . ? If not, I beg you to explain . . .[20]

Indeed, Shaarawi could not have been any less gentle in her protest to the British authorities in Egypt, for we understand from her memoirs that the Shaarawi family had a personal friendship with them and, of course, with all other Europeans there, as had all upper-class Egyptians.

Shaarawi herself had special admiration for European culture, manifested in her close friendships with her European teachers and with members of the European royalties. But her attitude to Europe was typically double-sided. On her trip there, her views of European civilization were shattered. She could not believe that Europeans, as "civilized and enlightened" as she thought they were, could resort to war, "the most brutal act imaginable" (*HY,* 102). Shaarawi, however, was greatly influenced by European thinking, without blind imitation. Her establishment of the girls' school was an act to prove that Egyptian women could do what Europeans did and without their leadership (*HY,* 94). She admired the Europeans but was not ready to give up her sense of nationalistic pride in being an Arab Egyptian.

Shaarawi's narrative is highly readable without much analysis or reflection. It reads as easily as a story from the *Arabian Nights.* There is obvious evidence that Shaarawi has read at least parts of that work. She refers to the splendor of the aristocratic atmosphere within which the annual charity fetes of Mabarat Muhammad Ali took place as "a splendour that evoked the days of Harun al-Rashid" (*HY,* 97), a name directly associated with the *Arabian Nights.*

Within her nonreflective narrative and gentle style, Shaarawi's writing cannot be described as an act of conscious self-formation through writing. Although there are scattered moments of self-exploration, what Shaarawi offers the reader is rather a narrative of self-presentation, using methods of self-clarification and self-justification. The reason why Shaarawi is not so philosophically self-probing can probably be explained in terms of why she decided to record her life story. One of her main motivations could be her wish to be remembered. She must have had, rightly enough, a sense of self-achievement. For Shaarawi had done certain things that she deserves to be remembered for. In fact, her accomplishments were recognized by the Egyptian state even in her lifetime. Shaarawi started a school for girls as early as 1910, the first in

Egypt to "offer general education rather than vocational training, such as midwifery."[21] She is one of the women who established the first Arab women's union. Although this union's ideology did not and could not have challenged the fundamental gender problems in Egyptian society at the time, Shaarawi's moderate feminism by today's standards was still revolutionary at the time. Through the union, she struggled to amend marriage and divorce laws, to encourage elementary and higher education for women, to end superstition, widespread at the time, and to campaign for public hygiene.[22]

Shaarawi's act of giving up the veil in public is in itself unforgettable. Although the veil was no issue for rural and working-class women generally, it was nonetheless a great burden for urban and especially for upper- and middle-class women. Shaarawi did not want history to forget her and all that she did. Neither did she want her beloved father's name to be associated with treason, being herself a highly nationalistic person. As I discussed earlier, defending her father's reputation must have been another motivation for writing her memoirs. If my speculations about why Shaarawi wrote her memoirs are correct, then it is possible to see why her narrative is far from being terribly philosophical. Shaarawi is not trying to understand her existence or to raise questions about the universe. Recording her life story can be seen as a kind of self-assertion.

HAREM YEARS

This view of Shaarawi's life is only possible through a reading of the original Arabic memoirs. The English-language version offered by Margot Badran offers a somewhat different view. Promoting an Arab feminist to English readers in the way that Badran does is undoubtedly very positive. However, in tailoring her book to her western audience, Badran inadvertently omits aspects of Shaarawi's life that are of great significance to Arab feminism. By first omitting then paraphrasing Shaarawi's words with regard to her father and his reputation, Badran marginalizes an issue which, as I have argued, is central to my reading of the memoirs as they appear in Arabic. Similarly, by choosing to cut out what she describes as Shaarawi's "fragmentary" discussion of her engagement in the Egyptian nationalist movement, opting instead for providing her own summary of Shaarawi's and other women's involvement in nationalist politics in an epilogue, Badran omits what I have tried to show is an important part of Shaarawi's concept of herself, namely, her political and nationalist public self.

I have already noted that *Harem Years* is actually a book by Margot Badran rather than by Shaarawi. If we go through the book from cover to cover we see that, out of 150 pages, only 77 pages are (supposedly) Shaarawi's direct words. The other 73 pages consist of a preface, a chronology, an introduction, a notes section, an appendix, a glossary, and 44 pictures. Still, the name of Huda Shaarawi is printed in big white letters as the author on the front cover of the book, matching those of the title, *Harem Years*.

Apart from a three-page introduction by Amina al-Said, the Arabic version is void of any other form of editorial interference. The cover page has an impressionistic painting of Shaarawi, and only her name and the publisher's name are printed there. Al-Said's name appears at the end of her introduction to the book.

Shaarawi does not seem to have given her memoirs any specific title. The title *Harem Years: The Memoirs of an Egyptian Feminist* was provided by Badran. A title functions as a device to announce a piece of writing and to point out its content. (Badran is an American academic who is very much interested in the history of feminism in the Middle East, especially in Egypt. *Harem Years* is part of her interest.) The secondary title, *The Memoirs of an Egyptian Feminist,* is printed in small black letters, matching those of Badran's name as the translator and introducer of the book. The word "harem" contrasts with the word "feminist," certainly for a western or a westernized reader. Moreover, the title *Harem Years* is very commercial. Apart from historians, anthropologists, and academics interested in the Middle East, few English-speaking people would want to read the memoirs of a turn-of-the-century upper-class Egyptian woman. The title has to be appealing, to attract as many buyers as possible. *Harem Years* is a clever choice. As I discussed before, the word "harem" has a special sensational tickle for a western reader, and not only an English-speaking one. It "conjures up a host of exotic images," as Badran herself admits (*HY,* 7). A title like *Harem Years* might evoke titillating, sensuous images of (probably) naked women engaged in sexual activities with a male master and among themselves.

A reader expecting to read such an account of a harem would be disappointed after reading *Harem Years*. For no such exotic images can be seen in Shaarawi's memoirs; sex simply has no place in her writing. So if Badran's intention is, and it might very well be, deliberately to use such an evocative title in order to allow for a new understanding of what "harem" actually meant in many circumstances like Shaarawi's, then she has done a good job. For Shaarawi's "harem" is only a space within which she has achieved more than many western free and unveiled women have done in their lifetimes.

Shaarawi's oppression, as represented in her memoirs, is no worse than that of many western women even today. "Harem" and feminism are not, after all, two opposing terms, at least as far as Shaarawi's situation is concerned.

Shaarawi's picture on the front cover of the book, which shows her as very feminine in her jewelry, with naked shoulders and an embroidered dress, can be explained as a breaking-out through that lattice window of the harem into the public world, which is exactly what she did in her own, though limited, way. The pictures throughout the book make it look more factual and documentary. They show Shaarawi at different ages, in varied poses and in different places; Shaarawi's mother, father, brother, husband, and friends; images of Cairo; Shaarawi's house; a women's demonstration; and a women's meeting. All these pictures are supposed to verify Shaarawi's account of her life.

One wonders, however, whether the reader needs this proof and whether these pictures make the reader believe the memoirs more than if the pictures were not there. Is it important that the memoirs should be read as factual? Is it truth that the reader of memoirs is looking for? The pictures make the act of reading easier and more enjoyable. A curious reader might also want to see how upper-class people dressed in those days or what a street in Cairo was like. The pictures function as a successful selling point, just like the title.

Badran clarifies her editorial position. She does not limit herself to giving the text a title, including pictures, and summarizing the political part of Shaarawi's memoirs; she also edits the text in a very visible way. She states in the "Preface" that she has arranged the memoirs into four parts for which she has provided headings. She also divides the parts into smaller sections with subheadings. Badran argues that she has had "to preserve the natural flow of the narrative" (*HY,* 3). In doing so, she transforms Shaarawi's text, perhaps inadvertently, into something that is different in tone and emphasis, maybe even in significance, from the original.

As I argue in Chapter 5, there is a kind of consensus among feminist critics that women's autobiographical writings challenge critical assumptions about autobiography as a genre, assumptions that have been basically developed through the study of male western autobiographers. One of the ways in which this challenge is materialized is when women "focus on relationships with others rather than as in men's autobiographies, on the development and successful accomplishment of the self."[23] Although Shaarawi goes on defining herself relationally to others, however, she manages to construct an image of herself as a woman who has successfully achieved an acknowledged public presence, in her own time at least. She therefore takes this merging presence even further to more publicity by the act of recording her own memoirs. We shall see that this sense of constructing an individual self, however rarely beyond the limits of relatedness to others, grows as we read more recent texts.

Conclusion

My reading of Shaarawi's memoirs and of *Harem Years* is by no means comprehensive of all the issues raised by this book. Shaarawi is representative of early Arab feminists, especially in that she was one of their leaders by virtue of being a president of the first Egyptian and Arab feminist unions. Her feminism was intellectually embedded in the reformist, and later the nationalist, movement of the time. Women's rights were fought for as part of the reformist Islamic argument. Women's liberation was also considered necessary for national liberation. Shaarawi was involved in both movements. Some of her feminist speeches and, more to the point, some of her actions can still be considered revolutionary even today. This is not because Arab feminism has not gone any further than in Shaarawi's days, for it has, but because Arab feminism today is facing opposition similar to that which Shaarawi and her fellow feminists faced at the turn of the century. Today Arab feminists are threatened by conservative Islamic forces which are probably more hostile to women's rights than those in Shaarawi's time. Casting off the veil, for example, is still a revolutionary act: many women are forced to wear the veil again or sometimes willingly wear it, either as a defensive strategy or out of belief. Although this is no cause for cheering, it is no cause for pessimism either. Things are changing all the time; women continue to fight in various ways to achieve more rights in spite of the opposition.

My book is about the ways Arab women express themselves and how these texts are presented to the west. Badran's version of Shaarawi's memoirs is one example of presenting the identity of a turn-of-the-century, educated, Muslim upper-class woman. Before considering other texts that show how women from different backgrounds represent and identify themselves, in Chapter 4 I discuss the theoretical issues related to the study of autobiography.

PART TWO **NARRATIVE THEORY**

Autobiography

Autobiography and Sexual Difference

We must reject the Autobiographical Tradition and its implicit divisions of autobiography into the literary and the non-literary. The variation of autobiographical traditions and their determinants—of, for example, class, race and gender—will have to be identified; autobiographies will have to be returned to a wider literary and cultural history; the use of autobiography by certain groups will have to be mapped; and contemporary autobiographical practice will have to be given attention—not referred back to some regulatory Tradition, but rather seen as a source of knowledge of what an adequate contemporary criticism of autobiography might be.[1]

Traditionally, autobiography has been studied and criticized from within a politics of genre that tends to be not only gender-blind but also class-biased and racially biased. Hierarchical values have always been implicit in gender distinctions, and class and race distinctions too, since Aristotle's *Poetics*. Western genre theory, according to Celeste Schenck, remains largely prescriptive, legislative, even metaphysical, for it preoccupies itself with establishing limits and drawing exclusionary lines in order to protect a supposedly idealized generic, sexual, and racial purity.[2] Perhaps it was not until James Olney's major contribution in *Autobiography: Essays Theoretical and Critical* (1980), extending the definition of autobiography to cover even lyric poetry, that autobiography was first liberated from the generic limitations imposed by traditional criticism. In such criticism, autobiography was viewed as a western invention—the roots of which were said to go back to the Renaissance, as the dawn of the age of modern liberal humanism of the western "man"—and was traditionally defined as a kind of "literary" or "aesthetic" narrative that tells the life story of a person, by "himself," from childhood to the time of writing. Autobiographies, or autobiographical texts as I prefer to say, of women, working classes, and nonwestern writers were banished from the "canon" or simply ignored.

My concern lies far from studying "great" autobiographies; in fact, as the opening quotation indicates, I am arguing for the inadequacy of a criticism based on a tradition of dividing autobiography into literary and nonliterary or rhetorical and empirical first-person narrative, for such distinctions, as Elizabeth Bruss argues, are "cultural artifacts and might be differently drawn."[3] My aim is to formulate a theory adequate to the varied autobiographical texts I have selected. In order to do so, this chapter first surveys approaches to autobiography, moving from the notion of the "completed" self and the "autobiographical pact," according to which autobiography was taken as a mere record or mirror of external reality, to the opposite deconstructionist position, which robs autobiography of any referential value and renders it pure fiction. Between these two extreme views lies the position for which I am arguing, which places autobiography in the field between truth and fiction. I also consider here notions of the self, the male version of the "unique" and individual self, and the opposite feminist version of the nonheroic and "collective" self, which proves more adequate to use in relation to some of the texts examined.

Perhaps it was not until the last two decades that conventional criticism of autobiography was challenged and new projects of studying "nonexemplary" autobiographies and the varying modes of writing the self came into existence. This chapter traces the major problems in the attempts that have been made to define autobiography in the conventional sense—the sense that implicitly or unconsciously (or occasionally explicitly) dismissed women's and working-class autobiographical texts as "nonliterary," denied even existence to nonheterosexual texts, and considered nonwestern texts to be mere imitations of western examples. Such criticism of autobiography is, in fact, what a critic like Edward Said is reluctant to accept. According to Said, criticism of autobiography (or of biography for that matter) is engaged in an act of elevating individuals above history and lifting the subject out of his/her time and society.[4] I believe that Said's worry is only relevant to conventional criticism of autobiography that is based on the theory of the uniqueness of the subject of autobiography or the "Self." His criticism is often invalidated when the writer of her self is a woman, especially when she is nonwestern. (Nonwestern, hereafter, is a shorthand term for a great variety of categories, including black people and ethnic minorities within western societies. It does not imply that all these different groups are the same or can be defined negatively simply through how they differ from the western, which itself embraces differences.) For as we shall see later, the kind of self constructed in most women's autobiographical texts is not singled out as a separate entity, standing independently on its own and defined in terms of its own merits.

Thus, a study of autobiographical modes that is based on cultural and sexual differences, on the one hand, and that takes into account the conditions of production and the role of the recipient, on the other, does not isolate the subject. Women, both in the west and particularly in other cultures, have extended the autobiographical mode, thus creating new and various forms of narrating the self such as memoirs, diaries, letters, interviews, essays, songs, and literary and sociological criticisms.

The "Completed" Self and the "Autobiographical Pact"

Perhaps the most conventional definition of autobiography is that based on the assumption that the writer of "his" "life story" is "he" who already has a clear understanding of "his" self before "he" expresses or transforms this image of "his" "completed" self into narrative.[5] Ross Miller, for example, suggests that

> [t]he pose of the autobiographer as an experienced man is particularly effective because we expect to hear from someone who has a completed sense of his own life and is therefore in a position to tell what he has discovered.[6]

What is highly paradoxical here is that Miller is commenting on *The Autobiography of Malcolm X,* who himself, according to Paul John Eakin, comes to realize at the end of his autobiography the impossibility of giving an up-to-date account of oneself that does not or cannot differ from or change when one looks back at oneself at different points in time. Incompleteness of self and the limitations of autobiography are what Malcolm X later discovers, yet Miller and others who studied the same autobiography, such as Barrett John Mandel and Warner Berthof, insist on defining the "good" autobiography as the one that succeeds in testifying to a "completed" self, already lived, known, and defined.

Philip Lejeune, considered the first to define and classify autobiography in the French tradition as a genre, also argues, according to Nancy Miller, for the "autobiographical pact": a "declaration of autobiographical intention, and explicit project of truth telling; a promise to the reader that the textual and referential 'I' are one."[7] Lejeune defines autobiography as the "retrospective narrative in prose that someone makes of his own existence, when he places the main emphasis on his individual life, in particular on the history of his personality."[8] As Sidonie Smith notes, although he later modified his essentialist and normative definition into a historical study of the way autobiography is read—that is, he came to realize that autobiography is as much a mode of reading as a mode of writing[9]—Lejeune's study remains gender blind.[10] The only implication for a feminist reading to be derived from his later definition is his realization of the significance of the conditions of reception. The role of the readers—and in certain cases the editor, the translator, or the interviewer—becomes as relevant as that of the autobiographer in feminist theory and in other modern theories, for the readers in their encounter with the text are rereading their own lives by association,[11] or even by contrast (as discussed below). For now I want to consider other challenges to the notion of the "completed" self or the "autobiographical pact," which look at autobiographical texts as hybrid forms that combine aspects of truth and fiction.

The Hybrid Form: Fiction and Truth

As early as 1956, the notion of the "completed" self was challenged by Georges Gusdorf, when he wrote his "Conditions and Limits of Autobiography." Since then, this notion has been further criticized on two major fronts, the deconstructionist and the feminist. Although Gusdorf studies autobiography as a "solidly established literary genre,"[12] a stance that this work is very critical of, he does not perceive autobiography as a mere mirror reflecting an image of a coherent already-lived self; it is rather an act of self-construction from memory:

> Autobiography is not simple repetition of the past as it was, for recollection brings us not the past itself but the presence in spirit of a world forever gone. Recapitulation of a life lived claims to be valuable for the one who lived it, and yet it reveals no more than a ghostly image of that life, already far distant, and doubtless incomplete, distorted furthermore by the fact that he who remembers his past has not been for a long time the same being, the child or adolescent, who lived the past. The passage from immediate experience to consciousness in memory, which effects a sort of repetition of that experience, also serves to modify its significance.[13]

Olney argues that an autobiographer has three strategic ways of employing the memory in the act of writing the self. He/she can either employ the memory in a "fairly ordinary but nevertheless creative sense," or abandon it completely, or "transform it out of all recognition."[14] Autobiography then exists somewhere on the line between fictitious narrative and historical truth.

Deconstructing Auto/Bio/Graphy

Poststructuralist, deconstructionist, and modern psychoanalytic theorists have challenged the notion of autobiography as a representation of a "completed" self even further. According to Jacques Derrida, Roland Barthes, and, notably, Paul de Man, the textual "I" has nothing to do with the "I" of the writer. The self ("auto") and the life ("bio") are fictions; there only remains the text ("graphy"), which in turn is to be deconstructed to "demonstrate the shadowiness" of even the existence of the characters involved on the page.[15]

In his "Autobiography as Defacement," de Man opposes generic definitions of autobiography on the basis that each autobiographical example turns out to be an exception to the norm. So far so good, but de Man goes on to argue (if I understand him right) two contradictory positions. He first states that a more fruitful approach could be that which looks at autobiography in relation to fiction. This is despite his claim that deciding what is autobiographical and what is fictional leads to similar difficulties as deciding whether a text belongs to the supposedly autobiographical genre or not. With all its difficulties or problems, I also want to maintain some kind of distinction between autobiography and fiction in order to be able to discuss different forms of autobiographical texts as well as fictional autobiography. However, de Man moves on to make an even more radical deconstruction of autobiography and suggests that it is as relevant to think that "the autobiographical project may itself produce and determine the life and that whatever the writer does is in fact governed by the technical demands of self-portraiture and thus determined, in all its aspects, by the resources of his medium" as to assume that "life produces the autobiography as an act produces its consequences."[16] According to de Man, then, the referent does not determine the figure, but the other way round. In other words, autobiography may not have any referential value at all. The subject is not even the autobiographical "I" but language itself. Language becomes both the object and the subject; it is the "theatre of self-expression and self-discovery."[17]

I find a kind of uncertainty or even contradiction between maintaining a distinction between autobiography and fiction on the one hand and dismissing any kind of reference to external reality on the other. Had de Man said that autobiography is merely fiction, which he does not seem to say, then I would have understood his nonreferential position, even though I do not agree with it. If autobiography is a hybrid form of fiction and factual report, which it is, then there must be some kind of reference to an external reality that is being retained in an autobiographical text in one way or another.

It seems that, looking back from Ross Miller to de Man, the criticism of autobiography has shifted from an early concern with life ("bio") to the self ("auto") and later to the writing ("graphy")—from the concern for finding out how true the life of the self is to dismissing all basis of referentiality and authenticity. Does this mark the end of autobiography? It might seem so; however, my own answer is no, it is not the end. For my approach is to reconstruct auto/bio/graphy into a new and adequate form. I believe that in each autobiographical text the "bio" (truth) and the "graphy" (fiction) both contribute, to different degrees, to the act of constructing the "auto" or self. To study the process of constructing this self, it is essential, first, to look at a theory of subjectivity that might serve the purpose.

Auto: Subjectivity in Process

Modern psychoanalysts, especially Jacques Lacan, have offered a new concept of subjectivity, which is "never sovereign by itself but only emerges in an intersubjective discourse with the other."[18] The self or the subject as well as the text can only be seen in relation to other selves or subjects or texts: "every subject, every author, every self is the articulation of an intersubjectivity structured within and around the discourses available to it at any moment in time."[19] With the proviso that discourses are produced from within a formation of social relations, this definition of subjectivity may adequately serve as a departure for understanding the kinds of constructed selves found in women's autobiographical texts.

In arguing for such understanding of subjectivity, I recall Smith stating that the autobiographer "situates herself and her story in relation to cultural ideologies and figures of selfhood" available to her.[20] But the female writer of herself, "aware of the vast areas of feminine experiences which have remained unexpressed, if not repressed,"[21] is engaged, according to Françoise Lionnet, in an attempt to excavate those elements of the "female self" which have been buried under the cultural and "patriarchal" myths of selfhood: in order to invent a more "authentic" image, the she/autobiographer has to invent her own myths and metaphors; by so doing she is engaged in a process of shaping her own self too. What I want to challenge here is the implication that there is a preexisting "authentic self" or an "essential self" waiting to be truly represented.

Linda Anderson, in "At the Threshold of the Self," also used the notion of subjectivity in process. She accepted the tautological nature of autobiography (argued for by Gusdorf and Olney)—the idea that the autobiographical self is a construct which "can neither have its origins anterior to the text nor indeed coalesce with its creator,"[22] because it entails, according to Anderson, a displacement of the past by language within the actual narrative. But at the same time, Anderson argues, criticism based on this idea fails to consider "how the writer, situated in language, is also inscribed in an order of sexual difference."[23] For Anderson, the production of actual narrative is not without ideological significance. When a woman writes about herself, she is immediately engaged in a double process of writing and rewriting the stories already written about her as a woman, as passive or hidden. By doing so, that is, by publicizing herself, she is challenging the very act of autobiography itself. A woman does not write about herself; she rather strives to. Writing for women becomes a double act of self-discovering and self-making. A woman struggles to find a discursive space within which she can create an image of herself not completely outside the roles assigned for her by her social conditions. As Anderson puts it, women's autobiography is a reaching both toward the possibility of saying "I" and toward a form in which to say it. Writing is a quest, a "process."[24] I would add that writing for women is a process and a quest for dialogue, social change, and the possibility of saying "we" as well as "I."

I have sketched, so far, four critical approaches to the study of autobiography. Before reaching my own formulation, I now want to discuss the position that challenges both the traditional definition of autobiography and the radical deconstructive one, a position that is more adequate in relation to women's autobiographical texts.

Referentiality: Autobiography and Truth

Sidonie Smith, in *A Poetics of Women's Autobiography,* also argues for the validity of the idea of the autobiographical "I" as being not completely the same as the "I" of the writer. All autobiography is not the same, according to Smith: the "autobiographical contract, that complex set of intentions and expectations binding the autobiographer and the reader together, is [not] as fluid as that which binds the fiction writer and the reader."[25] In contrast to de Man's theory of nonreferentiality, Smith argues that there is always a kind of truth in autobiography, which is "best understood as the struggle of an historical rather than a fictional person to come to terms with her own past."[26]

At the same time, she asserts, the autobiographer, by joining together facts of remembered experiences, enters into both the process and the product of assigning meaning to these experiences. For doing so, she adopts different means of emphasis, juxtaposition, commentary, and omission.[27] This is what Elizabeth Bruss (*Autobiographical Acts*) calls the autobiographical act.

Conventional criticism of autobiography, then, stressed the issue of reference or representation; for example, the notion that autobiography represents or tells the story of a "completed" self would mean that the writing refers to or represents something that preexisted independently of the text. From that peculiar case, I want to consider the issue of referentiality, from a stance opposite to de Man's. I want to retain referentiality, but I do not, of course, take the text as a mirror or a window. Writing is both construction and representation. In the act of politicizing and publicizing the private sphere, autobiographical writing depends on the reference to social relations, which is not fiction. Consider the following examples: how inadequate and, indeed unfair, it would be to apply de Man's concept of nonreferentiality of language to political narratives of any sort, especially those either written or even recited to some editor or translator or publisher who has a certain interest in listening to a story of an American Indian, or a black slave woman, or a Latin American who participated in the country's revolution against colonization, or a Palestinian woman imprisoned or raped by the occupiers, or an Egyptian dismissed from her job and jailed by her own government. Doris Sommer, in her "Not Just a Personal Story: Women's Testimonies and the Plural Self," challenges the deconstructionist concept of nonreferentiality in relation to testimonials by Latin American women like Domitila Barrios, Rigoberta Menchú, and Claribel Alegría, which are "speech acts of the most passionate and militant variety."[28] To doubt referentiality in such political acts "would be an irresponsible luxury, given the urgency of the call to action."[29]

In other words, to treat the sort of writing that we see in such testimonials, or indeed in most texts by underprivileged persons or groups, as if they had no reference to anything outside themselves or the texts would be to lose all the political force of such writing, which is an encouragement to take action. For deconstructionist reading, if understood in this way, leads to an apolitical position. However, this is not to suggest that autobiographical texts are utterly "correct" representations of "real" words or lives. As Sommer argues: "This is not to say that testimonials lack irony or that they doggedly defend a particular code of description or a single program of action."[30]

On the contrary, any narrative, including above all an autobiographical one, is engaged in different kinds and degrees of referentiality and construction. The history of a world war, for example, is a construction, an interpretation, but it definitely refers to things and actions that undoubtedly happened. Journalism and fiction are different interpretations of reality; and autobiography is neither only "fiction" or merely "actual."

Nevertheless, to raise questions of referentiality—of the relation of a text to external reality—on their own is perhaps to distort the whole autobiographical project; other issues have to be studied jointly in order to develop this project. Some feminists see that the adequate way to study women's autobiographies is to read the narratives as depicting the "journey of a female self striving to become the subject of her own discourse, the narrator of her own story."[31] Other critics suggest concentrating on the literary mode rather than the subject matter of autobiographies of previously unacknowledged types. David Murray's study of Indian, Hispanic, and Asian autobiographies in America is a good example. In such texts, argues Murray, the conflict between textuality and authenticity is particularly relevant, because "the cultural and social imbalances mean that the production of the text often operates to turn the speaking subject into an object, whether for study, entertainment, or the frissant of the exotic."[32]

Heroism within a Unique History of Autobiography

Traditional criticism of autobiography usually evaluates long "literary" narratives that tell life stories of acknowledged western intellectual figures at or toward the end of their careers. Autobiographies of St. Augustine, Jean-Jacques Rousseau, Henry Adams, Walt Whitman, François-René de Chateaubriand, John Henry Newman, André Gide, and Johann Wolfgang von Goethe, for instance, are supposedly the best examples for people wanting to write their life stories. But can anyone write "his" life story? According to such criteria, probably not. Someone whose autobiography is to be read at all is someone whose life has contributed to making the "history" of "his" time: "he" should be a hero. Only autobiographies that have "great" and "unique" stories to tell in a "great" and "unique" style are "good" ones. Moreover, having a "great" story to tell does indicate that one must enjoy a highly developed awareness of one's uniqueness of personality. According to Gusdorf, for example, the sense of individuality, the main condition for writing an autobiography, is a relatively new and local creation; thus "autobiography is not to be found outside of our cultural area; one would say that it expresses a concern peculiar to western man."[33] To have the "natural" need that the western "man" feels to look retrospectively at "his" past life, according to Gusdorf, is not a universal thing. When Mahatma Gandhi wrote his autobiography, he was borrowing "Western means to defend the East,"[34] says Gusdorf. For a culture such as the Indian culture, which does not encourage a consciousness of self, does not and cannot independently produce autobiography in the conventional sense.

Gusdorf even dates the birth of the conscious awareness of the singularity of each individual life back to the Copernican Revolution. For Gusdorf, this creation was not sudden or unprecedented. In contrast to the philosophy of classical antiquity, which was content with the "disciplinary notion of individual being and argued that one should seek salvation in adhering to a universal and transcendent law," Christianity came to Europe bringing

> a new anthropology to the fore: every destiny, however humble it may be, assumes a kind of supernatural stake. Christian destiny unfolds as a dialogue of the soul with God in which, right up to the end, every action, every initiative of thought or of conduct, can call everything back into question. Each man is accountable for his own existence, and intentions weigh as heavily as acts—whence a new fascination with the secret springs of personal life. The rule requiring confession of sins gives to self-examination a character at once systematic and necessary.[35]

Thus Christianity, according to Gusdorf, gave birth to the seeds of the concept of individual self—an interpretation that is, I suppose, generalized; for not all branches of Christianity might stress the individual's position above that of the community. Before Gusdorf, Ralph Waldo Emerson (in 1827) raised a similar generalized point about the spirit of Christianity, which, according to him, diverts people's attention from the outer world and directs them to look inward.[36] Gusdorf also argues that this sense of individuality culminated in the Renaissance, the age of "free enterprise in art as in morals, in finance and in technical affairs as in philosophy."[37] The Romantic era, with its "exaltation of genius, reintroduced the taste for autobiography";[38] but it was through Michel de Montaigne, in the sixteenth century, and Rousseau, in the eighteenth century, that the "virtue" of autobiography was completed, says Gusdorf. Then came the teachings of psychoanalysis to increase this "virtue" even more.

The concept of uniqueness, then, is the core element in Gusdorf's history of autobiography—a history that one can easily describe as first sexist and second colonial. It is sexist because such history does not include women in the west: it "consists of threads . . . selected from men's activities in war, business and politics, woven together according to a pattern of male prowess and power as conceived in the mind of man."[39] It is colonial because such making of history, from a western view, excludes nonwestern cultures as if the west had never been influenced by any of them. According to such history, and outside this illusory circle of "western man," then, there are either no autobiographies or "bad" ones. For unless there is an individualistic self at the center, the autobiography is a failure.

The emphasis on the autobiographical subject as an individual isolated being is not exclusive to Gusdorf but pervades most critical approaches to autobiography, even recent ones. Although Olney, for example, argues that the autobiographical self is created during the act of writing it, he nevertheless, according to Susan Stanford Friedman, invokes Plato in positioning the self as a "teleological unity" whose metaphors of circularity represent the isolated uniqueness of the individual.[40] One way to understand the autobiographical life, according to Olney, is "as the vital impulse—the impulse of life—that is transformed by being lived through the unique medium of the individual and the individual's special, peculiar, psychic configuration."[41] Even Elizabeth Bruss assumes an individualistic model of self and in her *Autobiographical Acts* only draws examples from a white male "canon": John Bunyan, James Boswell, Thomas De Quincey, and Vladimir Nabokov, all of whom represent themselves as unique individuals. Patricia Meyer Spacks, in her "Selves in Hiding," also argues that the writer of his/her autobiography claims the "authority of individual personal experience, asserting knowledge of that unique subject, the self."[42]

According to Friedman, the healthy ego, for psychoanalysts, always seeks to separate from others. Both Freud's and Lacan's concepts of ego-making are based on the supposition that the "ego results from a process that moves away from fusion and towards separation."[43] Thus, even psychoanalytic models of self are individualistic.[44]

In his short essay "Confessions and Autobiography," Stephen Spender argues that every individual has two images of self available to "him": first, as "he" is perceived by others from outside; and second, as "he" perceives himself from within. He goes on to argue that to write autobiography is to write about the second image of self, that is, the self which is perceived inwardly.[45] The implication of Spender's study, as of Gusdorf's, is that it is impossible for women and also for nonwesterners to write autobiography in his sense. Women in "patriarchal" systems always have been perceived in the eyes of men as the "Other" and more seriously have, under the weight of "patriarchal" culture, internalized or accepted the dominant male view of themselves. The great variety in the autobiographical writings by women, however, conveys a great number of ways in which women have sought to free their vision of themselves. Nonwestern people of either sex as seen from a western view would not be able to adopt Spender's model since, like women vis-à-vis men, they are constructed negatively as the "Other" of westerners. Similarly, or to an even greater degree, nonwestern people develop a variety of models that cannot all be fitted into Spender's categories.

The concept of the uniqueness of the constructed self is even significant for poststructuralist Roland Barthes. The self he constructed in his *Roland Barthes par Roland Barthes* claims uniqueness and a sense of heroism: "I am myself my own symbol, I am the story which happens to me; free-wheeling in language, I have nothing to compare myself to."[46] The individualistic concept of self, as considered above, raises theoretical problems when we realize that women, minorities, and many nonwestern peoples have different conceptions of self, self-creation, and self-consciousness. When we know that until very recently, even in the west, "singularity in women was hardly to be boasted of,"[47] we realize the need for a new concept of self that does not deny uniqueness completely. There have been several feminist attempts to formulate the kind of self we see in many unacknowledged autobiographical texts, a model that renders inadequate not only generic definitions of autobiography, notions of the "completed" self, but also the notion of the unique individual self. Before looking at such attempts, I would like to consider a set of questions dealing with various kinds of social references raised by some feminist criticism about the content of women's autobiography as different from men's, some of which unfortunately depend on conventional definitions.

Women's Autobiographies versus Men's Autobiographies?

According to Estelle C. Jelinek, in her preface to her collection *Women's Autobiography: Essays in Criticism,* before 1967 there was literally no criticism on autobiographies written by women except for works on Gertrude Stein. Her book, however, as pioneering and interesting as it might be, seems to acknowledge and indeed contribute to the conventional study of autobiography as a literary genre. The intention of the contributors, to "fill the gaps in the history and development of the genre itself and draw attention to the neglected contributions by women to the autobiographical mode,"[48] honorable to the cause of feminism as it might seem, tends to follow from a similar traditional attempt to canonize autobiography, in this case women's. By concentrating on examining autobiographical texts written by literary women who are already acknowledged at least by feminist standards (such as Lillian Hellman, Gertrude Stein, Maya Angelou, Anaïs Nin, and Kate Millett) or politically active women (such as Elizabeth Cady Stanton, Eleanor Roosevelt, Angela Davis, Golda Meir, and Emmeline Pankhurst), the writers of *Women's Autobiography* seem to consider such autobiographies representative models, either to follow or to avoid, for women wanting to write themselves.

Spacks, in her "Selves in Hiding," rejects autobiographies of Roosevelt, Meir, Dorothy Day, Emma Goldman, and Pankhurst—all politically successful women—on the basis that their texts have no self at the center.[49] Day, according to Spacks, had a "clearer" sense of self than the other women, yet she managed to lose it constantly.[50] Accepting the definition of autobiography as a genre of self-display, Spacks argues that these women failed "to a striking degree" to emphasize their own importance directly, and thus their autobiographies are opposite to what autobiography is:[51] self-assertion. The concept of self and definition of autobiography that Spacks is employing are clearly the traditional individual self and the conventional definition, both criticized in this chapter. Spacks fails to address the question of who those women are writing for, because such a question determines the way they write and what they write about. She also fails to understand that Roosevelt's interest in politics, Day's imitation of the saints, Meir's devotion to husband and child, Goldman's conversion of the anarchists' suffering to political inspiration, and Pankhurst's total identification with a cause which destined her and her daughter to risk and to physical misery can also be read as positions of strength, as a new way to identify the self based on different criteria than the unique ego, rather than understanding these situations as embodiments of modes of self-transcendence or self-denial,[52] as Spacks does.

Although there is no harm at all in devoting a whole book to English-speaking women, as Jelinek does, the problem lies in generalizing: the editor claims that even those who have written papers on Continental autobiographies have drawn similar conclusions about women's autobiographies, such as "the tendency of women to write in discontinuous forms and to emphasize the personal over the professional."[53] This suggests that women, no matter what cultural, economic, or ideological situations they speak from, always write similarly and on similar matters, but differently from men and men's subjects. That is obviously not the right way to approach the topic. Such separatist and oppositional kind of criticism is, for my purpose at least, not in the least fruitful. In spite of the problems I have mentioned and although the book does not "provide a metacommentary that would prepare for a theory of women's autobiography,"[54] *Women's Autobiography* raises important questions and draws historical analyses which are not to be dismissed without looking at them.

The history of English-speaking women's autobiographies from the seventeenth to the eighteenth century to be drawn from *Women's Autobiography* is a story of development from self-denial and apology for writing the story of a life to self-assertion and creating a self through writing it. Accepting Gusdorf's historical study of the origins of autobiography, Cynthia S. Pomerleau also locates the Renaissance in the age of self-consciousness, the social development which would produce the rise of autobiography toward the beginning of the seventeenth century.[55] Autobiography, according to Pomerleau, was nonexistent before then. She argues that women in seventeenth-century England did not question the superiority of men: they even took their own subordination for granted. This is doubtful. Pomerleau maintains that in their autobiographies women were proud not of their own selves but of a husband or a father or perhaps a son. Women in seventeenth-century England had less access to culture, education, and publishing than men did; they consequently had a smaller range of experience, so that their writing was on a smaller scale and touched on fewer subjects than men's. Seventeenth-century English women writers of autobiographies were aristocratic by and large and were expected to be devoted wives and caring mothers. They wrote about these roles. Women's lives were private; so were their writings.

Toward the beginning of the eighteenth century, Pomerleau argues, women were gradually becoming dissatisfied with their dependent positions but were not yet fully aware and able to rebel; so some of them took religion as an outlet for their emotions. It was the changes brought about by the eighteenth-century industrial revolution that had their effect not only on economic and social conditions but also on culture and its representations. The sense of dissatisfaction grew bigger. The muted pre-eighteenth-century voices found a way to express their growing anger. However, and despite this slight change in attitude, love and marriage remained the overwhelming subjects of women's autobiographies, though represented less idyllically.

In seventeenth- and eighteenth-century America, too, women chose a religious life to gain acceptance by the community while at the same time aiming to acquire some degree of independence, according to Carol Edkins. Her main contribution in her essay "Quest for Community: Spiritual Autobiographies of Eighteenth-Century Quaker and Puritan Women in America" is her realization that Quaker women's spiritual autobiographies were remarkable documents, with "telling patterns" of the community. American Puritan women such as Elizabeth White, Anne Hutchinson, Jane Hoskens, and Elizabeth Ashbridge did not express individual voices but mirrored "the community's struggle." One should not have one's expectations deflated by not finding highly individualistic and unique stories of spiritual questing, for those women did not write as rebels or "artists"; but they "searched very hard and sometimes very long for a niche" and "once having found it symbolically celebrated their sense of community via the written word."[56] As we shall see, three centuries later, women—not only in the English-speaking world but from many other cultures—still have the sense of solidarity and collectivity celebrated in their autobiographical works.

Collective Selves and Women's Texts

Helen Carr, in "In Other Words: Native American Women's Autobiography," says:

> Westerners have assumed that they can see and judge the inhabitants of the Third World more clearly than they do themselves; just as women have been traditionally evaluated by the male gaze. But in both cases the gaze has been myopic, selective, reifying.

She notes that "these autobiographies, with all their limitations, remind us of the need for sensitive agnosticism and for the acknowledgement of other subjectivities, other points of view."[57] Indeed so. For the texts I examine in this book are richly diverse in ways in which women from widely different cultural backgrounds have asserted their voices as active subjects, consciously or sometimes unconsciously, challenging the oppressive representations and actions of forceful hierarchies. Even sometimes from within a so-called traditional stance, as devoted mothers or dutiful wives, these women express different voices not only in regard to their individual situations but mostly in terms of a social group. Of course, this is not to be naively optimistic in forgetting or ignoring the limitations and self-delusions, "the inevitable strategies and complicities out of which particular individuals make their way to open up that culture which has bent their language and mental perspectives to new shapes."[58]

Writing, for women, becomes a way to provide spaces within which women can talk about the complexities and pluralities of their selves. The individualistic model, provided by male writers, especially in the west, becomes inadequate to the lives women lead. Women from different cultures have devised instead many routes to speak of themselves and for their readers, going beyond the constraints of traditional boundaries. Their contribution to autobiographical writings provides new methods of debating the status of the self and the nature of self-representation and of language. Thus, more complex perspectives are needed to study them.

Although there have been more studies on western women's autobiographical writings than on those of other cultures, the few books that have appeared in the last ten or fifteen years contain only a few essays dedicated to black women's and ethnic minority writing and a small number on women from other cultures in the world. *The Female Autograph: Theory and Practice of Autobiography from the Tenth to the Twentieth Century,* edited by Domna Stanton in 1984, was one of the first of its kind to raise pluralistic, theoretical, and comparative questions that strive to "undermine the generic boundaries that have plagued studies of autobiography, often resulting in extended lists of unconvincing criteria for differentiating various modes of self-inscription."[59] By assembling a "collage of pieces" from different cultures, modes, times, and fields, Stanton attempts to confront issues of "class, of race, and of sexual orientation [that] have only been sporadically addressed."[60] These issues were also later addressed by other feminist books. *Life/Lines: Theorizing Women's Autobiography* (1988), edited by Bella Brodzki and Celeste Schenck, poses interesting questions about the process that women go through from life to writing, such as:

> what strategies have women who "write [their] own lives" adopted, when confronting their world, to free themselves from the images of role personae and desire encoded in language? Have they moved beyond silence to speech, engendering through writing alternative motives and myths? And reached that authenticity in the weaving of a text which puts its marks on "literary" writing?[61]

Sidonie Smith's *A Poetics of Women's Autobiography* (1987) explores among other issues how, in autobiographies of women of color or of working-class women, ideologies of race, class, and even nationality intersect with and compound those of gender. Consequently, a woman finds herself

> doubly or triply the subject of other people's representations, turned again and again in stories that reflect and promote certain forms of selfhood identified with class, race, and nationality as well as sex. In every

case, moreover, she remains marginalized in that she finds herself resident on the margins of discourse, always removed from the centre of power within the culture she inhabits. Man, whether a member of the dominant culture or of an oppressed subculture, maintains the authority to name "his" woman. In her doubled, perhaps tripled marginality, then, the autobiographer negotiates sometimes four sets of stories, all nonetheless written about her rather than by her. Moreover, nonpresence, her unrepresentability, presses even more imperiously yet elusively on her; and her position as speaker before an audience becomes even more precarious.[62]

The Private Self: Theory and Practice of Women's Autobiographical Writings (1988), edited by Shari Benstock, situates the question of gender in relation to issues of race, class, religion, and historical and political conditions. It also raises questions:

> [W]hat is it about autobiographical writing that raises issues of the "private" in terms of the "self"; how is the "self" opened to question in the positioning act of writing? How does "private" situate itself in terms of the "public"? Are private and public selves forever opposed to each other? Does "self" position the subject in the singular? If so, how do "women" redefine the properties of the autobiographical? What roles do "theory" and "practice" play in such a grouping?[63]

Almost all the criticism on women's autobiographical writings agrees that they have the potential to challenge conventional conceptions of identity and its relationship to politics and writing. Such writings attempt to remove questions of identity from the exclusive ground of the psychological or interpersonal and to open questions about the relationship between psychic and social life, including intrapsychic, interpersonal, and political struggles. They try to unsettle the boundaries around identity not in order to dissolve them completely but to "open them to the fluidities and heterogeneities that make their negotiation possible."[64] Thus, the very theory that used to reject women's texts on the basis of violating this theory is challenged. Women have resisted, and continue to resist, the individualistic concept of the autobiographical self and have reversed the standard definitions of autobiography. The kind of self represented in most women's writings from different cultures goes hand in hand with the concept of the "social self" upon which Karl Marx based his theory of communism. For Marx also rejected the bourgeois liberal view of the self as an independent individual and considered the self in relation to social forces, though not merely a field of such forces.

The first theory that women's autobiographical writings resist is perhaps the theory of genre. Shari Benstock argues that women's autobiographical texts are "as individual as women themselves, and often resist easy classification."[65] They therefore pose problems for theory. But this is not to say that there is no such theory that can contain them. Theorizing women's autobiographical writings is possible and not futile when we think of theory as a mode of clarification open to revision and as a dynamic element in shaping our awareness of the significance and richness of autobiographical writings for women and when we are conscious of the complexity of the relations between theory and practice and the impossibility of dividing them into two separate spheres. Women's autobiographical writings, different as they might be, share at least two aspects: intention (i.e., different women wrote differently but always aimed at constructing a truer and more "authentic" image of themselves, as discussed below) and the kind of constructed self.

A more positive, and indeed feminist, way to look at women's sense of collective identity is to see it as Benstock does: as a source of strength and transformation. Sheila Rowbotham, writing from a socialist feminist position in her *Woman's Consciousness, Man's World* (1973), was one of the first not to interpret women's sense of collective identity as negative or as a symbol of weakness. On the contrary, she argues that women, not seeing their real selves in the reflections of cultural representation, develop a dual consciousness—the self as culturally defined and the self as different from cultural prescription.[66] The sense of alienation, then, caused by cultural representation of women leads women to find new forms and new consciousness of self. This new "consciousness" enables women to see themselves in a

> new relation to one another. [They] can start to understand [their] movement in relation to the world outside. [They] can begin to use [their] self-consciousness strategically. [They] can see what [they] could not see before.[67]

Nancy Chodorow's work on the psychology of gender socialization within the family (*The Reproduction of Mothering: Psychoanalysis and the Sociology of Gender*, 1978), argues, like Rowbotham's book but within a psychoanalytical context, that the concept of isolated selfhood is inapplicable to women. She asserts that, because "of the nature of the mother-daughter relationship, women's sense of self is continuous with others and that, unlike men, women experience themselves relationally."[68] The works of Rowbotham and Chodorow have been used by other feminists, such as Susan Stanford Friedman,

Mary Jean Green, and Sidonie Smith, to study women's autobiographical selves, arguing that:

> emphasis on individualism as the necessary precondition for autobiography is . . . a reflection of privilege, one that . . . excludes from the canon of autobiography those writers who have been denied by history the illusion of individualism.[69]

Friedman rightly notes that the importance of group identification has repeatedly surfaced not only in women's but also in minority group autobiographies. In theory and in practice, this sense of collective consciousness, according to her, enables individuals to move beyond alienation within the dominant culture to construct meaningful lives in writing and otherwise. Creating new, and indeed more authentic, images comes neither from completely dissolving the individual nor from within the individualist isolated self but from merging it with a collective group identity.

The collective sense is to be found not only in black autobiographies but also in other autobiographical texts of women from other cultures with different attributes. Sommer argues in relation to Latin American testimonials that the testimonial "I" does not claim typicality or presume a universal or essential human experience. It is not, nor does it claim to be, typical enough to stand for the "we" completely. On the contrary, the testimonial "I" achieves her singular identity as an extension of the collective: the "singular represents the plural not because it replaces or subsumes the group but because the speaker is a distinguished part of the whole."[70] Sommer notes that it is not mere preference on behalf of the writer of the testimonial to talk about herself collectively; it is rather dictated by the culture, "the colonized language, that, opposite to western culture, does not equate identity with individuality."[71]

Fox-Genovese also talks about the colonizing attitude of the west, in relation to "Afro-American and Third World Literature," which has already begun to challenge "the implied blackmail of Western white, male criticism."[72] The new western concept of "the death of the author," which threatens the western autobiographical project, argues Fox-Genovese, might "accurately reflect the perceived crisis of Western culture and the bottomless anxieties of its most privileged subjects."[73] It can hardly be applicable, however, to a culture in which most of its subjects and authors do not have "much opportunity to write in their own names or the names of their kind, much less in the name of the culture as a whole, [who] are eager to seize the abandoned podium."[74] This would be putting the cart before the horse; it is impossible that someone who had never had the chance to say "I" should be ready to abandon this "I" and accept such depersonalization and abstraction. It does matter who the writer is; after all, what is autobiography for women but finding a way to define the "I"? The concept of "the death of the author" proposed by Barthes in connection with canonical texts and empowering the reader vis-à-vis the text is inadequate to the kind of noncanonical, autobiographical texts I am concerned with. As Fox-Genovese puts it, to "read well, to read fully, is inescapably to read politically, . . . [for] political and social considerations inform any reading, for all readers are political and social beings."[75]

Conclusion

As in history and in the social sciences, women have been marginalized and excluded from literary traditions and institutions. Feminists find this final field of culture, ruled by men, to be "central to the hegemonic power of education";[76] education is one of the major battle fields for feminists. Thus, literary issues become an integral part of the feminist struggle. In fact, for a feminist like Mary Ellman, who is interested in "women as words," the political and the historical aspects of "patriarchy" can best be studied within literary texts.[77] My analysis of the texts shows that the strength of such texts is, first, that Arab women's writings, whether deliberately or sometimes unknowingly, violate literary traditions; second, that their stories can be seen, to a certain extent, as real testimonies to gender oppression in Arab societies; and, third, that their stories are the very site of dealing with such oppression.

Arab Autobiography
A Historical Survey

In the previous chapter, I traced the history and the major characteristics of autobiography in western literary traditions. In this chapter, I want to offer a similar sketch of autobiography within Arabic literary history in order, first, to challenge Gusdorf's belief that autobiography does not exist outside western cultures and, second, to explore the traditions and conventions within which the women writers and tellers of their life stories whose texts I am studying operate. As in western traditions of literary criticism, autobiographical studies have only recently been receiving attention from Arab literary critics, which is why my choice of references has been extremely limited.[1]

There is evidence in all the references I have come across that the earliest autobiographical text was written in the eleventh century by Ibn al-Mu'ayad. As in western traditions, though, the writing of other people's lives (called *sira* in Arabic, meaning biography) preceded autobiographical writing itself in Arabic literary traditions and dates back to the seventh century. The *sira* of the Prophet Muhammad, which has been written by several historians and writers, is considered the first full biography in Arabic literature. Beside the Holy Quran and the Tradition (Hadith, or the Prophet's sayings), the *sira* is the third source of Islamic law and conduct. But it is also read as the history of the success of Islam; for in it, biographers *wrote* about all the battles the Prophet fought and won against people of other religions and creeds at the time, who resisted the spread of Islam. The *sira,* however, did not come into existence out of the blue; it owes a great deal in structure to an already known pre-Islamic set of war narratives called *Ayyam al-Arab* (The Days of the Arabs). The Prophet's *sira* was also inspired by Persian royal epics and the Judeo-Christian hagiographies known to Arabs at that time.[2] After the Prophet's *sira,* biographers became interested in writing the *sira*s of other leading figures in Islam. They also compiled reference books, comparable to today's *Who's Who,* containing the life histories of many influential people. Gradually, around the eleventh century, some leading Islamic figures started writing their own life histories.

One critic, Muhammad Abdul Ghani Hassan, speculates on the reasons for the absence of autobiographical writing as such before the eleventh century. He wonders why Arab Muslims wrote biographies and histories extensively and artistically but rarely tried their hands at autobiographies. Arabs, he suggests, may have been so keen on their private lives that they did not wish to make them public by writing about them. And perhaps those of high rank or special position who led a public life did not write about themselves but left it for other people to write. For it is supposedly a moral characteristic of an Arab man not to talk about himself, saying "I" or "I did." Hassan finds it strange that an Arab poet can boast about "himself" in his poetry, saying "I" or "we," referring to "his" tribe, but a prose writer is not expected to sit down to tell an episode of "his" life. Hassan's speculations fail to throw light on the question of why Arabs suddenly started writing autobiographies in the eleventh century, if it was not customary for an Arab to boast of the self in prose. It is obvious that Hassan is restricting autobiography to its traditional definition offered by male western theorists.[3]

Hassan's approach is not unique. Other studies of Arab autobiographies are immersed in traditional western views of what an autobiography should be and who the best autobiographer is. Ihsan Abbas, a well-established and respected critic, although acknowledging the existence of many forms of autobiographical writings in early Arabic literary history, argues that they were mere collections of news, stories, and events witnessed by their writers. They all lacked the "unity of structure, the sense of time, and any development of character."[4] Only autobiographies that were written by celebrated twentieth-century Egyptian writers influenced by western traditions are "good" ones, according to Abbas.

However, one critic, Yahyia Ibrahim Abdul Dayem, in a 1975 doctoral thesis on autobiography in modern Arabic history, dedicated a chapter to a favorable discussion of early Arabic autobiographies. He divides Arabic autobiographies into two groups, those written before the sixteenth century and those written since the nineteenth century. Abdul Dayem argues that earlier autobiographical writings were as rich and as literary as modern ones. He classifies earlier autobiographies into six groups according to motives for writing: first, those written to excuse oneself or for apology (like that of Hanin Ben Issak); second, those written to explain one's philosophical views (like that of Abou Bakr Arrazi); third, those written to resolve emotional depression or conflicts (like that of Abou Hayan); fourth, those written as ideal examples (like that of Abdul Rahman al-Jawzi); fifth, those written to trace one's intellectual development (like those of Abou Arrayhan al-Beiruni and Abou Ali al-Hassan Ibn al-Haitham); and finally those written to recover certain memories (like those of Osama Ibn al-Munquiz and of Giovanni Casanova in the western tradition).

There were other forms of autobiographical writings in the early period too, such as memoirs, diaries, and confessions, although these forms were not yet named as genres. A form of writing which combined both biography and autobiography, in which the writer tells his own story while at the same time writing someone else's biography, also existed, like *Sirat Sultan Jalal Addeen* by Ali Bin Ahmad Nasawi and *Sirat Sultan Saladdeen* by Ibn Shaddad. An example of this form of writing in the western tradition is James Boswell's biography of Dr. Samuel Johnson.

Unlike other critics, Abdul Dayem argues that earlier autobiographies were as retrospectively reflective and daring as modern ones. Some of them were even attacked for disclosing personal views which contradicted or differed from dominating ideologies at the time (for example, expressing doubts about Islam, criticizing certain traditions, or speaking about desire and sensuality). Sometimes earlier autobiographies aimed at spiritual idealism. However, these kinds of motives did not affect the spontaneity of these autobiographies; on the contrary, most of them had enjoyable narrative styles. Aspects of time and place, verifying facts by enclosing historical records, and, above all, keeping the narrative literary and fluent were the main characteristics of earlier autobiographies, according to Abdul Dayem.

Autobiographical writings seem to have disappeared between the sixteenth and the nineteenth centuries—the period considered the "dark ages" by Arab intellectuals and historians—during which Arabic culture is said to have suffered decline, disintegration, and deterioration at all levels. The nineteenth century witnessed the revival of autobiography. Since then, critics seem to view autobiographies as mirroring the beginning of the search for a nationalist and Arab identity. Many autobiographies were published in Damascus and Cairo. The nineteenth century marked the beginning of the European intervention and domination of the Arab world. The influence of western cultures was felt on Arabic literature in general. Translations of western literary works were extensive, and many students completed their studies in European universities, as is still the case today. Critics argue that Arabic autobiography reached its aesthetic perfection with Taha Hussain's *Al-Ayyam* (literally, The Days), published between 1926 and 1955 in three volumes and in 1967 in one complete volume. Hussain, who received his higher education both in Cairo and at the Sorbonne, is now considered the doyen of modern Arabic literature. Since Hussain's autobiography, hundreds of autobiographies of literary value have been published.

In spite of western influence on modern Arab autobiographies, we see that the tradition of writing the self is also deeply rooted in Arabic culture. Thus, celebrating the self by writing about it cannot be viewed as an exclusively western invention. It has been argued that Islam, which is so predominant in Arabic culture, favors the community over the individual. This point is sometimes used to explain why Islamic cultures supposedly lack autobiographical writing; but that lack, as I have already noted, is imaginary, and the claim of such a lack is based on ignorance. Although I do not want to challenge the idea that Islam is the culture of the community rather than the individual, I do want to challenge the idea of a monolithic "Islam" about which it is possible to generalize.

I also want to stress that a major theme of Arabic writers, whether Islamic or pre-Islamic, has been to celebrate their freedom and their ability to do whatever they wished to do or go wherever they wished to go, no matter what dangers were involved or what obstacles had to be surmounted. Pre-Islamic writers often boasted of their individualistic achievements, such as surviving a fierce battle with a powerful enemy (be it a man or a wild beast), or having been able to make friendship with a "noble" animal like a lion, or having used wit and wisdom to escape execution. Islam did not kill this sense of individuality. In fact, there is an old Islamic saying which has become an aphorism that most Arabs chant: "Do not say who my father is or what my lineage is, for it is who you are and what you do that matter." I would argue that Arabic individualism is highly appreciated as far as it can be contained within the interests of the group. This containment does not make the Arabic sense of individuality less developed and, more importantly, does not make it less qualified to be a motive for writing one's life story than western individualism in Gusdorf's sense. Naming is probably one way of emphasizing the importance of one's communal existence. Arab ways of self-identification used to be, and still are in most areas, bound to the identity of the dominant bloodline. Arab names used to be a chain of names connected by the word "Ibn," meaning "son of."[5] Clearly, all this refers overwhelmingly to the work of men from the educated and usually upper-class elite.

Arab Women's Autobiographies

If literary criticism of Arab men's autobiographies is so scarce, criticism of Arab women's autobiographies is nonexistent. The references above are all to men's autobiographies. Not a single text by a woman is mentioned, as if it were taken for granted that such texts simply do not exist. One reference, however, argued in three pages that Arab biographers gave women full consideration in that they compiled some books on leading women. In the ninth century, for example, Tahir al-Khurasani wrote a book on *The Rhetoric of Women: Their Eloquence, Their Humor, Stories of Those Who Were Influential, and Their Poetry in al-Jahiliah and the Beginning of Islam.* In the eleventh century, Abu al-Muzaffar Muhammad b. Ahmad al-Abiwardi wrote *The History of Women.* Leading women were also included in biographical anthologies of leading men. In modern times, the Syrian writer Zainab Fawwaz wrote a biographical book on Arab and western women called *The Scattered Pearls.* Aminah (the Prophet's mother) and Walladah (the Andalusian poet) were among the Arab women included, as were Queen Margaret of England and the Austrian empress Maria Teresa among western women.[6] Since Fawwaz's book, many women have written biographies of other women, usually well-known literary and historical figures, such as poets, warriors, queens, princesses, and the Prophet's mother and wives.

The first references to Arab women's autobiographical writings do not occur until the beginning of the twentieth century. The lack of published material, of course, is no evidence that Arab women did not write about themselves before this century. Above all, there has been no effort to trace this kind of women's writings, and it is beyond the scope of my book to do so.

This book studies a broad range of autobiographical texts by twentieth-century Arab women. These women are very diverse in that they live in varied socioeconomic circumstances and have different intellectual and educational backgrounds, from the highly educated to the illiterate; thus, they offer a spectrum of voices. They are writing, or telling, their stories within different contexts which may already have their own distinct sets of values, distribution of power, and norms of interaction. These contexts include structures such as the family, class, profession, village or city, and country in which these women find themselves. Within these structures, women (and men for that matter) are taught certain conventions, traditions, and morals, which in most cases deeply influence their behavior, their conceptions of themselves and of everything surrounding them, and their relationships with other people.

Placing each woman writer or teller of her story within her relevant context is essential, for her act of writing or telling is directly informed by it. The family seems to be the dominant context for most, if not all, of these women whose texts are examined here. Their consciousness is mainly embedded in familial ideologies, although other networks of social relations (such as friendships and circles of acquaintances through jobs) also affect them deeply. Although the act of writing or telling one's life story in itself is an act of self-acknowledgment in one way or another, these women could only assert their identities when they sought a departure from the restrictions of the family. The more daring the departure is, the clearer the sense of identity is.

Each text raises special questions relevant to it. However, there are also common issues in all the texts. In their self-writing, or self-telling, how far do these writers transcend or trespass beyond the boundaries and traditions of the cultures they are writing or telling within? Do they challenge or violate this culture, or do they try to save it? What strategies do they adopt in the passage from life to self-writing or self-telling? Is the act of writing or telling a way of freeing themselves from the traditional roles and images represented in their language? By breaking the silence, have they engendered new language, new motives, and new roles? Have they achieved a new power or authority that has enabled them to change their circumstances? To what extent is the writer or teller of her story the subject of her text? To what degree is the narrating "I" self-conscious or collective and socially identified? To what extent is the act of publicizing the self, through writing or telling it, a breakthrough from oppression to rebellion and possibly liberation?

Taking autobiographical writing as a form of story-telling, especially in an Arabic context, makes it difficult to avoid referring to a major story book which has inspired writers of different genres, Arab and western, for centuries. The narrative of *The Arabian Nights* is a story of salvation,[7] a theme particularly relevant to my thesis. Through the act of telling stories—that is, through the medium of the reproduction of words—Shahrazad managed to save not only her own life but also the lives of hundreds of potential wives of Shahriar. Death is conquered by narrative; silence is broken by discourse. Narrative becomes indispensable for life. Shahrazad's "cogito, ergo sum" becomes "I narrate, therefore, I am." How far is Shahrazad, then, an adequate model for these women whose texts are studied here—or do they go further than she did?

A study of *The Arabian Nights* as anti-*sira* and anti-biography is relevant here to argue that women's acts of self-narration challenge men's ways and traditions of displaying the individual self in writing.[8] *Sira*—the first model of biographical and autobiographical writing in Arabic literature—enjoys a multiplicity of characters, plots, and actions. Its narrative can be described as linear, however, in that everything centers on the main person whose *sira* is being narrated, whereas Shahrazad's narrative is circular in that it does not center on one climax. This is probably due to the fact that *sira*'s main raison d'être is to glorify a certain man, whereas Shahrazad's main purpose is to entertain the sultan in order to divert his attention from wanting to kill her to wanting to listen to her never-ending stories. Shahrazad herself, the heroic figure of *The Arabian Nights,* is a model of the idealized feminine woman in Arab Islamic cultures. She is an attractive, educated, well-brought-up daughter of a high-ranking official.

Shahrazad takes the place of the masculine hero of the *sira*. Instead of the battlefield on which the hero of the *sira* proves himself, Shahrazad carries out her struggles and her victories in a boudoir, while sitting in bed. She is armed with narrative and discourse. The hero of the *sira* is a man of great deeds; Shahrazad is a woman of great words. In *sira,* life is effectively transformed into narrative; Shahrazad does the opposite: she transforms narratives into life. When a woman writes her own story down on paper or tells it to others, she is asserting her autonomy by ordering her life into a composition and to that extent moving toward feminist consciousness, though, of course, some women achieve more than others through the act of self-writing or self-telling. Shahrazad is just an example. The texts discussed in this book come near or, better still, go further than Shahrazad and her narrative.

Authors and Editors

The voices or narratives of these women are all autobiographical but are produced in different forms: autobiographies, memoirs, interviews, and fictional autobiographies. Some of these women wrote their autobiographies or memoirs because they themselves wanted to; others were asked by someone who was interested in knowing about them, whether for research reasons or for personal ones; some famous and public women were interviewed to tell the story of their success or were asked to explain their personal views on different issues. Some texts were originally written in Arabic and were introduced to English readers by translators. Others were directly addressed to an English-reading audience by their original Arab writers or editors.

All these texts, then, can be described as being bicultural or even multicultural for different reasons and in different ways. Translation is one factor, for translators are never innocent of implementing their own linguistic and cultural conventions and assumptions in the texts they translate. Most of these texts are "hybrid products" or "multi-voiced,"[9] in that they are all edited, though in varying degrees. All texts are invisibly edited by the writers or the tellers of their stories, who usually, having a sense of audience in mind, shape their texts carefully and choose what is to be revealed and what is to stay hidden. Other texts are visibly edited by the translators using different techniques, such as giving the texts titles; arranging them into chapters and giving them headings; adding prefaces, introductions, epilogues, or footnotes; providing pictures; or omitting some material considered insignificant or not marketable. In spite of all that they do to the texts, these editors usually tell the reader that the text is the autobiography or the memoir as written or told by the "subject" herself, unaltered and unchanged. The editors or translators do not usually acknowledge their role in infusing their own lives into the supposedly autobiographical texts. My cross-cultural study of these texts addresses the effect of editorial interference—visible and invisible—on the reception of such texts, especially in that they are embedded in at least two cultures.

The chapters in Part Three are arranged according to the density of editing in each text. In other words, they start with the most heavily edited texts, where the voices of editors/translators are dominant, and end with the ones in which the voices of the original writers of their life stories are most audible. Chapter 6 looks at three recent anthologies of interviews conducted by academic women who tape-recorded other women from Arab countries: *Khul-Khaal, Doing Daily Battle,* and *Both Right and Left Handed.* The interviewees are of different ages and come from varied social, economic, and intellectual backgrounds. Most of them are illiterate, though of various but mainly working-class backgrounds. It is this last group of women which most interests me, for there are very few autobiographical or biographical texts by or about illiterate and working-class women in modern Arabic literature. Hence these anthologies provide a platform and a microphone for the women who have been voiceless and underrepresented. Therein lies their potential value.

Chapter 7 examines *Mountainous Journey, Difficult Journey* by Fadwa Tuqan (1917–), an upper-class Palestinian self-educated poet, translated in part by Donna Robinson Divine. Although the text is heavily edited, the role of the editor—who is also the translator—is less visible than the role of the writers of the anthologies of interviews discussed in Chapter 6, who are not presented as editors. They are more adequately called writers than editors in any case, because they have doubly written the so-called stories of the interviewees: they have not only translated from Arabic to English but, within the same process, have also translated oral dialects into written forms. Unlike English, spoken Arabic can be extremely different from written Arabic, which entails this double process of translation.

The last chapter discusses a fictional memoir, a political memoir, and a travel book by Nawal el-Saadawi (1931–), most of which are available in English. Saadawi is one of the Arab writers and women best known to western readers, for her books have been translated into many languages. Saadawi's texts are less heavily edited than all the previously mentioned works. The fact that she is a well-known writer could be one of the reasons why the translators of her books do not try to introduce, explain, and illustrate, as in the previous examples. Visible editing, then, is limited to translating. Saadawi herself, however, consciously or unconsciously, plays the part of the invisible editor of her own texts.

As a cross-cultural study of texts embedded in at least two cultures, this book examines the modes of production of texts. Given my interest in a modified Marxist and feminist theory, I also study the modes of oppression in every text, concentrating on the interaction of class and gender. And because I have chosen autobiographical writing, I examine the modes of self-representation in each text. These three theoretical pillars are the main basis of my applied analysis in the following chapters.

PART THREE

ANALYSIS OF TEXTS

CHAPTER SIX

Anthologies

In this chapter I examine three books published in the 1980s: *Khul-Khaal: Five Egyptian Women Tell Their Stories,* by Nayra Atiya;[1] *Doing Daily Battle: Interviews with Moroccan Women,* by Fatima Mernissi;[2] and *Both Right and Left Handed: Arab Women Talk about Their Lives,* by Bouthaina Shaaban.[3] As their subtitles indicate, all three books contain life stories of women from Arab countries. These books fall into one category not only because of their subject matter but also because they raise similar sets of questions relating to their technique and conditions of production. This chapter looks at the three texts jointly and makes some general points (which do not all apply to all of them to the same degree) before examining each text on its own.

In explaining my own position in relation to reading these anthologies of interviews I offer a critique of the process of stereotyping and generalization drawn from these anthologies by the authors/editors themselves (as in *Khul-Khaal*) and comment on how readers also tend to generalize even without editorial prompting (a process discussed later when analyzing the other two texts). Nonetheless, I still think that these same texts, read carefully, are potentially good sources of knowledge. I do not read these anthologies ethnographically—that is, I do not take the interviewee as typical of Arab culture, which I already know to be too complex to be represented by these women alone. However, I can still draw some conclusions, which necessarily entail some kind of generalization, about how a common culture affects self-image. "Common culture" here does not refer to a monolithic Arab culture as such but to the similar social and economic conditions which some of the women share. This discussion also examines how class and economic positions interact with gender in these anthologies and produce different forms of oppression (my generalizations, I trust, are not harmful and do not entail the risk of stereotyping involved in the cruder kinds of ethnographic reading).

Textual Strategies: Control and Dialogue

To start with, each of these books is multiauthored, in the sense that each one contains life stories of the interviewees and of the interviewer herself to different degrees. Although they are multiauthored, only one name is presented on the cover of each book as the writer. This is justified insofar as the interviewed women did not themselves write their stories but told them orally to the interviewers. Nor did they initiate the telling of their stories, without which these books would have been impossible; their stories were instead solicited by academic Arab women (Nayra Atiya, Fatima Mernissi, and Bouthaina Shaaban, respectively), whose names we read under the titles of the books. These books are also multiedited or at least doubly edited. Selectivity, which is necessarily practiced by any person who decides to record personal autobiography or memoirs, is here imposed according to specific criteria upon the interviewed women, who (at the request of Atiya, Mernissi, and Shaaban) answered certain selected questions about their lives. This is not to deny that the women themselves also, consciously or unconsciously, practiced selectivity. For they too must have chosen what to reveal in their answers and what to keep hidden. Generally speaking, all people exercise a strategy of deciding what to say depending upon whom they are addressing or who is likely to read or hear them.

The question of the implied or intended audience is especially relevant to these books. For they all are edited, structured, produced, and translated—in a word, textualized—for potential western readers. But the books have not been published in Arabic at all; Atiya and Shaaban translated the interviews and published them in English. Mernissi originally wrote her book in French, which was later translated for English readers by Mary Jo Lakeland. The fact that these books were published in English and French makes them more ethnographic material than simply life stories of Arab women. I use the term "ethnographic" not in the sense that the interviewed women are taken by Atiya, Mernissi, or Shaaban to be the "savage," "primitive," or "tribal" "others" who are the subjects of many ethnographic studies. The authors'/ editors' intention cannot be said to be the same as that of a western ethnographer who merely seeks the knowledge of an "other," usually perceived as "inferior," for private or public reasons or both. For besides wishing to display some kind of an alternative knowledge to western readers, the editors of these anthologies also aim—as their first objective, so they claim—to allow a public "voice" for the women who have been unrepresented or underrepresented. An English or French reader is still bound to read the interviewed women as "exotic others," however, and thus read their stories ethnographically.

Whether intentionally or not, these books are made polemical. On the one hand, the titles and subtitles present the books as stories of individual Arab women; in their introductions, the interviewers themselves declare their objective of wanting to break the silence of the underprivileged by allowing them a voice through which each of them can express herself freely and publicly. On the other hand, another objective for Atiya, Mernissi, and Shaaban, as they themselves admit, is to reveal to western readers their limited and mystified knowledge of Arab women. These works include the stories of many different women, from the illiterate to the professional (in Atiya's book there are no professional women as such, but two women went to preparatory school). The writers of these books, especially Shaaban, hope to show the diversity of conditions of Arab women and to present them as powerful and always struggling to better themselves by the means available to them, in contrast to what has been believed about them in the west. Demystifying the harem, which (except in some areas) nowadays hardly exists beyond western fantasies and discourse, is one of the main aims of these texts. Thus, these books offer a kind of knowledge about Arab women in general. The voices of these women cease to be voices of individual women; their stories are presented to be read and remembered mostly as typical of Arab women.

The number of women whose life stories are included in each book also contributes to their typification. Five women are interviewed in *Khul-Khaal*, twelve in *Doing Daily Battle*, and several dozen in *Both Right and Left Handed*. It becomes difficult for the reader to remember whose story is whose, either because the stories are so similar (as in Atiya's book) or because of the large number of women who are assigned limited space for their stories (as in the other two books). Moreover, the names of the women in *Khul-Khaal* are concealed under false ones, which makes them even more into types rather than individuals to be distinguished by their real names.

Furthermore, the nature of these books is dialogic: they are based on the question/answer model of interviews. Atiya, Mernissi, and Shaaban have conducted "discourses," an adequate term for such interviews borrowed from Emile Benveniste, whose definition of discourse as "a mode of communication in which the presence of the speaking subject and of the immediate situation of communication are intrinsic" is relevant to my reading of the three texts.[4] According to Benveniste's definition, discourse should not be read outside its specific situation or occasion, in which "a subject appropriates the resources of language in order to communicate dialogically."[5] The women in their answers did not transcend the immediate context and the limited situation in which dialogues were communicated through language. The use of "I" (which necessarily implies a "you"), and of other deictic indicators (such as "this," "that," "now," and so on) signals "the present instance of discourse rather than something beyond it."[6] In Benveniste's sense, then, discourse cannot or should not be interpreted outside its situation. But Atiya, Mernissi, and Shaaban did interpret the interviewees' discourses through the process of transforming them into texts. This process is called textualization, which is defined by James Clifford as a process through which unwritten behavior, speech, beliefs, oral tradition, and ritual come to be marked as a corpus, a potentially meaningful ensemble separated from an immediate discursive or performative situation.[7]

Textualization, then, is the shaping and preparation process which precedes interpretation of a discourse. I want to add to Clifford's comments that the process of textualization implies within it some kind of a conscious or unconscious generalization and typification, which also might lead to falsification. A textualized discourse may be turned into evidence of a generalized context, a cultural one. The textualization of the dialogic mode makes a type of a person. The subjectivities of the interviewed women are dissolved in the texts, but to varying degrees. In *Khul-Khaal,* textualization is taken to its extreme, whereas preserving the format of question and answer, as in the other two books, limits the extent of the process of textualization.

Before examining the extent of typification through textualization in each book separately, I want to argue that the convention of these kinds of texts (which are based on orally told stories conducted through interviews) was used by ethnographers as early as the nineteenth century. This method became valuable to anthropologists because it gave "the imprimatur of authenticity to their observations of the lifestyles" of the various "native" groups.[8] An American Indian, for example, may be interviewed over a period of time by a "white" ethnographer (who sometimes lives in the same household or nearby and probably learns some of the Indian's language) for the purpose of publishing a book, presenting it as the memoir or autobiography of the interviewed Indian as written by him/herself.[9] The question/answer model is, of course, repressed in a first-person narrative, and the narrative is usually supplied with many footnotes and pictures as well as forewords, introductions, appendices, and glossaries, usually with the help of a translator whose role is equally obscured. The interviewer, who is also the editor and probably the translator, denies any significant interference and, in effect, effaces him/herself in an attempt to claim full neutrality, sincerity, and authenticity in the disguised descriptive ethnography. Atiya's text fits adequately in this structure (as explained later).

Recent ethnographers, who have realized the need to announce themselves as the actual writers and interpreters of such so-called autobiographical accounts, keep the basic interview model in the final production of their texts. Presenting the discursive process in the form of a dialogue between two individuals somehow balances the authority of the ethnographer, it is claimed. That is, it gives a voice to the interviewee, whose knowledge as the other is sought—a voice which is no less distinct than that of the interviewer. This new mode is supposed to lessen the ethnographer's authoritative representation of the "other"; it does not completely stop typifying the "other" as a representative of a culture, however, although it does so to a lesser extent than in the repressed dialogic model. An example of such recent ethnographic material is a book called *Tuhami: Portrait of a Moroccan* (1980) written by Vincent Crapanzano, who questions ethnographic authority from within the discipline.[10]

Although the texts I am using are not written for ethnographic disciplines, in form, at least, they fit in this area. Like ethnographic books, these kinds of texts have had an increasing market in the west since the 1950s and form a new type of knowledge for westerners, who for centuries have been studying and speaking for the rest of the world. Their classification as books on social conditions of women in Arab countries brings them even closer to ethnography. Technically speaking, Atiya's book fits in the first model, whereas Mernissi's and Shaaban's books fit in the second. One main difference between ethnographic writing and the texts I am reading is that the writers of these texts are not foreign to the areas where they are conducting their interviews. They are western-educated Arab women. Their intention to present their material to westerners, however, makes their situation almost similar to that of American and European ethnographers who seek knowledge of what they usually see as (inferior) "other" cultures. Although the women interviewed in these books are not "the other" as such for Mernissi and Shaaban, they are so for Atiya, who went to Egypt as an adult woman from the United States. But, of course, even within one geographic area "the other" may be constructed through class, education, and dialectal difference.

Khul-Khaal: Repressed Dialogue

Khul-Khaal was first published in 1982 by Syracuse University Press in New York and was republished by Virago in London in 1988 with an afterword by Nawal el-Saadawi (I am using the London edition here). The book also has a foreword by Andrea B. Rugh, a professional American anthropologist, who reads the book from this standpoint. These stories "provide a mine of information for anthropologists and others seeking an understanding of Egyptian culture," she comments. Rugh makes generalizations from these five stories about "Muslim women" at large, although one of the *Khul-Khaal* women is Christian. She concludes from her reading, for example, that "the possibility men have to divorce fairly easily, however remote that eventuality, hangs like a cloud over the heads of Muslim women" (*KK*, xii), as if all Muslim women were living in fear of divorce and there were no Muslim women who would prefer a divorce to a marriage they were not happy in. Rugh also repeats some of the women's claim that "[m]oney and sex are the most basic problems discussed among Egyptian women" (*KK*, xii) as if it were the ultimate truth. Referring to Dunya's first husband, Hagg Ali, Rugh calls him instead "the Libyan" four times in her foreword; this makes him more of a stereotype than an individual.

Rugh does criticize western generalizations about "eastern people"— for example, that they have a "fatalistic nature" or that their women are "suppressed" and "passive." She explains that reading *Khul-Khaal* will correct some of the misrepresentation and misunderstanding of Egyptian and "Muslim" people. Rugh goes on, however, to romanticize the stories of the five Egyptian women. According to her, these women have "extraordinary natural perception about the world in which they live" (*KK*, vii), and they are philosophers. Such condescension is an underestimation of these Egyptian women, although Rugh is trying to prove the opposite. The term "natural" in itself implies underestimation, and calling them "philosophers" when they are being commonsensical implies that they are not even expected to have common sense. These women are "talented storytellers," but again Rugh generalizes this into a characteristic "particularly developed among the folk of Egypt" (*KK*, viii). The term "folk" romanticizes, generalizes, and dehistoricizes.

Rugh, then, reads *Khul-Khaal* as "an encounter with a new culture" (*KK*, xix), as she says. In her attempt to present the book to western readers, she makes Dunya, Suda, Om Gad, Om Naeema, and Alice stand for Egyptian, if not Muslim, women: the names of these women (false anyway) do not matter anymore. Instead of reading these accounts as life stories of individual women, the reader is led to generalize from them a knowledge about the culture that these women are made to exemplify.

Atiya was born in Egypt but moved to the United States at eleven, only to return to Egypt as an educated adult woman at thirty-three. Although she spoke Arabic, Egyptian society felt strange and foreign to Atiya. Writing

Khul-Khaal was her way of understanding Egypt. In her "Preface," she writes:

> I felt I was being allowed a privileged peek into a society I knew almost nothing about and which I longed to understand, as much as I longed to become intimately acquainted with an Egypt I had left to go to the United States some twenty-five years earlier. (*KK*, xxiii)

Although she is not an anthropologist herself, Atiya's situation is similar to Rugh's; for she, too, seeks knowledge of Egyptian society. Atiya denies that the five women are "representative of all Egyptian society" or "any particular social class or type of person" (*KK*, xxviii). But among all the stories that she collected on her tapes, she chose the five that touched her most, whose "richness of detail . . . added perspective to [her] efforts to understand Egypt and [her] people" (*KK*, xxviii). Atiya's selective and emotional reaction, which is different from the objective stance of "knowledge," indicates that these women are typified, to herself most of all; for through their stories she claims to have understood Egypt and the Egyptian people, and from them she draws a number of generalized conclusions. Atiya includes forty photographs in her book, which, she says, do not identify the five women but are meant to illustrate the texts. The reader looking at the photographs of men, women, and children is liable to take them as being representative of Egypt. The photographs, then, add to the process of typification.

Atiya tape-recorded these stories over a span of three years (1976–1979), yet the idea of publishing them is supposed to have been suggested by Rugh. Atiya also claims detachment from the stories: she says that she does not wish to make an analysis but prefers to leave the task for anthropologists and sociologists. Such a claim tends to conceal that the stories are her production more than anybody else's and that interpretation is already implied in her very writing and translation of them. Atiya did not have the women tell her their stories in one session. As she herself said, she met these women on many occasions, during which she recorded incidents and episodes of their lives. Yet Atiya collected and combined these elements as if they were "narrated" as complete stories. She admits editing the stories before translating them into English. Translation in itself changes a great deal: it "may render bizarre, exotic, downright irrational what would have been ordinary in its own context,"[11] as Crapanzano argues. Atiya's interpretation is carried out within a complex process: first, asking certain questions; second, editing fragmented stories; third, translating them; and, finally, producing the book *Khul-Khaal*.

The subtitle of the book, *Five Egyptian Women Tell Their Stories,* reads as if these women actually told their stories themselves. In spite of all the efforts to convince the reader that the book is a spontaneous telling of women's lives as they were told, however, the book is clearly Atiya's intended version of such stories, which should be kept in mind for any kind of reading.

Doing Daily Battle: Transparent Dialogue

Mernissi presents *Doing Daily Battle* in a much more straightforward way than Atiya. The subtitle is not disguised: it simply says *Interviews with Moroccan Women,* which conveys the real nature of the book. Unlike Atiya, Mernissi keeps the question/answer model in her final production of the book. Mernissi, herself a sociologist, does not try to efface her personal motives— nor herself for that matter. She declares early in her introduction that the objective of the book is to break the ancestral silence of Moroccan women but also to see how Morocco appears through the words of its women. The implication is that the book is intended as knowledge about twentieth-century Moroccan women, but with no denial by the writer herself. It is meant to show the reader, first, that the harem time is almost over—only one of the twelve women (Batul Binjallna) spent her life in an actual harem—and, second, that Moroccan women have a different story to tell about their lives and about their society than that told by men. But who is this knowledge addressed to?

Having been first written in French then translated into English, *Doing Daily Battle* is clearly addressed to western readers. The introduction and the footnotes give details to readers who are presumed to know either very little or nothing or who have distorted knowledge of Morocco. The "Glossary" is particularly addressed to those who know no Arabic at all. French is widely spoken among the Moroccan educated elite, who also are potential readers of Mernissi's book. As a rhetorical device and as a way of anticipating "his" response, Mernissi pretends to address herself particularly to an intended reader who belongs to this last group (whom she calls "Mr Terrorist") and who, she claims, would reject her book on the basis that the interviewed women are not representative of Moroccan reality. "Mr Terrorist" stands for the men who monopolize the symbolic values of Arab societies. "Terrorist tactics" are adopted by these men, according to Mernissi, whenever a woman stands up to express herself, either by stopping her or by denigrating what she says. Mernissi explains to these men (who also reject feminist ideas as "imported" and hence contradictory to the local "cultural heritage") that, although her women are not claimed to be representative of Moroccan women, their stories are real. Many "terrorist" men in other Arab countries speak only Arabic, however, and would not have Mernissi's message passed on to them.

While Atiya tries to conceal herself in her book, Mernissi avoids self-effacement in two ways. First, she introduces herself fully to the reader, summarizing her own story, unlike Atiya, who keeps herself unknown to the reader except for the publisher's eleven-line summary of her life. By telling her story, Mernissi equates it with the stories of the women in her book, while Atiya looks detached and aloof. Second, Mernissi does not try to disguise herself by omitting her questions and diffusing the dialogue into a first-person narrative, as Atiya does. Mernissi even admits that she was not objective in her attitude toward the women she interviewed: most of them were illiterate, and she says that she had a special affinity with them because she remained illiterate herself until the age of twenty. Mernissi refers disapprovingly to the objectivity of the "research technique" she was taught in French and American departments of sociology and anthropology. She also admits her "intervention in the preparation of the words of interviewees for the printed page" (*DDB*, 19).

By preserving the question/answer model, Mernissi preserves some authority for these women and also some sense of identity. The answers are not taken out of context; nor are they generalized into complete stories. Thus, these women are not presented as typical, as are the women in Atiya's book. Mernissi's aim of depicting the stories of the women as facets of Moroccan reality, and not as the Moroccan reality, can be said to be achieved.

Mernissi considers her book an initiative toward understanding herself as well as the women she interviewed. This claim may very well be true, and I do not wish to dispute it. In fact, most people who have done this kind of research claim that they themselves go through a process of self-examination and self-understanding during and after the interviews. Crapanzano, for example, admits that he learned much about himself and his world through his encounter with Tuhami and argues that fieldwork of this kind must be understood as a process of continual discovery and self-discovery.[12] The point I would make in relation to Mernissi's claim, however, is that she gives no tangible evidence for the reader to see her self-discovery taking place in the pages of her book. In other words, she does not translate for the reader the process of self-comprehension that she claims is taking place in her consciousness, whereas the third book I want to consider does exactly this.

Both Right and Left Handed: Integrated Dialogue

Shaaban presents her book *Both Right and Left Handed* (published in 1988) as part of her struggle for "mutual self-discovery among women" (*BRLH*, 2). She achieves this not only by telling her own story, and with more details than Mernissi, but by full reciprocation in her conversation with the women she meets. "Conversation" is a more adequate term to describe Shaaban's dialogue with the women than "interview," because although she (like Mernissi) preserves the question/answer model, she does so in a narrative mode. Mernissi registered her interviews in a formal and journalistic way, identifying questions with the letter "Q" and answers with "A." Shaaban preserves the dialogic mode as a novelist does. Technically speaking, her book reads as an autobiography. Shaaban herself can be read as the main character, who is seeking self-understanding by the detour of comprehension of other women, the other characters. Unlike Atiya and Mernissi, Shaaban tells the reader about the time and place of her conversations with the women and explains when and through whom she met them. She describes the women themselves, how they dress, how they behave, and what they feel. She even introduces side plots, like quoting the conversation she overheard at the bus stop between two unknown women.

Above all, Shaaban reflects upon herself. Every now and then, she flashes back to her own life and her relationship with her husband and her family, by narrating an incident or by comparing her own situation to those of the women she talks to. This technique makes Shaaban equal with the women she meets, more so than Mernissi. Apart from being the writer of the book, Shaaban does not seem to be practicing authority, which could make the women look like inferior others whose stories are narrated with fascination and an awareness of difference (as in Atiya's book). The women in Shaaban's book (as in Mernissi's book) might still be read as more typical than individual because Shaaban too selects the theme questions; however, the large number of women and the diversity of their stories make them more representative of their societies than, say, five Egyptian women whose stories are presented as almost the same.

There are also situations where Shaaban is engaged in a conversation with more than one woman at a time. This makes her book a real "attempt to enable a number of women caught up in a burning moment in history to share experience with others" (*BRLH*, 2). Shaaban, though, has in effect limited the audience that could share her experience and those of the women in her book to English readers. Her stated purpose in publishing the book is

to enable other Arab women and Western women to share something of
my experience, and to hear for themselves the voices of these women—
fighters and professionals, politicians, devoted wives and faithful mothers of martyrs. (*BRLH*, 1–2)

But, of course, the number of Arab women who can read English is very
limited; the majority of them will not be able to share the experience Shaaban wants them to. This is a point I want to make in relation to all three
books I have discussed in this chapter. Atiya, Mernissi, and Shaaban have limited the effect of their books by not publishing them in Arabic, a language
they all know very well. Yet there are some publishers, such as Al-Saqi Books
in London, that support feminist writing and publish such books. Had they
been available in Arabic, these books could have contributed to the cause of
Arab feminism. Reading these books in an Arabic context, given their potential value, would have fewer of the problematic aspects of the ethnographic
use discussed above.

Shaping the Dialogues: Themes

Thus, we see that the themes around which these three books center cannot
be voluntarily and freely chosen by the women interviewed but are consciously and knowingly selected by the writers of the books. Rugh tries to ab-
solve Atiya of deliberately choosing the themes of marriage, death, and circumcision, claiming that "the vivid details of these events have naturally
flowed out of the narrative, not selected by [Atiya], but chosen by the women
themselves as the subjects around which to organize their discourses" (*KK*,
xxi–xxii). In Atiya's "Preface," however, we sense some kind of confession
that she herself chose these topics. Atiya, fascinated by the experiences that
Dunya went through, chose to "round out" these common experiences by
making them the center of her intended book. Mernissi does not deny that
she aims in her book to see how the Moroccan women perceive "three phenomena: sex roles, the marital couple, and contraception" (*DDB*, 5). Her
questions are directed toward these issues.

In Shaaban's book, the topics are varied and carefully chosen according to
each woman's educational background. Unlike Atiya and Mernissi, Shaaban
did not ask the women she met only about their personal lives but brought
them into serious discussions about different issues. There are discussions on
family upbringing, interfamily and arranged marriages, motherhood, hetero-
sexuality and homosexuality, relations between husbands and wives, mothers
and sons and daughters, traditions, religions, education, professions and ca-

reers, the law, politics, feminism, the dichotomy between the private and the public and between theory and practice, comparisons between the position of western and Arabic women, and so on. The women include the illiterate and the highly educated, those who work as mothers and wives only and those who combine professions with these roles, the young and the old, the submissive and the rebellious or the feminist, the liberal and the militant. I am not trying to set these books up along a spectrum of truth/falseness as such, but I want to show how they differ not only in form (as explained earlier) but also in content.

There are no complete life stories in these anthologies; there are rather extracts of lives. Each woman is interviewed within a limited time, and a limited space is assigned to each woman's story. Moreover, the types of questions addressed to each woman dictate what she tells about her life. Hence, questions related to the representation of self (which are addressed in the following chapters in relation to memoirs and autobiographies) cannot be examined in relation to the short extracts in these anthologies. Although the stories are fairly short and organized in accordance with certain questions, I want to look at the issues these women raised in their accounts and also the issues raised by the way they presented their accounts or the way these accounts have been presented for them by the editors.

I read the "voices" of these women as calling for political action and change, when they talk about the necessity of education, when they complain about their arranged marriages, and when they publicly describe certain sexual practices which contribute to their oppression. Their spelling out of sexual issues can be read as an act of publicizing what is perceived in their societies to be the most "private" and taboo of all matters. I see the practice of female circumcision and the ceremony of the bride's defloration both performed in a semipublic way as a contradiction in a society which considers sex a taboo question. Spilling the female child's blood at circumcision and displaying the bride's virgin blood at defloration turn the female body into an object of control and a device to publicize the honor of the family in its men's interest. In these anthologies, the women publicize these "private" issues by talking about them too, but in this case in their own interest.

Change through Work and Education

Most of the women who "speak" in these books and who are illiterate and from the working class do not offer a strong sense of individual self in the western sense of the term, though as noted later there are signs of self-reflection on their position. That is to say, they do not talk of themselves as independent individuals or of their lives as being of their own making, although it must always be remembered that a different impression might have been produced had they been asked different questions. These women often attribute their "miserable" lot to fate or destiny, in accord with conventional religious teaching. However, they do not seem to be totally submissive to such fate, for they themselves acknowledge the need for change through education and work, and there are moments when they appear to aspire to a way of distinguishing themselves from others. Aware that if they sit at home without work their poor families or husbands cannot look after them, these same women go to look for work everywhere, no matter how far from home, in contrast to the traditional role assigned by middle and upper-class men, which confines women's work to the private realm of the household.

Learning a skill or a trade is essential for most of these women's and their children's survival. For some women, paid work is necessary for more than just survival. Nazha, for example, could not have continued her education had she not worked during vacations and after school hours. Necessity, however, is not the only reason why some of these women go out to work. Dawiya al-Filaliya (born in 1913 in Morocco) did not like her second husband's preventing her from working outside the home, although he could afford a comfortable life for her. For her, work was a means of socialization and integration with different people (*DDB*, 94). Suda, a Sudanese Egyptian, did not mind doing any type of work, even work as a maid, a job which she had to deny doing because her male guardians considered it "shameful." For Suda, any job is good as long as it gives her a "clean piaster." Work provides her with economic independence, which gives her the right to choose when and whom she will marry. For these women, whether it is to spare them the humiliation of begging or dying of hunger or to support their education or even just to be able to communicate and socialize with more people, paid work provides them with some kind of independence, authority, and respect, making them less liable to be oppressed and exploited by their men. Om Gad, for example, who helps her husband at the garage workshop, is the manager of the household financial affairs. Every now and then, her husband gives her all the money they have made, and she looks after the spending and the savings. Had he not trusted her ability to do so, he would never have given her control of the family's finances.[13]

Speaking in the 1970s and 1980s, these women are also aware that education can provide them with better-paid jobs and more humane conditions at work. Those who missed the chance of going to school are very keen on their children's education, for both sons and daughters. Dawiya admits that when she was young she did not know that education was important for her daughters; she did not enroll the eldest and accepted that the younger should leave school because she did not seem to be interested and because Dawiya thought that education would not help her daughters to find a job. But later she realizes that "an educated girl is somebody. A trade is also useful, but an education is more important" (*DDB*, 104). For Zubaida, too, education makes "somebody" of a girl. She was forced to leave school at the age of eleven, so she was trying hard to ensure that her daughters continued their education. For Alice, education and having a profession, for a woman, mean "not only self-support but a chance to have a say in things that matter to her" (*KK*, 39). This thirst for education is an essential part of the life stories of Fadwa Tuqan and Nawal el-Saadawi (examined in the following chapters). Among the working classes especially, this interest in education is part of a rising consciousness which is rapidly spreading even in the remotest areas in the Arab countries. It is surely a great help and hope for Arab feminism; for education helps people to question conditions that they would have taken for granted before.

The educated women are, first, more conscious of themselves and of what they have achieved and, second, more gender-conscious than their illiterate sisters. Abla, for example, is proud to have gotten her academic job in the History Department in Damascus University in 1947, when most urban middle- and upper-class girls were doomed to "suffer the boredom of spending their time in total isolation at home waiting for eligible husbands" (*BRLH*, 32–33). Abla talks about social discrimination against women in every field and criticizes "the degrading and outdated laws" of the country. She acknowledges the improvement in women's position since the seventies but pleads with all women to continue the struggle for "real equality."

Makboula Shalaq is a lawyer who made history by being the first Syrian woman university student in 1941. She criticizes the dichotomy between what men preach and what they practice. Like Abla, Shalaq admits that Syrian women have proven their capacity and creativity in every field, yet they "are still regarded first and foremost as cooks and cleaners and only secondarily as creative workers" (*BRLH*, 45).

Thorea Hafez is proud to talk about her participation in the nationalist struggle for women's rights. She tells the story of the time in 1943 when she gathered with other women in the main square in Damascus and they publicly took off their veils.[14] Hafez compares the past and the present and sees that Syrian women have achieved complete equality, especially now that the law has been reformed to women's advantage. She goes on to draw a rosy picture of the situation. Hafez is, of course, talking from her upper-class position and overlooks the situation of other women whose poverty can prevent them from deploying the law on their side. This point is raised by Amal, a law student, who thinks that the law in Syria is "illiberal," remote from social reality and biased against women, as all the judges are men. Amal also perceives that the main problem from which Arab women suffer is the dichotomy of "what seems to be and what actually is, of our public and personal lives" (*BRLH,* 68). This important issue will be raised again by Fadwa Tuqan and Nawal el-Saadawi.

Family, Class, and Feminist Consciousness

To say that the more educated have more feminist consciousness is not to say that the illiterate women are not aware of any kind of oppression related to their gender. Malika, for example, who was never enrolled in school, sees marriage as an institution where women are oppressed, although she expresses it in her own simple terms. Had her father been alive (the father stands for social and emotional security, as discussed below) and had she had a well-paid job, Malika says that she would never have wanted to get married. She prefers to work for her mother and herself rather than to serve a husband (*DDB,* 122).[15] However, what we notice from the illiterate working-class accounts is that they are more aware of the problems they suffer as poor people rather than as women. In other words, class-consciousness is more striking than gender-consciousness in their accounts. Om Gad's class-consciousness, for example, is clear in her argument about her daughter's marriage. She wants her to marry a man of their own class; she does not want a middle- or upper-class son-in-law who would ridicule and humiliate them (*KK,* 22). Om Gad's gender-consciousness is very limited. There are a lot of stereotypical statements in her story. She thinks that her son is "a real man" because nothing moves him (*KK,* 7) and that "men are never afraid" (*KK,* 14). Om Gad is aware that "a girl's life is difficult," but she thinks that this is the case in "every sort of family and among all nationalities" and does not "know why" (*KK,* 17–18). In other words, she is aware that a girl suffers more than a boy, but this awareness is overshadowed by her worry about her poor family's survival.

Working-class women may not develop a clear gender-consciousness, as the educated middle- and upper-class women may; however, they are more likely to develop not only a maturer class-consciousness than middle- and upper-class women but also a feeling of solidarity with the women of at least their own class. In the absence of any form of health insurance at work, Dawiya al-Filaliya, who worked in a hand-made carpet workshop, speaks about how the women workers hide the sick ones in the middle of the wool and do their work so that the boss will not notice any reduction in production, which is his main concern (*DDB*, 99). Alice, conscious of her middle-class position, praises the working class's feeling of collectivity and readiness to unite and help each other, in contrast to middle-class "selfishness" (*KK*, 52).

Educated or uneducated, upper-, middle-, or working-class, aware of their unjust conditions or not, class- or gender-conscious or both, these women do not speak about themselves independently from their respective families. The family/class position is the milieu within which these women (and the women whose texts are studied in the following chapters) tell their stories. The family remains the main social unit in all Arab countries. The extended family is the old form, which still exists; however, the new form, which consists of a married couple and their children only, is rapidly taking over in most Arab countries, especially in the cities.

Whether extended or not, the family still plays a controversial role in Arab women's lives. In the family, many if not most women experience the first forms of discrimination from their fathers and brothers. Yet at the same time, for many women, these same figures (fathers and brothers) can be the first source of social protection and support. The father either symbolizes utter oppression for some or is idealized by others, especially in his absence—or, more paradoxically, both simultaneously. The women in *Khul-Khaal* think that their lives could have been much better had their fathers been alive. We have seen how Shaarawi idealizes her dead father, whereas, as we shall see later, Tuqan tells how unjust and discriminatory her father was to her. The brother also can be the source of either more oppression or more support and help or both. If it was not for her brother, who had to leave school and look for a paid job, Nazha Zannati and her children could have not survived after the death of her husband. Shaaban's brother, however, caused her a lot of suffering. The brother relationship is a major theme in most Arab women's life stories and is studied in the following chapters as well. This is why the women in these anthologies (and in the following chapters) weave their life stories around their families and their family relationships.

Women Oppressing Other Women

The male members of the family may very well be the first oppressors of women; nevertheless, the women themselves are not completely innocent of all blame and responsibility. For they themselves exercise some kind of discrimination and even oppression, one could say, upon their own daughters, thus perpetuating the very problem they have been suffering from. Twenty-year-old Leila, from Damascus, tells how her mother discriminates against her, although she is her only daughter. The mother had herself rebelled against her own family and eloped with a man and as a consequence was "cut off from her social milieu." Yet, Leila comments, her mother loves her five sons, while having a "nervous, erratic relationship" with her only daughter. Moreover, while stipulating to her sons that they could marry any woman of their own choice, the mother has tried to force her daughter into an arranged marriage, according to Leila. Leila tries to excuse her mother, though, because she needed an outlet "and there was no-one around her on whom she could exercise authority except" Leila (*BRLH*, 69–70).

Egyptian Om Gad was proud and happy when she had "four men" who "filled the house with their presence. Their comings and goings were my joy. They made me feel needed and gave me hope in the future" (*KK*, 10). But she does not mention anything special about her three daughters. Om Gad is a simple woman who might not see anything wrong with preferring boys to girls, perhaps because she sees everybody else doing so. But what excuse can Alice, a middle-class educated woman, have when she admits that she prefers sons to daughters? Her marriage experience led to her "blind hatred" and "distrust" of all men and to regret that she ever married, as she repeats on many occasions, and she intelligently criticizes the social injustice against women in her society. She even seems to be conscious that preferring sons to daughters is not a very good thing (although she does not admit it overtly), for she says that there is one good thing to be said in her husband's favor—namely, that he prefers daughters to sons (*KK*, 42).

Bodily Mutilation

Preferring sons to daughters, or discriminating between them, is only one form of many ideological contradictions which are to be traced in almost every Arab woman's life. Arab feminists have yet to liberate themselves fully from all the effects caused by centuries of oppression. Ideological contradictions of this kind sometimes materialize in physical forms of oppression such as the tradition of circumcision, which is still in practice in some areas in Egypt, the Sudan, and other African countries, among Muslims and Christians alike. Although a complete stranger to this tradition, I do not hesitate to call circumcision a mutilation of the female body. Doctor Saadawi, who herself experienced it, was one of the first people to criticize this operation and call for its prohibition because of the pain and danger it inflicts upon women. The five women in *Khul-Khaal* describe this "unforgettable" experience in its horrid details, which I prefer not to quote here because of their sickening effect. It is enough to say that Suda describes it as an "ordeal" and as "hell." All of the women were circumcised in the presence of their mothers, who in their turn had been circumcised too. Having gone through the pain and torture they so vividly remember, these women helped to pass the same experience to their daughters.

Alice recalls the experience with severe criticism. On the one hand, girls are brought up and prepared for their future role as wives who have the duty of sexually entertaining their husbands; on the other hand, they themselves are not supposed to enjoy sex, for circumcision "makes it harder for a girl to enjoy sex," according to Alice (*KK,* 41). Even Alice, however, took her eldest daughter to be circumcised, although she went to a doctor to make it less painful for her; when the doctor told her that the operation was illegal, she resorted to a midwife. But Alice did regret doing that and saved her younger daughter, who was fortunate enough to be born at a time when this operation was becoming less and less popular, especially in urban areas.[16]

The same operation is supposed not to affect women's sexual desires according to Om Gad, although she still describes it with similar painful details as Alice and the other women do. For Om Gad thinks that an uncircumcised girl is "disfigured" (*KK,* 13). She does not say whether she was sexually affected or not. But even if she was not, this does not mean that Alice is wrong. Medical research has shown that circumcision does affect women's sexuality because the operation destroys very sensitive parts of the woman's sexual organs. One could argue that Muslim and Jewish boys are circumcised too. However, the effect of the operation has never been reported to have negatively affected men's sexuality in any way. On the contrary, boys are usually proud that they are circumcised. For them, it makes them clean and virile. Above all, the difference lies in the different anatomy of men and women, which means that female circumcision can lead to more infections and diseases as well as physical pain.

Another kind of bodily mutilation, which I had never heard of until I read *Khul-Khaal*, is the bride's deflowering by the hand. The *Khul-Khaal* women recall the disgust, pain, and humiliation they felt when they were deflowered on their wedding night. In Arab and Muslim countries, in rural areas in particular, the honor of the family is still measured against the virginity of daughters before marriage. In some cases for a marriage to be complete the bride's proof of virginity, a bed linen or a piece of cloth stained with her blood, has to be shown to everybody concerned. The convention of wedding parties in these countries has helped this tradition to continue. For wedding ceremonies, celebration, and consummation take place in the bride's or bridegroom's parents' house, where the mothers of the wedded couple check the wedding bed in the morning. Until very recently, some brides have paid with their lives as punishment for failing the test. Some were pressured to commit suicide rather than live as outcasts for the rest of their lives.

This tradition, it must be said, is gradually dying. Arranged marriages are becoming less fashionable. A man and a woman can choose to marry anyone they want provided their respective families agree. Even when the families do not agree, a man and a woman can elope and get married somewhere else: Beirut was a place where lovers fled when all other Arab countries were still very strict as far as marriages were concerned. Whether arranged or unarranged, wedding consummation no longer has to take place in the parents' house. People who can afford it travel for a honeymoon after the wedding party; in that case it is only the groom who decides what to do if he finds out that his bride is not a virgin. Today Arab men have different attitudes toward this issue. The question of women's virginity before marriage is still important to many. Some men do not marry women they have been in love with and slept with before marriage, on the grounds that a woman who sleeps with a man before marriage may also sleep with other men before and after marriage—she would be considered loose. This is why some women who lose their virginity before marriage resort to a doctor who can amend their hymen just before the wedding is to take place. Again, women are exploited by these same doctors, who charge them a great deal of money and blackmail them as well, for it is an illegal operation.

This discussion might seem a diversion, but it is not. I want to show that the way the *Khul-Khaal* women were deflowered must be one of the most traditionalist and, I dare say, ugliest ways. The women were not even left alone with their husbands on the wedding night. The deflowering—which was performed using the finger, either by the husband himself or by an old woman relative—was witnessed by a host of women relatives, including the mothers of the bride and bridegroom. The main cultural contradiction here is that sex is one of the taboos in Arabic cultures. Few would talk about sex publicly, especially within the family, yet the way the *Khul-Khaal* women are treated on their wedding nights makes it appear as if this sexual action were a public event. Moreover, I consider this way of deflowering a kind of mutilation because the women themselves describe it like this. Om Gad, at thirteen, had not yet developed breasts or menstruated when she was married to a man twice her age. After the nauseating deflowering, she was left "limp" and "afraid," yet the husband went on mounting her all through the night (*KK*, 15). Alice complained that she "was sore for about ten days" after her wedding night (*KK*, 38).

The other two anthologies do not raise the issues of circumcision and deflowering, except for a brief reference to deflowering in Rabi'a's story. Answering Mernissi's question: "Did [your sister] accompany you in order to bring back the panties?" Rabi'a said: "I wanted it to be done by a doctor." Rabi'a was married at a distance to a man in France. She traveled with her sister from Morocco for the marriage consummation. Someone has to bring back proof of the bride's virginity when the marriage is consummated away from the parents, which is what Mernissi meant by "bring back the panties." I would not have understood Rabi'a's answer had I not read *Khul-Khall*. Rabi'a wanted her deflowering to be done by a doctor, because she was frightened. This reference indicates that the same tradition of hand deflowering is also practiced in Morocco; but the women in *Doing Daily Battle* did not talk about it, no doubt because they were not specifically asked to do so.

Uncovering Sex and Sexuality

The question is: would the *Khul-Khaal* women have spoken about circumcision and deflowering had they not been deliberately asked to? Huda Shaarawi recorded her own memoirs before she died, entrusting her cousin to publish them. Shaarawi was an Egyptian and lived one generation before the oldest woman in *Khul-Khaal* (1879–1947). Circumcision and hand deflowering must have been in practice then, but she referred to neither of them. Shaarawi, however, was an aristocrat, whose style of propriety and gentility would have made it difficult for her to refer to any sexual/physical experience she might have had. She recorded her memoirs in the 1940s, whereas the *Khul-Khaal* women (most of whom are working-class) were interviewed in the 1970s and the 1980s. Fadwa Tuqan, a Palestinian, did not touch upon any sexual/physical matter, although her autobiography was first published in the 1970s. Until recently, this shyness about sex and anything to do with it has been characteristic of Arab women's writings.

The fifties marked a kind of revolution in this field: the Egyptian Nawal el-Saadawi published both scientific research and fiction criticizing the sexual oppression of women, for which she was censured by some Arab governments as a promiscuous woman. A Lebanese woman, Leila Baalbaki, published a novel (*I Live*) in which she described the sexual satisfaction felt by the heroine and was put on trial for offending decency by the Lebanese authorities, then considered the most liberal among Arab countries. Since that time, a number of brave Arab women writers have been taking the questions of sex and sexuality beyond just criticism to a much more open and positive advocacy of women's right to sexual pleasure and fulfillment, including Ghada al-Samman (Syrian), Hanan al-Shaikh and Huda Barakat (Lebanese), and Sahar Khalifa (Palestinian).[17] Homosexuality and lesbianism are now being uncovered and written about, and premarital sex can be explored in writing as well as in reality. Sexual pleasure, not only oppression, is also described. Some Arab governments still heavily censor such writings as corrupt, but things are constantly changing.

In *Both Right and Left Handed*, Shaaban herself ventures into uncovering lesbian practices among some Arab women. She writes about the women she has seen in a back room at the hairdresser's in Damascus. She also asks one of her interviewees whether she has thought of making love to her friend. Om Muhammad, an illiterate woman who had just celebrated her sixtieth birthday at the time of the interview, was married to a man who already had a wife. After some tension in the beginning, the co-wives became "friends." Om Muhammad was relieved when her husband "took the unilateral decision not to sleep with [her]" (*BRLH,* 63). Answering Shaaban's question, Om Muhammad tells how one cold night she and her "friend" slept together and how much they enjoyed it:

> As usual, we felt close and intimate. Our legs touched, we hugged and we kissed each other, and suddenly our hearts started beating fast. We started panting, feeling all the warm blood in the world thrust into our veins. (*BRLH,* 65)

The women in *Khul-Khaal* do not speak about their own sexual desires. When they speak about sex, they refer to other women and seem to be inhibited about talking about their own sexuality. Om Gad thinks that women should be "reasonable" about sex and that it is shameful for women to ask for sex. She complains that there are some women who

> just want a man all the time. Others don't. There are some women who want a man with them morning, noon, and night. If a night passes when he hasn't "bathed" with her, as we call it, she becomes angry, nervous, and ill-humoured. (*KK,* 13)

It is also shameful for the woman in Suda's story who used to complain about her husband who had not slept with her for some time. She thought it was humiliating to ask for sex: "What can I do? Am I to sell myself? Do you think I can stoop so low as to say 'Come to me I want you?'" (*KK,* 75). Suda tells the story and sounds appalled when she comments that Egyptian women were obsessed with sex and money (*KK,* 79). Sex, for women who are forced into marriages at an age when they do not even understand the meaning of the word, is perceived as no more than a marital duty. In *Doing Daily Battle* and in *Khul-Khaal,* most of the women were married before they had the chance to have any kind of love relationship. In that case, "sex is hateful, and a girl approaches it with fear," according to Alice (*KK,* 38).

The inhibition about talking about one's own sexuality among working-class women does not match the view expressed by middle- and upper-class women, who assume that working-class women are uninhibited about their bodies. Tuqan, for example, as we shall see in the next chapter, expresses her admiration for the working-class women whom she used to see in the Turkish bath moving around freely with their bodies naked, whereas the richer women seemed embarrassed to do the same. This phenomenon can be explained as a result of not only having to work with other women during the day because of poor working conditions but also sharing other bodily activities, such as bathing and sleeping, at home with other female members because of lack of enough space for each woman to have her own room. Lack of privacy at work and at home lessens some of the women's inhibitions about their bodies, without their necessarily losing inhibition about their own sexuality.[18]

The lack of premarital love in these women's lives is not the only reason why sex is perceived as a burden (by Om Muhammad) or as shame (by Om Gad). The hardship of everyday life also contributes to limiting the sexual lives of these women. As Alice comments, women need to love but also to be financially secure and bodily comfortable to be able to enjoy sex:

> When a woman has no problems in her life and she loves the man she is married to, then sex is a pleasure. But if there is struggle or daily hard-

ship connected with any part of her life, she resists it. It becomes intolerable to her. There is no sweetness in loving if you are in financial straits. (*KK*, 38)

Most of the women in *Doing Daily Battle* have to work long hours in bad conditions in order to survive. Sex would not be the main issue in their life stories. It is significant that the only woman in *Khul-Khaal* who spoke about sex—Alice—connected it with class position and is a middle-class woman who, although a working mother, did not have to work long hours in bad conditions. The working-class women, by contrast, did not make a big issue of sex. Om Gad, for example, seems to be more submissive about the whole issue; having gone through a painful deflowering on her wedding night, as she describes it, she simply got "used" to her husband's demanding sex all that night.

Women like Om Gad do not seem to be aware that there is any kind of oppression in circumcision, hand deflowering, or the institution of marriage as a whole. Circumcision is a tradition which many of them pass to their own daughters. Om Gad's main concern, in regard to her daughters, is to "place [them] happily in some man's house" (*KK*, 9). Women like Om Gad, who believe strongly in traditions, do not see how their oppression as women could be different from that of the men of their own class. The similar bad conditions that both the men and the women of the working classes share make them brothers and sisters in suffering. Working-class women's sympathetic attitude toward the men of their class seems to inhibit any awareness of distinct gender oppression being practiced upon them. The lack of education and the belief in superstition and black magic, as we see in these anthologies, help these women to overlook their own suffering as women. It seems that women are more likely to be aware of their own oppression when they are educated and when they have the luxury of working and living in conditions that provide them with some kind of privacy and some spare time (privileges enjoyed by middle- and upper-class women). Education opens women's eyes to the falsity of many beliefs held as unquestionable traditions or else presents alternative values and lifestyles, leading to inner conflict; and comfortable working and living conditions give them the time to think of themselves, as I have argued.

Exchange of Women?

I have commented on the women's differing educational and class positions; of equal importance is the historical process of economic changes and cultural shifts that allows older traditions and newer practices, older modes of thinking and newer ideals, to coexist in one society. The practice of male and female circumcision but more particularly the practice of the semipublic deflowering can be seen as characteristic of marriage as a system of exchange between extended families. Such a system of exchange may be described as patriarchal inasmuch as the token of exchange is the female rather than the male body. The ritualistic significance attached to virginity and the much more drastic intervention in the female circumcision of the body (compared to male circumcision) reduce the young woman, more than the young man, to an object of value being exchanged.

The existing arranged marriages in Arab countries might be described as reminiscent of older times when the tribe or the extended family was (as it still is in some Gulf countries) the basic unit of the society. In such a society, the interest of the tribe or the family is above the individual's interest. The bodies of both men and women are completely taken up as social objects to enhance social alliance between families or tribes. In my feminist reading I am concerned with the much more drastic interventions and control of women's bodies evident in such practices as female circumcision, rather than with men's bodies, but the interrelatedness of the social control of women and men should be noted.

The idea of the exchange of women in marriage was discussed by Friedrich Engels in *The Origin of the Family: Private Property and the State* (1884) and by Claude Lévi-Strauss in *The Elementary Structures of Kinship* (first published in 1949). Engels argues that since antiquity, throughout the Middle Ages and up to modern times, marriage for the people who usually count as society (the free men and women and later the feudal and then the bourgeois classes) has been "arranged by the parents and the partners calmly accept their choice."[19] Marriage in this sense becomes "a contract, a legal transaction" by which women, especially, are exchanged. With the advancement of capitalism, the dependence of marriage on economic considerations has become complete: for the bourgeoisie, marriage "is a political act, an opportunity to increase power by new alliances; the interest of the house must be decisive, not the wishes of an individual."[20]

Claude Lévi-Strauss, as a structuralist, also views the exchange of women in marriage as universal. In *The Elementary Structures of Kinship*, he sees women being treated, like words, as signs that can be exchanged. The difference is that women, unlike words, are persons and thus have a different kind of value. According to Lévi-Strauss, women are seen under two incompatible aspects: on the one hand, as the object of personal desire, thus exciting sexual and proprietorial instincts; and, on the other, as the subject of the desire of others, and seen as such, i.e., as the means of binding others through alliance with them.[21]

The exchange of women, which he believes takes different forms, "direct or indirect, general or special, immediate or deferred, explicit or implicit, close or open, concrete or symbolic," acts to establish kinship structures.[22] Lévi-Strauss, of course, overlooks the role that women themselves play in such matchmaking arrangements. In some cases in Arabic societies, mothers are completely responsible for finding husbands for their daughters and fathers have only to approve of the mothers' choices.

The attitude of older women and mothers, when they are eager to match-make for their daughters and when they consciously or unconsciously perpetuate certain sexual practices, can be explained on two levels. On the economic level, these women are anxious that their daughters get married, for husbands are supposed to look after them. If circumcision is seen as necessary to guarantee husbands for their daughters, and if semipublic defloration is perceived as important to be sure of the honor and reputation of the family, then mothers have little choice in helping to practice them on their daughters. On the ideological level (the mental representation of material relations), mothers think that by preparing their daughters for acceptable marriages and by finding them what they see as suitable husbands, they are doing the best for them. Moreover, celibacy is discouraged in Islam. What is actually symbolized by turning the female body into a ritualistic object might have been forgotten; but the ritual is still significant as marking womanhood, even if, paradoxically, it also removes from women the possibility of sexual pleasure.

I want to argue that some Arab women are still being exchanged in arranged marriages, although the old significance of enforcing alliance between families might have been forgotten. I am not trying to decry all arranged marriages. However, I am certainly against not only the concept of exchanging women as objects but also the idea of deciding their future partners for them. Love might not be a feminist issue for American or European women; but it certainly is for many Arab feminists, who until recently have not had the freedom of choice, inasmuch as choice implies having autonomy and control over one's own body. Some might argue that love, which is an individualistic conception and is glorified as the height of self-expression and self-experience, is, yet again, an import from the west. This is simply not true, for love is one of the major themes glorified in Arabic literature for centuries. Lovers in pre-Islamic poetry, though, were usually not allowed to marry each other, especially when their love became known in the tribe.

The opposition to marriages based on love matches, especially when they clash with the interests of the families concerned, was shared by western societies as well until the beginning of the twentieth century. Engels argues that throughout antiquity "love relationships in the modern sense only occur . . . outside the official society,"[23] that is, among slaves. Except among slaves, love affairs were found only as "products of the disintegration of the old world and carried on with women who also stand outside official society, with . . . foreigners or freed slaves."[24] For free men and women, marriage "was arranged by the parents and the partners calmly accepted their choice."[25] Love affairs occurred among them, but in the form of adultery, according to the same source. In the Middle Ages and in modern times, Engels contends, marriage continues to be based on economic considerations rather than on individual and emotional relationships, especially among the upper classes. In twentieth-century societies, his distinction between bourgeois and working-class marriages cannot be maintained, because of the vast changes in social and economic structures. In Arabic societies today the two systems—love matches and arranged marriages—are practiced side by side, especially where the nuclear family is taking over. In this case, changing consciousness and desires lead to conflict and make traditional practices look more problematic.

Conclusion

Khul-Khaal: Five Egyptian Women Tell Their Stories, Doing Daily Battle: Interviews with Moroccan Women, and *Both Right and Left Handed: Arab Women Talk about Their Lives* are important mainly because they provide a voice for illiterate and working-class women who otherwise would not have been heard or represented. The life accounts of these women, however solicited, can be used for comparisons and contrasts with the life stories of upper- and middle-class educated women in the following chapters (which specifically look at the interaction of class and gender oppression to see how images of self vary according to the social, economic, and educational backgrounds of women). Although the life accounts or extracts in these anthologies are not long enough to show self-reflection, there are signs of reflection in them. The women, especially the illiterate ones, have shown a desire for change, although they do not seem to be completely capable of it themselves. Instead, they see that some of their aspirations are achieved through their daughters. It is evident that change is taking place, even in Om Gad, the illiterate woman who seems to perpetuate certain oppressive traditions without questioning them. Her insistence on educating her daughters in itself is a conscious or at least semiconscious admission of the need for change. Class consciousness may foreground gender consciousness in most illiterate and working-class women; but, with education spreading fast among younger generations of women in most Arab countries, gender oppression is becoming a major issue for them.

I would not go so far as to say that change has led to liberation; in fact my main thesis is that full liberation is yet to be achieved by even the most conscious feminists in Arab countries. The basic reason is that feminist consciousness is not enough on its own to liberate women; adequate social, economic, legal, and political revolutionary changes should take place too. Considering the circumstances of the women in these anthologies, however, I see a potential Shahrazad in each of them—a muted Shahrazad perhaps, for these women could not have spoken without the articulate Atiya, Mernissi, and Shaaban. These women and my mother have given birth, though, to maturer Shahrazads, who are growing in us and even more in our daughters to come.

My discussion of these anthologies has been predominantly based on the modes of production and modes of oppression, because of the way they are presented. My study of modes of self-representation has been limited both by the way in which the texts were produced and edited and by the content. I could not look at the images of self-construction in the interviewees' short accounts of their lives, which are responses to certain questions addressed to them by the editors/writers. The following chapters, which examine more complete versions of autobiographies and memoirs, offer a balanced discussion of the three modes.

CHAPTER SEVEN

Fadwa Tuqan's
Mountainous Journey, Difficult Journey

Fadwa Tuqan, almost a contemporary of Huda Shaarawi (whose memoirs, *Harem Years,* are examined in Chapter 3), is known to Arab pupils through their poetry textbooks. Her name is associated with Palestine and therefore with the Arab nationalist cause. Arab schoolchildren grow up with an almost mythological image of Tuqan as a resilient woman who fought against British and Israeli imperialism by the power of her poetic discourse. She stands as a public figure whose poetry is as highly valued as that of the "great" male poets of the Arab world. Tuqan's autobiography, however, comes as a shock to the Arab reader, who had associated her name with politics. For it discloses the unknown side of Tuqan, the woman who always found it difficult to be engaged in the political life of her country. Political poetry, which gained her fame, is not where Tuqan excels, as she emerges in her autobiography to tell us. While Tuqan is allowed a public voice as an acknowledged poet, the irony is that, instead of affirming this public voice, she has created a more personal one in her autobiography.

As in my reading of *Harem Years,* my reading of *Mountainous Journey, Difficult Journey* considers both the Arabic and the English texts. The editorial intervention, especially in relation to the English translation, is shown to be at its extreme in this particular example. This chapter is divided into four main sections. The first section, on modes of production, considers issues of the production and distribution of Tuqan's autobiography in its Arabic and English forms. Sections 2 and 3, on modes of self-representation and modes of oppression, are based more on my reading of Tuqan's original Arabic text. Section 4 compares and contrasts Tuqan's autobiography and Shaarawi's memoirs.

1. Modes of Production

Mountainous Journey must have been read by more Arabic readers than *Harem Years,* because it has been reprinted three times, whereas *Harem Years* has been published only once and its distribution outside Egypt has been limited. *Mountainous Journey* was first published in serialized form between 1978 and 1979 in a Palestinian journal, *Al-Jadid*, which is not very well known outside Palestine; however, *Addouha*, a widely distributed monthly Arabic magazine, published Tuqan's autobiography in 1984, introducing each part as the main article in the volume. One chapter, titled "My Poetic Experience between the Past and the Present," was introduced as "an invaluable and indispensable contribution to the understanding of the development of modern Arabic literature."[1] After that, *Mountainous Journey* was published as a book and reprinted three times, most recently in 1988. A leading Palestinian poet, Samih al-Qasim, wrote a foreword for the book under the heading "Discovery and Discovering"; he considers Tuqan's autobiography one of the best, for no autobiography since Taha Hussain's *Al-Ayyam* has been as honest, frank, original, and literary as Tuqan's, according to al-Qasim.[2] Keeping in mind that Arabic culture reveres poetry, the voice of al-Qasim, a renowned male poet, is significant in publicizing this autobiography.

For English-speaking readers, however, only extracts from the original text are translated and included in an academic book, *The Female Autograph: Theory and Practice of Autobiography from the Tenth to the Twentieth Century*.[3] A paperback book entitled *Harem Years* is more likely to be picked up from bookshop shelves than a hard-cover specialized academic book such as *Female Autograph*. Out of 239 pages of Tuqan's autobiography, a mere 13 pages are translated in this American book. *The Female Autograph* (published by the University of Chicago Press in 1984) investigates women's nontraditional literature in a pluralistic, comparative, and theoretical manner. Domna Stanton's strategy as the editor of the book is to "undermine the generic boundaries that have plagued studies of autobiography, often confining them to lists of unconvincing criteria for distinguishing various modes of self-inscription" by assembling a "collage of pieces" from different fields, modes, cultures, and eras.[4]

Tuqan's text, or text fragment, is translated and introduced by Donna Robinson Divine and included in a part called "Emblematic Places." Divine has made a poor choice in the five passages of Tuqan's autobiography that she translates, which do not give the reader any indication of who Tuqan really is and what her autobiography conveys. Divine takes out of context certain passages which do not make sense when read on their own. She calls her translation "Mountainous Journey—Difficult Journey: The Memoirs of Fadwa Tuqan." There are also headings for every passage, which Divine seems to have provided (the version of Tuqan's autobiography which I read has no subtitles at all). For a book like *The Female Autograph,* Divine could have translated a much more adequate passage, like the one in which Tuqan writes about her search for her own date of birth (which was lost because she was never registered as born) or the one in which she writes about where her name comes from. The passage called "Shykha," for example, does not make sense at all standing on its own in English; it merely gives the impression that Arab women are either controlled and suppressed like Tuqan or fundamentalist and oppressive like Shykha.

Divine's translation is also problematic, to say the least. It is flawed with mistakes and distortions, missing phrases, and misconstrued sentences.[5] In her introduction, Divine rightly states that Fadwa "notes ironically how many people claim to be descended from the family lineage of Muhammad"; but she goes wrong when she then claims that Tuqan "proceeds to speak with pride of her family lineage and its connection to Muhammad."[6] What Tuqan actually says is "at any rate, what is certain is that the family I belong to does not relate to any prophet,"[7] and nowhere in the book have I found anything like Divine's claim.

Another example of incorrect translation is the passage where Tuqan writes about the time when she used to like watching people at prayer. Divine translates: "while their facial expressions were quite different, they all began at a speedy pace, then humbled themselves without paying attention to anything but God. My heart and spirit were moved as I watched the worshippers pray formally and slowly."[8] The equivalent in Tuqan's words is, as I translate it: "I saw differences in the expressions on their faces and the way they prayed. There was the speedy one who looked as if he were not thinking of what he was doing, and the humble, attentive one, and the one who was completely absorbed, heart and soul."[9] Reading the Arabic version makes one clearly understand that although Tuqan is very philosophical about the question of believing or not believing in a God, she always enjoyed listening to the Muslim call to prayers and watching people pray, especially when they seemed to be "honest" about it. Reading the English translation, however, makes the reader think that Fadwa must be ironical when she describes how people are praying.

The English translation concentrates on the total negative effect of the scene. For the description of the body movement of people doing the Islamic prayers in the translation (with hands "raised behind the ears, then brought instantly above the head and finally to the right side . . . bowing the torso to the front; raising the body and lifting the head . . . kneeling down . . . Raising two index fingers")[10] without hearing what is being said—combined with the use of the term "theatrics" twice—seems more funny than devout and pious, as Tuqan wants to convey it. Divine appears to be haunted by religion and to be trying to add a religious atmosphere to Tuqan's text even when it is not there. For example, she translates "a term derived from the name of a Persian musical instrument which looks like a dulcimer" as "a term derived from the Persian word for God."[11]

Divine's translation should therefore be treated with the utmost caution. She uses Tuqan's autobiography in her essay on "Palestinian Arab Women and Their Reveries of Emancipation"; here too, she makes contradictory judgments. Divine claims that Tuqan's life "illustrates how the process of change may be animated almost entirely from within the tradition."[12] She argues that

> women like Tuqan had very little exposure to the philosophical literature of Europe. It was largely the resources of Arabic literature available to them that served as a reservoir of serviceable images and metaphors to explain their feelings about their societies, families, and selves. Driven by a sense of desperation as strong as that of the Palestinian men who urged social and political change, yet provided with fewer cultural outlets, women were forced to develop more internally and authentically Arab and Palestinian solutions.[13]

There are two main problems with this paragraph. First, it is wrong to claim that the women had no knowledge of European philosophical literature. Although there were (and perhaps still are) fewer educated women than men, those who read were just as exposed to western knowledge as men were, both through formal education and through available translations. Tuqan's autobiography itself is evidence of how widely read she is. The number of names of European writers that she knows equals the number of Arab names. Divine herself later argues in the same essay that Tuqan has developed a personal understanding of the Marxist notion of "consciousness":

> From Marxism, Fadwa Tuqan could meditate on the word "consciousness" until it fostered a new and different meaning. For her, consciousness became a word descriptive of a sense of self, of personal desires, and of the structure of life.[14]

The second problem is in claiming that Tuqan is included among the women who represent "internal and authentic Arab and Palestinian" identities. With all her political knowledge, Tuqan's autobiography is a highly personal quest. She continuously states how hard it has been for her to be involved in the Arab or Palestinian nationalist struggle. How could Tuqan, of all women, then be made an emblem of an authentic Arab self?

2. Modes of Self-Representation

ALIENATION: SOCIAL CONSTRAINTS
AND INDIVIDUAL ASSERTION

As noted in Chapter 5, there is a consensus in feminist theory that women tend to assert some kind of a collective identity in their autobiographical writings. I have argued that this is true in some cases but even then only up to a point. For the moment people start writing or talking about themselves, they are creating an egoistic space of some kind. However, this ego can either be magnified, as happens in most men's texts, or diminished in order to give way to a more collective ego or self, as happens in most women's texts. Tuqan's autobiography is an ideal example for the study of the irresolution of identity. It can be read as a quest to find the *self* between asserting her egoistic self, on the one hand, and desiring to be part of a more collective entity, on the other.

Tuqan's sense of achievement is made clear from the very beginning. She describes herself even before birth as "the tree which clings to the earth, as if encompassing in the essence of its being the spirit of determination, counter-challenge."[15] Tuqan is nevertheless quite humble about who she is and what she has achieved. Her prologue to her autobiography begins:

> During my literary life, I always felt uneasy when I was questioned about my life. I knew it was because I was never happy about my life; for the tree of my life had given very few fruits, and my soul was continuously eager for better achievements and wider horizons.[16]

In the same prologue, however, she explains why she has written her autobiography, to show:

> How I could, within my capabilities, surmount what was impossible to overcome had it not been for the strong will and genuine desire to go on striving for the best, and had it not been for my insistence to give meaning and better value to my life than that already planned for it.[17]

The sense of accomplishment in spite of hardship is clearly expressed. Tuqan is aware of her individualism or even egoism; and her autobiography is an insistent apology for her inability to be a sociable person, as she herself confesses. She is always aware of the need to be a member of a social group but also finds it very difficult to sympathize with this very group which has caused her unhappiness. Time and time again, Tuqan writes about her lonely self, caught in this persistent conflict. She states very clearly that she has never been able to be entertaining company for people and that her only and best friends are always her own self and her books; self-love has dictated Tuqan's behavior all her life.[18] She lived at a time when her country was not at peace. Since her birth, Palestine had been living through crises of occupation and war. Tuqan's family was very much a vital part of Palestine's political life. Her father, uncle, and brothers were all directly involved in political leadership, demonstrations, and upheavals. When Tuqan witnessed a mass demonstration, a protest, or the arrest of a member of her family, for example, she writes that she felt sympathy for the people involved. However, her feelings for the community never lasted for more than a few minutes. In such circumstances Tuqan cries not for the people and what happens to them but for herself, because she is not able to engage herself and her feelings completely with the people. Early in her life, her brother and friends used to advise her to break through the circle of herself and venture outside it, but she always failed to do so. She writes: "[M]y poetic attempts were always circling round my emotions and my private pains."[19]

Mountainous Journey is a narrative of self-revelation and self-evaluation. Unlike Shaarawi's memoirs, Tuqan's narrative is very retrospective from beginning to end. Nevertheless, like Shaarawi, Tuqan also talks a lot about the people who influenced her most throughout her life. In fact, Tuqan dedicates her book to those who "played their role in my life, and disappeared in eternity."[20] Whereas I had to surmise why Shaarawi wrote her memoirs at all, Tuqan makes it very clear from the beginning why she decided to write her life story:

> Why did I write this book then, in which I disclosed aspects of my life which I never liked? With all sincere humility, I say that this life, with its little accomplishments, never lacked the severity of struggle.
>
> The seed does not see the light before it digs a difficult crack into the earth. And my story is a story of the struggle of the seed with the hard rocky earth; it is the story of struggle against thirst and hard rocks.
>
> Perhaps in it, people would see rays of light to help them in their own difficult journeys. And I would like to add this fact: the struggle for self-fulfillment is enough at least to fill our hearts and give meaning and value to our lives. No harm if we lose the battle—we just have to make sure never to surrender.

The powers of evil, be it metaphysical, social, or political, always work against *man* and try to destroy *him,* but *he* stands against such powers with all pride and resistance in spite of *his* weakness [my emphasis].[21]

Tuqan, then, is fully aware that her life story, a story of continuous struggle and resilient will, is unique:

The iron frame that our families mold for us prevents us from escaping it. I was always fervent to get out of that climate and those unbreakable and unreasonable traditions, which destine women to triviality. The time is that of oppression, depression, and dissolving into nothingness; the place is the prison of the house.

There are people who come to this world and find it all very easy and simple, and there are those who find it difficult and thorny.

It was on the difficult road that the unknown left me, and from there I began my difficult journey.

I carried the rock and the tiredness, and I had to go up and down endless rounds. No great dreams help, even will alone is not enough . . .

I have realized that work is the other side of the dream and of will . . .

And I have decided to deal with a multisided coin: will and action.[22]

Tuqan would like other people, especially women who might be in circumstances similar to hers, to benefit from her own experiences. It is made clear to readers from the very beginning that they are not going to know everything about her:

I have not opened the whole closet of my life, for it is not important to reveal all particularities.

There are dear and valuable things that we like to keep hidden deep in one corner of our souls away from curious eyes, so we have to keep the curtains drawn to protect them.[23]

Although apparently conscious of the uniqueness of her story, Tuqan nevertheless never represents herself as a genius. Indeed, the main narrative in her autobiography is the story of a self-made poet and the difficulties that she faced in her life.

Tuqan continues to have this conflict. But she also knows why she cannot be very much involved with the people and why her feelings have been centered on herself. It is the sexual discrimination that Tuqan has experienced since her childhood which prevented her from wanting to belong to such society. She knows that her inner self can only become complete within a social group, but this group is there behind the walls which are besieging me, and between them and me lie long centuries of the "harem" world . . .

My father was the first one who planted the seeds of this conflict, which stayed with me during my poetic experience . . . I always felt completely lonely, and no one was there to share my misery, except for my own being, my being was torn and tortured . . . The heart was mine too, it was also melancholic and it was crushed . . . My calamity was becoming more complicated . . . The greater my misery and my depression grew, the more egoistic and individualistic I became. My existence within the closed "harem" made me shrink into myself, which became my own prison.[24]

It was not until 1967, with the Israeli invasion of Nablus and the rest of Palestine, that Tuqan felt that she was a member of her society.[25] Her political or rather nationalist poetry before 1967 was, according to her, devoid of genuine feelings; it was merely artificial, rhetorical words engraved on rocks.[26] But after the great disaster of 1967 which shook the whole Middle East, Tuqan says, her feelings were suddenly awakened, and nationalist poetry poured out of her heart.

Tuqan might seem like a terribly egoistic person who was only moved by major disasters, but her experience can be seen as the experience of many Arab women; she is just being honest about it. In fact, Tuqan raises a vital issue that many feminists, even today and even in the west, have not been able to resolve. It is the dilemma that women face when wanting to rebel against the very source of their oppression, only to find out that the first people they are estranged from are family members, those supposedly closest to them. Her autobiography, in this sense, raises the issue of how far women can actually define a female identity within a tradition that suppresses it.

Thus, while Tuqan was always seeking to be embedded in a wider social network, she also struggled hard to create an "individualistic" or "egoistic" person of herself, a seemingly contradictory attitude for which she felt guilty. Tuqan can call herself egoistic, but I would describe her inability to become an active and socially oriented person as a characteristic alienation, in Marxist terms, caused by the very class and gender problems she had to live with. Many Arab women in circumstances like Tuqan's suffer this dilemma: while wanting to escape the social isolation imposed upon them by the family and wanting to achieve some personal independence in order to build self-respect, they become antisocial or antisociable. Women who do manage to break through the boundaries of their family/home, which Tuqan constantly refers to as the "prison," face more discrimination and more restrictions in the bigger "prison" of society. Alienation is the most expressive term to describe the case of Tuqan and many other women like her.

Tuqan's understanding of humanity and of life in general has affinities with Marxist thinking whether she is aware of it or not. Pondering on the existential argument that "man is free, and that he alone can weave the fabric of his existence," Tuqan wonders whether "man is rather a prisoner of his conditions, circumstances, time, and psychological and physical formation."[27] This of course is a Marxist view. Analyzing her own conditions, Tuqan writes with a dialectical understanding of life comparable to a Marxist position. She notes that if it were not for the oppression and the injustice she experienced in her life, she might not have had the strong urge and will to create a poet of herself; that is, the more she was oppressed, the more defiant and determined she grew.

3. Modes of Oppression

FAMILY OPPRESSION

The instability and depression which characterize Tuqan's life in her autobiography are introduced from the very beginning. "I came out of the darkness of the unknown into a world which was not prepared to accept me": this is how Tuqan starts her autobiography.[28] The reader's attention is immediately shifted to her mother. Contrary to the reader's expectation (and especially an Arab reader's, knowing how much Arabic culture reveres the mother), Tuqan presents her mother as her main source of oppression, very much like Shaarawi's mother: "[M]y mother tried to get rid of me during the first few months of her pregnancy, she tried again and again, but she failed."[29] Tuqan's autobiography problematizes, demystifies, and subverts not only the ideal of motherhood, "a quasi-sacred activity and the life dream of virtually all Middle Eastern women," but also "the mother herself, her power, and the idea of matriarchy."[30] However, the image of the mother is not completely subverted in Tuqan's text. The representation of the mother fluctuates in the following pages between blaming her for wanting to get rid of Tuqan before birth and for not showing her love after her birth on the one hand and trying to justify her action on the other. The sense of blame is obvious: "[My mother] had ten children. She gave birth to five boys and five girls. But she never tried to abort any until it was my turn."[31] Tuqan was number seven. The sense of justification is obvious in the following sentence: "[S]he was tired of pregnancy, of giving birth, and of breastfeeding. She gave birth every two and a half years. She was only eleven when she got married, and she was only fifteen when she had her first baby." Her mother was "the generous earth," and "it was time for her to rest."[32]

Tuqan continues to find excuses for her mother's "cold" attitude toward her. She thought that her mother associated her with bad luck because her father was arrested by the Israelis when she was born. To justify her discrimination, Tuqan notes that her mother was probably frustrated. As a baby, she never hated her mother. She was affected by a story that her sister used to tell her about the children whose mother died and who were treated very badly by a wicked stepmother. Tuqan dreaded the idea of being brought up by a stepmother like the one in her sister's story and prayed that her mother would never die.

Tuqan does not remember any affection or care from her father either. According to her, he did not stand by her when her eldest brother decided that she was never to go to school again and never to leave the house without escort after he saw her accepting a rose from a young boy. For her father, Tuqan claims, she never had any feelings; but in his old age, in his illness, and when he was jailed, she secretly prayed for him. After his death, she even admits missing him terribly, and she wrote him an elegy, although she claims that he never showed her any love even when she was almost dying of malaria.[33]

SOCIAL AND ECONOMIC OPPRESSION

Tuqan is aware that the problem of discrimination does not lie just within the boundaries of her family. She knows it is a social and an economic issue. Early in her life, Tuqan was closer to her aunt (her mother's sister) than to her own mother—not only because her aunt showed her love and attention but also because she felt her aunt's house was healthier, since a lot of social activities used to take place there. She describes her aunt's husband as "not a fundamentalist, nor a slave to traditions."[34] Thus her aunt was free to have many women friends to visit and to go out with. Tuqan is particularly aware of the fact that her aunt and her husband were not as rich as her own family and that richer people are more strict. She writes: "I always wished I was the daughter of my aunt and her husband, and I hated the fact that I belonged to my family . . . I would always have preferred to belong to a less rich family but more free."[35] Tuqan also criticizes her fundamentalist old aunt, al-Shaikha, for being an advocate of class supremacy. In the public bath, where she sometimes went with her mother, Tuqan noticed how the rich women used to get special care from the staff. She also admired the women of the lower classes because they were not at all inhibited about moving around the bath with their bodies naked: "I liked the spontaneity of those women who enjoyed a climate of more freedom and more honesty than that of the bourgeoisie, which was hypocritical and false."[36]

Tuqan is also critical of Arab men's double standards of morality and of conduct. She first criticizes the way children are brought up. Tuqan was prevented from going to school because she accepted a flower from a boy. Most Arab societies condemn relationships between the sexes even at an early age. Not only did Tuqan metaphorically have to wear a "scarlet letter" for a long time, but she was also prevented from going to school. Since that "tragic" incident, she never felt good about herself; she felt guilty for something she should not be made to feel bad about in a "healthy" society:

> And there was planted a bad idea about my soft and innocent self. I became used to walking with my head down not daring to look into their faces, which attacked me every morning with sulking and hatred.[37]

Boys and men, however, are not as restricted as girls and women are. When Tuqan wanted to learn English, some of the family heads, like al-Shaikha, objected, so Tuqan's father supported them to avoid a dispute over such a matter. She criticizes the men:

> They wore European clothes, and spoke Turkish, French, and English. They ate with forks and knives. They also fell in love, but ambushed us whenever any of us tried to fulfill our humanity in the most natural ways of development or was ambitious for something better. They represented, at best, the inertia of the Arab man and his inability to keep a homogeneous unsplit personality. They continue to represent the split in the Arab man's personality into two halves: half with progress and response to the spirit of the age and keeping pace with contemporary ways of living, and the second half paralyzed, possessed by the accumulated selfishness of the eastern men's stubbornly selfish treatment of their women relatives. And so everything was suffocating me, even the walls of the ancient house I felt were pressing on my chest. How I wished to sleep under the sky, no ceiling above me, no walls around me, and no relatives beside me.[38]

Tuqan raises another important issue here, for Arab feminists at least: some Arab men who claim to support the women's rights cause can still be strict with the women in their own families. It is acceptable for other women to be singers or dancers, as long as they are not one's wife, sister, mother, or daughter. Tuqan's father, for example, was fond of music and of singing, but he would not let his daughter sing or play music.[39]

CLASS-CONSCIOUSNESS

Tuqan's written life story is a narrative of her conscious desire and attempt, within her means, to escape the boundaries of the family/class position within which she was raised. She was constantly aware that her family (which, as she herself describes, was patriarchal, extended, and harem-like) practiced "unjust discrimination" against its women and so caused their unhappiness. Being part of the "bourgeoisie," the Tuqan family adhered to the moral standards of "respectable" families and kept its women at home, preventing them from being active members of the society in which they lived, she complains. Lower-class women, however, led healthier lives, according to Tuqan, because they were freer and more active in their social life. She is explicitly critical of upper- and middle-class ways of life as being "contradictory" and "hypocritical." While her mother, for example, was a member of a women's union in Nablus, she was not allowed to attend the meetings or to participate in the demonstrations. While the family traditions prohibit women from leaving their houses, joining a women's union in name only is supposed to give prestige to the family. Although the political dimensions of such unions, which were formed by the national bourgeoisie, were limited to arranging demonstrations, sending letters of appeal and protest, and holding conferences, Tuqan stresses that it was the rural and working-class women who—being unveiled and having the freedom to be actively involved—were able to fight to achieve the union's actual objectives. They were the ones who risked their lives in transporting weapons and food to the "revolutionaries hiding in the mountains."[40]

Tuqan's criticism of the family/class position clearly has affinities with the classical Marxist analysis of the "woman question" or, more precisely, with the arguments of Engels: though middle- and upper-class women were materially better off and less exploited than lower-class women, they were more oppressed in being enclosed in the household and hence less able to fight for social change. The fact that Tuqan never married can be seen as an expression of her rejection of the family institution, where the oppression of women is practiced with no outside authority to question it. She perhaps did not want to create the space where such oppression might be perpetuated.

4. *Mountainous Journey* and *Harem Years*

There is a reference to Shaarawi in Tuqan's text. Tuqan's mother was an active member of a women's group in Nablus which had joined Shaarawi's General Union of Arab Women in 1929.[41] Like Shaarawi, who was one of the first Cairene women to take off the veil, Tuqan's mother was the first woman to take off the veil in Nablus.[42]

Comparison of *Mountainous Journey* and *Harem Years* reveals both common factors and differences. First, for both Shaarawi and Tuqan, childhood is the most important time in their lives. It is this period that they write about most, with more detail and openness, perhaps because it seems far away in the past, which distances them from it and makes them more frank. Both Shaarawi and Tuqan, in their relatively extensive sections on their childhoods, stress that the major features of their personalities were shaped in that period. Although both were brought up in rich families, which were able to provide their material needs, neither of them was happy in childhood because of the sexual discrimination they claim to have experienced. Thinking of committing suicide, as in Tuqan's case,[43] and wishing to fall severely ill, as in Shaarawi's, were ways of expressing rebellion and attracting attention.

Second, after childhood, the story of self-determination begins. Having been forced into an early marriage, Shaarawi performs her first feminist act by separating from her husband for a few years, during which she continues her private education and forms the basis for the women's union that she later establishes with the help of the women friends she has made. Tuqan is not forced into an arranged marriage but is forced to leave school. Having no means to challenge the family's decision, she can only have the will and determination not to submit. Unlike Shaarawi, Tuqan does not have private teachers; thus to allay her thirst for education she must depend upon herself and her brother. With the help and supervision of her brother Ibrahim, a poet in his own right who became her teacher, Tuqan not only educated herself but made a great poet of herself. Apart from her poetry, her autobiography is evidence of her wide-ranging reading. Tuqan quotes dozens of names of western philosophers, writers, and poets, including Friedrich Nietzsche, Søren Kierkegaard, Ezra Pound, T. S. Eliot, Karl Marx, Friedrich Engels, Oscar Wilde, and William Blake, together with a host of Arabic ones. Again, the brother's support is the main factor in making Shaarawi's and Tuqan's plans succeed. Like Shaarawi's, Tuqan's love for her brother is beyond description, and her gratitude for his help is expressed throughout her book.

Third, sexuality and sex are taboo subjects in both *Harem Years* and *Mountainous Journey,* though Tuqan ventures to refer to the growth of her female body early in her adolescent years:

> I noticed the florescence of my body . . . I was scared and ashamed. The growth of my breasts . . . embarrassed me, so I tried to hide them. I went on observing this matter with great shyness as if it were a shameful sin I deserved to be punished for.[44]

One can see Tuqan's implied criticism of the neglect of sexual education for children in her society, in which sex is not to be discussed. Whereas Shaarawi speaks only about her love of her brother, her father, and Umm Kabira, Tuqan at least tells the story of her first love at the age of eleven or twelve. She writes that she "knew nothing about love at all, for this topic was not spoken about in front of us: the children."[45] The family members, typically, react very badly, for their honor depends on their women's chastity and virginity; the fact that Tuqan is so young does not make the issue any different. She is not to leave the house for any reason anymore because the brother has seen her receiving a flower from a sixteen-year-old boy.

Tuqan explicitly criticizes this social and sexual censorship throughout her book, yet she censors her own sex life. For this is the only love story that she writes about, although she stresses on different occasions that love "engulfed her existence forever." She writes about love only as a concept, as an abstract idea without which life is unbearable. Tuqan must have had love relationships later in her life, but she does not write about them. In contrast to the people whose names she reveals, Tuqan hides two men's names: one she calls "A. G.," and the other is referred to as "The Strange Friend." She never raises or answers the question of why she never married. Thus we see the limits of openness to which either Shaarawi or Tuqan could go.

Fourth, as I have argued, Shaarawi's text is more a testimony to her achievement than an act of self-formation or self-creating through the medium of language itself. She is already made outside discourse; her narrative does not reflect upon her life or reveal hidden areas of herself, as is the case in *Mountainous Journey.* Tuqan's autobiography is very much a story and an act of self-formation in language. Although Tuqan, like Shaarawi, has an already constructed self in life, she reforms it and re-creates it in language. By being reflectively retrospective, analytical, and critical of the conditions of her life, she reveals the unknown side of herself (unknown to her reader, of course); but by doing so she is also involved in this process of knowing the self through rebuilding it in language.

Fifth, Tuqan's self-formation through the very medium of language is her feminist act of liberation. For she tells how she has been always unable, even as a grown woman and a well-known poet, to defend herself against injustice and to stand up for her rights. By narrating the story of her "inability" to speak up for herself, however, she has negated her silence and has liberated herself in language. Both Shaarawi and Tuqan achieve some kind of liberation, but through different means: Shaarawi through action and Tuqan through words. While Shaarawi is an active Shahrazad whose actions, not words, were the means of her relative liberation, Tuqan is a literary Shahrazad whose liberation lies in the words of her autobiography rather than in her actions. There is no doubt, though, that Tuqan goes beyond Shaarawi, as I hope my discussion of their texts has made clear.

Sixth, I have argued that Shaarawi's liberation is limited; so is Tuqan's. For Tuqan's language itself is somehow caught in the standards drawn by men. For example, she still uses the traditional method of referring to the human being in general, using the masculine pronouns "he," "his," and "him." Examples of this can be seen in my translation of some of her text throughout this chapter. Furthermore, Tuqan herself is aware and admits that her "hatred" of her society has been "negative," for she could not actively participate on the social level,[46] as Shaarawi did, for example.

A seventh point is that whereas Shaarawi's language is simple and straightforward and her narrative highly descriptive and rarely reflective, Tuqan's language is highly literary and sophisticated and her narrative very reflective, analytical, and philosophical. Thus, Shaarawi's memoirs are clearly addressed to anyone who can read. But Tuqan's autobiography, which may be also intended to be read by any literate person, can be appreciated more by a highly intellectual reader. This is due not only to the narrative form but also to its content. Tuqan writes a great deal about the development of modern Arabic poetry in her time, raises arguments about poetics, discusses some poets (both men and women), and quotes many names that the ordinary reader is not likely to have heard of. Whereas *Harem Years* is almost simple reportage of a life story with hardly any analysis or criticism, *Mountainous Journey* is an analytical book, richer and more complex for an Arabic reader. There is something here for almost everyone. Even if readers are not feminists and do not care about the representation of the social injustice that Tuqan has experienced, they will appreciate Tuqan's language. If they think Tuqan is too critical of her society and its traditions, they will find comfort in discovering that she is just as critical of another society in which she enjoyed living for three years: England. If readers do not care about poetry and how Tuqan became a poet, they will enjoy her philosophical questioning of the universe. And if readers do not care about any of these things, they will find the story of a Palestinian city under occupation interesting.

The lack of any philosophical details in Shaarawi's text can be explained by the fact that writing one's own autobiography is different from reciting one's life story to someone else to write. Shaarawi's Arabic was not advanced enough to write her own autobiography. Had she written her autobiography in a language she knew well, as Tuqan did, then she would surely have produced a quite different text from the one we have.

Conclusion

My analysis of Tuqan's autobiography is in no way complete; nor does it consider the entire original text. My references to the original are primarily intended to bring out contrasts with the extract available in English. With that proviso, I have raised the issues that relate to the general subjects of my thesis. The significance of modes of production—translation, publishing, distribution—is clear, especially when it comes to translating extracts from a text. Divine has used her problematic translation of Tuqan's text, manipulating it and making some wrong judgments, all of which served her own purposes. The concentration on the question of religion also serves certain "Orientalist" and colonialist views of Arab women. The question of identity for women is problematic and cannot always be solved by appeal to the sense of collectivity with which all women are supposed to identify. These texts illustrate one dilemma for Arab feminists: how difficult it is for women to break away from the family and its traditions, because this same family is where they experience love and affection on the one hand and oppression and discrimination on the other: one brother tried to isolate Tuqan, another to open the road of success and fame for her.

I would also like to make this last point. Tuqan is no doubt aware of sexual and class discrimination in her text, as I have shown in this chapter. All in all, however, her autobiography does not strike the reader as the autobiography of a feminist. It is the autobiography of a poet rather than the autobiography of a woman. Her "journey" is the journey of a self-made poet and the difficulties she faced and not the journey of a feminist. In other words, feminist issues are not given priority in her text; they are not straightforwardly and deliberately raised. Apart from the way Tuqan presents her text, the fact that she is already accepted and renowned within the Arab male literary tradition has probably contributed to the way her text is received by readers. Arab readers see Fadwa Tuqan as a poet before they see her as anything else. Samih al-Qasim's introduction to Tuqan's autobiography also plays a significant role in presenting it as the autobiography of a poet. Al-Qasim compares Tuqan's poetic odyssey to the autobiography generally considered the best in Arabic literature: the autobiography of Taha Hussain, a leading figure in the canon of modern Arabic literature. Moreover, it is not at all wrong to argue, as does Fedwa Malti-Douglas, that al-Qasim's introduction to Tuqan's text comes as the male's voice legitimizing that of the female. The voice of the renowned male poet is giving the right to speak to a female poet. Tuqan herself does not seem to mind being legitimized by the male literary canon; she must have allowed al-Qasim to write his introduction. Besides, in her autobiography, she writes about the exhilaration and pride she felt every time she was compared to great male poets.[47]

Tuqan's autobiography is accepted in Arabic tradition as a literary text. Most of the reviews written about it approach it as such, and the feminist aspect of the book is hardly raised. The following chapter looks at three texts by Nawal el-Saadawi, who, unlike Tuqan, is not as appreciated in the Arabic literary tradition in spite of the many novels, plays, and short stories that she has written. Saadawi's feminism is the main object of criticism. It seems that the refined literary veils covering Tuqan's feminism are more acceptable than the naked feminist features of Saadawi's writing. But which is more effective?

CHAPTER EIGHT

Nawal el-Saadawi

Introduction

Chapter 6 looked at three anthologies of interviews with Arab women whose stories and voices were heavily determined by the textualization of their spoken words carried out by the editors, who were themselves the interviewers. Chapter 7 discussed a written autobiographical text by an Arab woman and an extract from it translated, edited, shaped, and presented to western readers by a western writer. This chapter examines various modes of writing in which different rhetorical devices for saying "I" are used by one Arab writer, Nawal el-Saadawi.[1]

I am dedicating a long chapter to this one writer for many reasons. First, Saadawi is one of the most prolific feminist writers in twentieth-century Arab countries. She has published books on a wide range of topics relating to contemporary problems of Arab societies. She has also tried various forms of writing such as short stories, novels, plays, and essays in order to express her vast range of ideas. Second, she is almost the first Arab woman to raise the issue of sexual oppression publicly in a daring manner; before her, only forms of social, economic, and political oppression were discussed by Arab feminists. Third, she is a very controversial writer, having been fiercely attacked by critics and her writings having been banned by some Arab regimes. Finally, she has become one of the best-known Arab women writers in the world, for her works have been translated into English, French, German, Italian, Dutch, Danish, Swedish, Norwegian, Greek, Portuguese, Urdu, and Persian.

It is useful, first, briefly to lay out Saadawi's social, educational, and professional background, for her writings and her position as an international figure are very much influenced by it. Nawal el-Saadawi was born in 1931 in a little village (Kafr Tahla) in the Egyptian delta but was brought up in the biggest Egyptian city (Cairo) by "parents of two different classes."[2] Her father was an only son to his poor mother, who sacrificed for his education while not being able to do the same for her daughters. Saadawi has frequently referred to her grandmother, whom she admired and whom she thought of as "Isis, the Egyptian goddess of knowledge . . . and Eve, who in mythology came from the tree of knowledge."[3] As a university graduate, her father married a Cairene upper-class woman, Saadawi's mother, who as the daughter of the director-general of army recruitment was educated in French schools.[4] Saadawi is always proud to announce that she was brought up in an atmosphere which encouraged education and knowledge.[5] She particularly expresses her gratitude to her father for giving her some kind of freedom and for encouraging her education. Saadawi's acknowledgment of her father rather than her mother is not so much a sign of sexual discrimination as it is a sign of alliance with working-class positions. Since she was a child, Saadawi had always been conscious of the class division in her society, echoed in her own family, because they were poor village people, according to her.[6] Her sympathy, then, was directed toward her paternal relatives represented by her father, whom she refers to more than to her mother. Her class-consciousness, as well as her gender-consciousness, is present in all her writing.

Saadawi's gender-consciousness is also linked to a major theme in her writing and in her life: the tension between art and science. She claims that she always loved literature and writing but was also good at science. When she finished school she was torn between studying literature or doing science. She chose to do medicine because the "Faculty of Medicine took the best students, those with highest grades";[7] she became a doctor in 1955. The conflict between art and science, a theme which recurs in Saadawi's interviews and writings, is an issue for many educated Arab women. In some Arab countries even today, women have to fight the basic battle to prove that they can be just as clever as men can be. Alongside her profession as a general practitioner, and then as a psychiatrist, Saadawi has also written and published prolifically, thus combining the love of both art and science in a dialectical way. On the one hand, her medical profession has given her a lot of material for her writings and insight into the human body and mind, which she sees as essential for every writer.[8] On the other hand, she has researched and published many articles on medicine, psychiatry, social problems, and public health. In a way, her work as a doctor and a psychiatrist is what is special about her as a feminist writer, for her scientific and medical knowledge and her firsthand experience with people must serve to validate her research on the oppression of Arab women.

Combining a medical career and writing has not always gone smoothly for Saadawi. The sensitive and taboo issues which she has raised have caused her problems in both her medical and writing careers. After publishing *Woman and Sex* (a pioneering and daring book on sexuality and gender) in 1972, she was dismissed from her job in the Egyptian Ministry of Health. In 1981 she was imprisoned by Egyptian president Anwar Sadat for her outspoken criticism of political corruption. While she is still widely read by Arab youth and by open-minded people, she also continues to be censored by many Arab regimes, some of which do not allow the distribution of her books at all. Her name has even been put on a death list by some extremists.[9] In her own country, she is blacklisted on television and on radio and is censored in the national newspapers.[10] Such problems of censorship, blacklisting, and persecution are suffered by many Arab writers like Saadawi, for they are considered a threat to conservative regimes. But other Arab regimes do not mind her books being distributed; some even invite her for conferences, public lectures, and television interviews. Syrian television, for example, often interviews Saadawi; and, according to her, she has been welcomed in Damascus, Tunisia, and Yemen for various cultural and medical events.[11] It must be said, though, that some Arab regimes who usually claim that they are democratic use writers like Saadawi who are already popular among the people for appeasement and propaganda purposes.

As a writer, Saadawi has also suffered exploitation by some publishers. When I asked her about the range of distribution of her books in Arab countries, she could not give exact details; whereas she knew that all twenty-seven of her books had been reprinted many times in Cairo and Beirut, some publishers, whom she called "thieves," had reprinted many of her books and sold them without any contract with her. There are also people whom Saadawi calls "smuggling merchants" who photocopy books and sell them without the permission or even the knowledge of their authors.[12]

Contrary to her reception within the Arabic cultural environment, Saadawi has enjoyed a good deal of favorable western press coverage. Almost all her books have now been translated into English, not to mention other languages. Various specialized magazines and pamphlets (such as *Third World Quarterly, Marxism Today, New Society,* and *Women's Review*) promptly print positive reviews of each newly published translation of Saadawi's books. Moreover, national political newspapers such as the *Times* and the *Guardian* regularly publish interviews with and articles written by Saadawi. Both the BBC and Channel Four interview her on her fairly frequent visits to Britain. Saadawi herself has been building up her international reputation. She travels around the world, giving interviews and participating in conferences and debates.

Saadawi has been considered a controversial writer by Arab critics and by

Arab governments. They disagree on the quality of her literary style; but most of them agree that her research work and criticism have been constructive.

1. *Memoirs of a Woman Doctor*

Saadawi was by no means the first Arab woman feminist writer; nor was her *Memoirs of a Woman Doctor*,[13] one of her earliest books, the first Arabic feminist text. Saadawi was a brave and daring writer, however, in being the first outspoken woman activist to write about women's sexuality. This subject had not yet been raised by any Arab male or female supporters of women's rights in the way that Saadawi did in the late 1950s when *Memoirs* was first published.

Memoirs, though it might have seemed outdated in the late 1980s when it was first published in English, can be considered the first radical Arabic feminist text. It is revolutionary both in relation to gender representation (that is, the image of women represented in the text) and in relation to class, though on a lesser scale. Above all, the book should be seen as an individualistic quest for self-realization. Although *Memoirs* is a fictional autobiography, I read it as embodying the earliest concerns of the feminist Saadawi before she moved into her general struggle to liberate women. In *Memoirs,* I see the relative liberation of a writer who, having affirmed the rights of individual women to autonomy, addressed the issue of poverty, and asserted her own private self, ventures into the public sphere in later writings.

I wish to express my respect for Saadawi's view that no "literary critic has the right to confuse a novel with an autobiography."[14] Saadawi thinks that art and literature cannot spring only from an artist's private life. Otherwise she could not have written a single story; nor could she have written about the authority of the father and the oppression of the mother, issues of greater importance for her than one individual's private life.[15] Art, according to Saadawi, "springs from the 'greater consciousness' or the 'higher consciousness' not the subconscious";[16] thus, she gives greater importance to the experiences of people around her than to her own in writing her books. Saadawi has written that her own life has been free of the problems and difficulties essential for writing an autobiography.

I view *Memoirs* as a fictional autobiography, unlike *Harem Years* and *Mountainous Journey, Difficult Journey.* I still, however, wish to maintain a distinction between fiction and autobiography, knowing that each employs devices of the other genre. Saadawi herself admits that there is both reality and imagination in the book, and the reality in it is very similar to the reality of Egyptian women today (*MWD,* 8). Whether the life of the heroine represents the experiences of Saadawi herself or those of any other woman of the time, the experiences are probable rather than fantastic. The text is written with the verisimilitude of the realist mode. This is not to say that I am interested in measuring the truth in the book; instead I am more interested in the strategies used to develop a textual self. The following discussion looks, first, at motifs in the book with a view to tracing the development of a feminist self; and second, at the ending of the book, which I see as a bridge between the private and the public. This transition from complete inhibition about the individual self to acquiring a global interest in people's oppression culminates in *My Travels around the World*.

THE GENDERED CONSTRUCTION OF THE BODY

Short as it is, *Memoirs* can be a rich sample of motifs for a feminist analysis: the construction of gendered subjectivity; the role of the family in transmitting oppressive social gender roles and the subjugation of women in an unjust society; and women's awakening or the development of feminist consciousness. Most of these issues can be examined through the motif of the body, which has been carefully built up in a dialectical structure. The narrative develops in a dialectical movement through the polar opposites of death and rebirth: the deconstruction and reunification of the body. The narrator's sense of herself as a woman is immediately connected with feelings about her body and the bodies of other people. The human body as a corpse on the dissecting table is literally deconstructed in order to be, yet again, unified. The ending of the text is controversial: as we shall see, it can be read either as putting an end to conflict by unification or, as I argue, as just another step in the zigzag process of constructing a personality which can be endlessly contradictory.

Memoirs begins with "conflict" (*MWD*, 9) and ends with "relief" (*MWD*, 101). Between the two is the long and painful process of a woman's struggle to achieve her identity in a society that tries hard to dictate what this identity should be. The book also challenges the social dualistic construction of notions like femininity versus masculinity, woman versus man, sister versus brother, mother versus father, body versus mind, and nature versus science.

In *Memoirs*, the heroine (henceforth referred to as "she") as a child was used to being called "Girl" by her mother, who probably called her brother by his name. She has also not been given a name by the writer, probably to stress the point, raised in the "Author's Note," that the book is regarded by the writer "as a fair description of the moral and social position of women in that period" (*MWD*, 8); that is, the narrator stands for Egyptian women or at least for educated, urban women in the 1950s. The absence of the name of the narrator in *Memoirs* is equivalent to the absence of the birth date of the narrator of Tuqan's autobiography, who is also not named until later in the text. Tuqan names her narrator Fadwa Tuqan when she is thirteen years old, when she writes her name on her copybook used for studying poetry under the supervision of her brother Ibrahim, having been prevented from going to school by her eldest brother.[17] It is as if the act of naming, at the time Tuqan started her relationship with poetry, marked her real birth.

The beginning of *Memoirs*—the dramatic act of coming into the world—is reminiscent of the beginning of Tuqan's autobiography. Like Tuqan's, the narrator's birth is not welcomed. The narrator of *Memoirs* is in conflict with her femininity; the act of narrating as well as the outcome of the narrative bring a resolution to this conflict. From the very first page, we encounter specific details that show how gender is socially determined. The narrator has to let her hair grow long and be plaited; her brother has his short and free; she has to tidy up her own bed and that of her brother, who is neither requested nor expected to reciprocate; she has to ask permission to go out, while her brother comes and goes whenever he wishes; she has to learn the etiquette of eating, whereas her brother eats roughly and noisily; she has to watch her movements lest her skirt uncover her thighs, although her brother jumps around freely. Tuqan as a child also used to be scolded by her religious aunt when she wore short dresses, being told that she and her mother were going to go to hell because she showed her bare legs.[18] It was shameful for a girl to uncover her thighs. The word "shameful," mentioned three times in one page, is very significant, for according to Islamic tradition a woman's body is wholly sexual and thus shameful while only a man's sexual parts are shameful.

If a girl's innocent childhood is associated with shame, what about adolescence? Her body, formerly perceived as shameful, now becomes unclean. A woman's body is doomed to be disparaged by society. Menstruation! What horror little girls feel when they first experience it. As the responses of the English writer Mary Barnes suggest, such shame is also characteristic of other societies:

> . . . when my body got fat and it got periods and breasts I hated all that. I wouldn't wear a brassiere and I demanded to know why didn't boys have "it," periods . . . I was about the age for it to happen . . . I was frightened. I daren't speak of it. I looked at other girls and wondered if they got "it"—periods.[19]

In *Memoirs:*

> I saw something red . . . Fear gripped my heart . . . locked myself in . . . to investigate the secret of this grave event in private . . . I took to my

room for four days running. I couldn't face my brother, my father or even the house-boy . . . Was this unclean procedure the only way for girls to reach maturity? (*MWD,* 11–12)

Simone de Beauvoir tells us in *The Second Sex* that "Anglo-Saxons call menstruation the 'curse'; in truth the menstrual cycle is a burden."[20] George Tarabishi, in *Woman against Her Sex,* claims that

> certain primitive tribes . . . used to isolate menstruating women, putting them in quarantine for the duration . . . believing that the blood was taboo and seeing the woman as possessed by evil spirits until purified. Indeed most religions have considered women to be unclean during menstruation.[21]

He further illustrates the point:

> The church in the Middle Ages forbade women entering a place of worship during menstruation. In Judaism, the woman is considered unclean during this period. Whoever touches her, or even the place where she has been sitting, will be impure until sunset.[22]

According to Islam too, the woman is considered unclean and is not supposed to pray or touch the Holy Quran or practice any religious ritual while in menses. This notion of uncleanliness inhibits most, if not all, women in many countries such as Egypt even today. Even when women themselves do not really believe in this attitude, instead of taking menstruation as a simple biological activity, they feel uneasy and sometimes isolate themselves. Thus, menstruation becomes a real burden every month and another source of psychological oppression.

It is interesting here that the narrator herself refers to menses as being "unclean" and as a "curse" (*MWD,* 12). In addition, mentioning "God" four times in two pages (*MWD,* 11–12) points to the religious attitude toward women's bodies. This socioreligious determination of femininity leads to what feminist theory calls the alienation of women from their bodies. This alienation is expressed in *Memoirs* in two ways: first, ignorance: "I knew nothing about my body" (*MWD,* 22); second, hatred and rejection: "I hated my nature" (*MWD,* 22). The feminine body, as constructed by society, dictates a woman's movements and activities. Instead of being the physical extension of the woman's inner self, through which she enjoys contact with the outside world, the constructed body becomes a prison that limits the possibilities of her existence and usually obstructs her happiness:

> I felt as if I was in chains—chains forged from my own blood tying me
> to the bed so that I couldn't run and jump, chains produced by the cells
> of my own body, chains of shame and humiliation. I turned in on myself
> to cover up my miserable existence. (*MWD*, 12)

This stage of rejection and hating the self as female, however, whether conscious or unconscious, does not last forever. For many women like the heroine of *Memoirs*, a new stage of awareness begins when they decide to discover their bodies and thus learn how to accept and even be proud of themselves as women. Unfortunately, not all women, even today, have or are given the chance to overcome the rejection and to contest the negative and limiting meanings assigned to the female body. Many women brought up in patriarchal and chauvinist societies, especially illiterate women, are brainwashed forever; the rejection of their femininity stays with them as long as they live. Though the heroine of *Memoirs* does not give credit to outside factors in her decision to be different and to uncover the deception of society, she tells us that she has chosen to challenge the system that makes women dependent, if not parasitic, fragile sexual symbols. She chooses to discover herself and thus the people around her.

Through studying medicine (how appropriate!), the science of the body, she is boldly introduced to the nakedness of the human body, both male and female. Medicine will put her in control of men's and women's bodies. She will transcend her body. It is interesting to note that medicine, in its liberal and symbolic power, was the absolute heart of the western feminist battle in the education sphere. Opening the medical profession to women was one of the main objectives of the suffragettes in Britain.[23] In *Memoirs*, the need to challenge was also another reason why she wanted to do medicine. Although it is no longer unusual to see women doctors in most Arab countries today, in 1950s Egypt it was very rare for women to study not only medicine but science in general. Fortunate girls who had access to education were supposed to study arts or languages; science was only for clever people, for men. To go to a medical faculty in those days was in itself a revolution. In *Memoirs* she wanted, as she herself asserted, to prove to everybody (beginning with her own family and especially her mother) that she could be at least as intelligent and efficient as a man:

> I was going to show my mother that I was more intelligent than
> my brother, than the man she'd wanted me to wear the cream dress for,
> than any man, and that I could do everything my father did and more.
> (*MWD*, 22)

It is interesting to note that the writer not only makes her heroine a scientist but also makes the man with whom she is to be united an artist; sexist representation would usually reverse the roles. The reversal of this situation in *Memoirs* challenges the whole idea of what society determines a woman can do and what a man is capable of. This also has implications for reading the love story between the narrator and the third man she meets as a success story involving a relationship between science and art versus the relation between science and science; her first relationship with an engineer and her second with a physician both fail.

A woman scientist (thesis) and a man artist (antithesis) are subsumed in one synthesis by making the man and the woman meet at the end of the text. This kind of plot strengthens the dialectical structure in the text. Some readers, especially male ones, might find the preceding quotation and other similar passages to be too assertive in their rhetoric. The objection would be that (as George Tarabishi has argued of Saadawi herself), by appropriating the male role, the narrator is trying to be like a man, to compete with men in terms of the values that men have set up. Within the text itself, quite apart from what a male reader might think, this position of denying the female role and seeking to enter the man's world is later relativized and overcome; but it is a very important and necessary stage in the development of the narrator's female consciousness. Moreover, as women's roles increasingly change, such hard and fast notions of the man's world or behavior appropriate to gender are bound to change. The narrator herself rejects her earlier attitude when she realizes that it is not enough to compete with men. So it is a one-sided reading—unfair and inadequate—to stress, as Tarabishi does, the fact that all the narrator wants is to be a man. It might be useful to recall that Michel Foucault argues in *Discipline and Punish: The Birth of the Prison* (1977) that the exercise of power leads to rebellion. This is exactly what happens in a society like Egypt or any other where women are commonly and strongly believed to have half or even a quarter of the brain of a man. It is no wonder that a woman would want to reject this belief in such assertive rhetoric as in *Memoirs*. When the narrator says that she is more intelligent than her brother, she does not mean that women are cleverer than men. She just means that some women can be cleverer than some men, which is simply true.

DECONSTRUCTING AND RECONSTRUCTING THE BODY

Through practicing medicine, the narrator literally deconstructs the human body, male and female, on the dissecting table and metaphorically deconstructs the social meanings given to the body. Scientific knowledge, including medical knowledge, is the key to proving that the physical or biological differences between a man and a woman have no mental or intellectual extensions. The fact that a man's body looks different from a woman's body does not mean, as it is sometimes believed, that his brain is different or superior to hers. Science proves that, although nature creates male and female bodies, it does not dictate that the one should be superior to the other. Men make men of themselves and make women of females, a process in which many women collaborate. In other words, society, not nature, makes men and women. This is the message we get from *Memoirs*.

It is quite obvious that the heroine's conflict with femininity at an early stage is not a conflict against nature but against society. She is fully aware that it is society that determines femininity and masculinity. There are many references to this awareness. For example, she asks why "had my mother made all these tremendous distinctions" and "why had society always tried to convince me that manhood was distinction and an honour, and womanhood a weakness and a disgrace?" (*MWD*, 25). The references to real people in certain societies are enough to prove her awareness of the social determination of gender and to prove that her battle is against social laws and not her own nature as a female, as some critics of Saadawi such as Tarabishi claim. "It's difficult for a woman to combine being beautiful with being clever" (*MWD*, 55), says the first man she marries, a scientifically educated engineer. The author's explanation of why people think like this makes it clear that the narrator is aware that gender is socially determined:

> From early childhood a girl is brought up to believe that she's a body and nothing more, so her body becomes her main concern for the rest of her life, and she doesn't realize that she's got a mind as well which must be looked after and encouraged to develop.
>
> Because men, who hold the key positions in life, don't want women to be anything more than beautiful, stupid animals whose legs they can lie between when they feel like it. Men don't want women as equals or partners; they want them to be subordinate and to serve them. (*MWD*, 55–56)

If this is social law, made by men, then why not fight it when it is so unjust to women, who constitute half of humanity? So the narrator fights the supposed laws of gender. She demystifies what has been made holy by society. It is part of the process of demystification that she, being a doctor, sees the human body not as a unified subject but as an assembly of material tissues. The description of the male and female bodies is made disgusting in order to achieve the aim of showing the contrast between what society has made of a man's body, on the one hand, and a woman's body, on the other, and what science has literally proven these bodies to be. Society has made a man's body "the terror of mothers and little girls" (*MWD*, 25); the scalpel shows her this body "covered with hair and the inside full of decaying stinking organs, his brain floating in a sticky white fluid and his heart in thick red blood" (*MWD*, 26). On the dissecting table, what attracts men in a living woman becomes a "piece of old shoe leather" (*MWD*, 26), the hair which is thought to be "a woman's crowning glory which she carries on her head and wastes her life arranging . . . fell into the filthy bin along with other unwanted bodily matter and scraps of flesh" (*MWD*, 27). There has always been a link, of course, between hair and sexuality.[24]

Science has proven to the narrator that "women are like men and men like animals" (*MWD*, 23). But this is not enough on its own; science cannot answer all questions or solve all mysteries—like death, for example. Under the rule of science she lives among living people whom she sees as mobile corpses; what kind of monstrous life is this? She could not go on like this, bound all her life "to illness, pain and death" (*MWD*, 35). A moment of rebirth occurs when she acquires the awareness that women are like men, animals and mortal creatures; this is manifested in her conflict against constructed femininity. But now she is acquiring a worldwide awareness that puts her more into the socialist sphere of feminism, for she tells us: "The focus of the struggle inside [her] widened out from masculinity and femininity to embrace humankind as a whole" (*MWD*, 38). To do that she has to look for a new direction, for science "toppled from its throne and fell at [her] feet naked and powerless, just as man had done before" (*MWD*, 39). From the world of reason to that of emotion, from science to art, nature is perceived in a different way.

In the bosom of nature, the narrator is reborn; she experiences new ways of living. She becomes closer to her own body, to her "naked self." She even learns how to enjoy eating, drinking, laughing loud, and lying down on grass, thus challenging the advice her mother gave her when she was a little girl. She no longer feels inhibited when "the gentle breeze lifted [her] skirt over [her] thighs" (*MWD*, 44). Her body is not "shameful." She finds her own body as experienced by herself, not as understood by men. By stripping herself "bare of the medical and scientific knowledge," she learns how to love people around her. Probably the most important change is that she no longer sees her patients as a "loose assemblage of discrete parts" (*MWD,* 43). She sees the human body in its integrity again, as "a whole person" (*MWD,* 45). We have seen how Huda Shaarawi liked to take refuge in the garden. Indeed, it has been argued that, in women's writing, nature "becomes an ally of the woman hero, keeping her in touch with her selfhood, a kind of talisman that enables her to make her way through the alienations of male society."[25] Having spent time in nature, the narrator of *Memoirs* returns to her family in the city filled with love of life and people, letting both her soul and body face life as it comes. She goes back to practice medicine with a new spirit, new outlook, and new understanding. She sympathizes with the sick and cries for them and becomes aware of the suffering caused by poverty, moving from a general humanism to a socialist awareness.

MARRIAGE AND/OR MEDICINE?

The narrator decides to give expression to her sexuality for the first time. Is it time to unite with a man, and at what cost? The first marriage relationship is significant because of two interrelated points that are essential for feminists: the marriage contract itself and the role of the woman as mother. She has to reconcile herself to a contract that treats her as a commodity, an article of merchandise, for the sake of the man with whom she agrees to unite, for whom the contract is "just a formality, nothing more" (*MWD,* 26). The (Islamic) marriage contract the narrator has to sign is shown to amount to more or less buying and selling a woman. In this regard, *Memoirs* is much more radical than *Harem Years,* for Shaarawi does not question her marriage contract, as her type of feminism does not object to all religious ideologies and practices. In *Memoirs,* the new husband soon proves that he does not believe that the marriage contract is just a formality as he had claimed. Something so basic and essential for a woman's self-respect has to be reconciled, and for what? For a man who turns out to be a typical reactionary traditionalist, for whom a woman is only respected when she is a mother or acts like one.

The term "mother" symbolizes, foremost, ultimate sacrifice, endless giving, giving up the self for the sake of the family, for the husband and children. The role of the mother is heavily celebrated in Islam; according to the Prophet, "Paradise lies at the mother's feet" (Hadith). In fact, this issue of the mother (as against the witch or the prostitute) is one of the main issues that feminist and nonfeminist defenders of Islam have to deal with in relation to the question of women. Childless women are not very much respected in

Arabic countries. Divorce, which the Prophet says is one of the most abhorred actions that God "himself" legalized, is granted to a man whose wife is barren. This is not to deny that Islam also grants divorce to women whose husbands are sterile; however, barren women suffer not only from being unable to bear children but also because they are women. In *Memoirs*, the rejection of the first husband, who wanted a wife who would utterly replace his dead mother, is a rejection of the whole institution of marriage, according to which women are seen merely as potential mothers. This is a feminist triumph. Thus, we see that the first attempt at unification has failed; but although unsuccessful in one sense, the outcome is victorious in a feminist sense.

A very important issue for feminists (especially those whose background of struggle is somewhat like Egypt's, where women have not yet achieved their liberation or equal rights as such) is touched upon in this paragraph:

> How dare they, these people who handed themselves to me body and soul, whom I saved from ruinous illness and death? What right had they to object to something in my private life, or to tell me their opinion? I was the one . . . Had they forgotten, or did they think that when I took off my stethoscope and white coat, I put aside my mind and intelligence and personality? How little they knew! (*MWD*, 67)

A woman is a woman—this is what an average Egyptian or Arab would say. In such societies, professional women who have some kind of independence can only enjoy being somehow equal while at their workplace. In her everyday social life, a professional woman is treated almost like any other woman or "housewife." The heroine of *Memoirs*, being a famous doctor though a divorcee, is an example of those fortunate women who have at least the economic or financial resources to be able to live independently of the family. A single or a divorced woman is supposed to live with her family until she marries or remarries; only women with money and a strong personality can separate from the family. Within the family in most Arab societies, a feminist woman is bound or expected to make a lot of compromises, due to family ties and duties. Compromise is a problem for feminists in obstructing or slowing down the pace of the women's liberation movement.

In *Memoirs*, there is no compromise:

> . . . I wanted a perfect man like one in my imagination and a perfect love and I wasn't going to abandon either of these goals, however long it meant I had to be alone. "All or nothing" was my abiding principle and I'd never accept half measures. (*MWD*, 71)

As a divorced woman, the narrator has to put up with the gossip around her, as characterized by the educated man's (the doctor's) view: "once a woman's been married, she's much more liberated than a young virgin" (*MWD*, 74). What he means by liberated is, of course, easy-going or rather cheap; this is why she answers him "angrily":

> My emancipation doesn't stem from a physical change within my body. Any restrictions on my body aren't because I fear for an insignificant hymen which can be torn by a random blow and restored by a surgeon's needle. I impose my own restrictions on myself voluntarily, and exercise my freedom, as I understand the word, in the same way. (*MWD*, 74)

Having considered what type of obstacles a feminist may face in such societies, it is perhaps legitimate to say that to look for a "perfect man" or "perfect love" is a romantic hope but to find one is even more of a utopian dream. Nevertheless, Saadawi lets her heroine find the ideal lover she seeks. What is the significance of this ending? Has it anything to do with the fact that *Memoirs* first "appeared in serialized form in the Egyptian magazine Ruz al-Yusuf in 1957" (*MWD*, p. 7)? What type of ending is this, closed or open? What is the effect of such an ending on the reader?

THE ENDING

Before reading the ending of the book, one must remember two significant points. The first is that the book was originally published in serial form in a magazine, which justifies reading the ending as a happy one, as I argue. The second point is that since the book was censored and has never been published in its original and complete form, the ending could have been different, for all we know. However, one can only read the ending of the published book, for it is the same whether in Arabic or English.

The ending of *Memoirs* can be read at least in two different ways. First, if we take the last line—"I buried my head in his chest and wept tears of quiet relief" (*MWD*, 101)—to mean just giving up her autonomous existence for the sake of "the ideal man," then the passage can be read as the rather conventional happy ending of romances. This view would be in keeping with the fact that *Memoirs* was published in a woman's magazine: the ending may be meant to mix pleasure with a feminist message for young women. The second reading goes beyond the last line to doubt how significant the man is at the end and also sees the ending as politically loaded. In the light of the last scene in the poor man's place, the "relief" the narrator felt at the end can be understood as arising from the high level of socialist awareness acquired by the doctor in that scene. When the poor dying man was handing her the money, she felt that

> it was not honourable, just or logical for a doctor to take a fee from a patient. How had I held out my hand all these years and taken money from my patients? How had I sold health to people in my surgery? How could I have filled my coffers from the blood and sweat of the sick? (*MWD*, 99)

She realized then that it was not an achievement to be rich and famous and that

> being a doctor wasn't a case of diagnosing the illness, prescribing the medicine and grabbing the money. Success didn't mean filling the surgery, getting rich and having my name in lights. Medicine wasn't a commodity and success was not to be measured in terms of money and fame. (*MWD*, 99–100)

The narrator recognized that being a doctor meant giving health to all who need it and that success meant giving what she had to others. In other words, she understood that she should be giving and not just taking, both as a doctor and as a woman. In fact, the last thing she was seeing at the end was not her lover's face but the

> cramped basement room, the dirty mattress on the tiles, the pool of blood, the haggard face, the hollow eyes and that long skinny arm stretched out towards me clutching the knife that had cleaved my mind and heart in two. (*MWD*, 100)

She calls the new awareness "truth"—before this she was "blind" to it. The socialist "truth" she acquired as a doctor treating the poor man is juxtaposed with the moment of personal and erotic fulfillment in the embrace. This combination could be read as conveying something rather like the feminist slogan "the personal is political," after all. She has seen the light again, another moment of rebirth that goes hand-in-hand with uniting with the beloved man. Could the final "embrace" be taken as a feminist failure or even death? Perhaps for separatists only. There is no evidence that this man is the man with whom the narrator will stay forever. Perhaps the relationship will end sooner rather than later—the reader does not know for sure. But she has seen the "light," and it would be very difficult for her and for the reader to pretend that it never happened. This is why the second reading of the ending is more strongly grounded in the text than the first.

FEMINIST CLASS-CONSCIOUSNESS

The question of class is nowhere clearer in the text than in the contrast which can be drawn between the miserable place of the poor man and the place in which the narrator herself lives: the flowers, the painting on the wall, the servant, the oven and the cake. The question of class and money is also connected with the earlier question of abortion. The poor girl who has nobody to support her, who has been cheated by a rich man (she was in his service) and who also has a father or a brother or an uncle waiting for her in the village to avenge the honor of the family—that is, to kill her—is another symbol of poverty and also of the worst form of oppression that is practiced upon women. Abortion is taken to be a violation of the "hippocratic oath" of doctors by critics like Tarabishi, who argues that the doctor should "struggle within the existing legal and medical structures to legalize and legislate for abortion. This is supposedly the democratic and radical solution to the problem."[26] Saadawi herself rightly answers such criticism:

> The heroine of *Memoirs* does not open her surgery to death through the medium of abortion . . . She intervenes to save . . . the unmarried pregnant girl who begs for her help because she knows that the girl is innocent and that the real criminal is . . . protected by society. The question, then, is not that she lives by performing abortion but that . . . she is debating the problem of rape.[27]

STRUCTURAL ISSUES AND CONCLUSION

Considering that Saadawi wrote *Memoirs* in her twenties, at a time when she had not yet been introduced to any western feminist writing,[28] one notices a considerable maturity in her dealing with the question of gender. Her feminist awareness in this early book can be described as ahead of that of many western feminists of her time. As far as her class-consciousness is concerned, one can say that, although the story in *Memoirs* centers on the subjectivity of an educated and relatively privileged heroine developing from girlhood into womanhood, the ending of the book shows clear signs of a more general interest in the public world and the lives of other people (men and women), especially the importance of medicine for the poor.

Finally, I would like to focus on the production and form of the book. The Arabic version is not introduced in any way to the reader, nor is its genre specified; it is left to the readers to read the book as they wish. A title page precedes the cover, followed by the text itself. This is probably why *Memoirs* has been always read as an autobiography by Arab readers, especially those who do not read a lot of criticism. This could be due to the association of the terms "Memoir" and "Doctor" in the title with the name of Saadawi, who was first introduced to the Arabic audience as a medical doctor. The Arabic version, however, includes some black-and-white drawings which are reminiscent of early romantic novels. These drawings are not included in the English translation of the book. Instead, it includes an introduction by Saadawi, probably to ensure that the same confusion should not happen again, in which she states that the book is fiction and not an autobiography. The publishers, Al-Saqi Books, also present the book as a novel on the back cover.

What could be the implications of reading a book as fiction rather than as an autobiography? I tend to agree with Barrett J. Mandel that readers need to know whether the book they are reading is fictitious or factual, for it does make a difference in terms of how the book is to be read. Reading an autobiography as fiction is

> a total denial of the reader's experience. It is simply a fact that readers turn to autobiography for the kind of satisfaction that one derives from reading something true rather than fabular.[29]

As a researcher on Saadawi who has read almost everything that she has written so far, I can, up to a point, distinguish what is autobiographical from what is fictitious in *Memoirs*. I am not interested in doing such an analysis, however, because (as I have made clear) it is not factual truth that I am tracing in my study of women's autobiographical writings but the strategies that women adopt when talking or writing about the self and the issues that are of most importance to them.

As far as the language and style of the book are concerned, Arab critics of Saadawi often accuse her of writing in a mediocre language and simple style, as if great literature could only be written in sophisticated language and a complicated style. The author has this to say to those critics:

> Egyptian and Arabic societies in general cannot stand ambiguity; they need complete clarity and simple vocabulary without complexity and multi-meanings. Sometimes I have to be simple in my style and language so that more Arab readers could understand me. In some novels, I am freer in that I do not bother too much about clarity, as in *The Fall of the Imam* and *The Children's Circular Song* . . . two advanced novels in terms of the artistic form and content. However, some readers found them too ambiguous and complex to understand.[30]

Writing in simple language is no sign of literary incompetence; it is rather a very good thing, considering the number of Arab men and women whose level of literacy is not too high. This is a way to reach as many readers as possible, especially given that feminist writing still has to be encouraged in Arab countries, in order to be effective in bringing about social and political change. Finally, I would like to raise the following points about translation. According to Catherine Cobham, who translated *Memoirs,* it was the easiest book she had translated from Arabic up to that time. She did not have to contact the writer about any difficulty or query, which was not always the case when she translated other books. Nor did she have to approach the publishers, Al-Saqi Books in London, who commissioned her in the first place. The one comment that Cobham had about *Memoirs* was that it was "too politically/sociologically slanted for something which purported to be a novel," and she admitted cutting down the number of rhetorical questions.[31] Being politically loaded, as is the case in most of Saadawi's writings, is no flaw in *Memoirs.* Saadawi herself admits that she cannot be neutral in her writings, for she has attitudes and opinions which she seeks to convey to her readers.[32] I cannot see how feminist writings of any kind, whether fiction or otherwise, can avoid being political, for it is the political message and the implied call for change which characterize such writings.

2. *Memoirs from the Women's Prison*

When Saadawi's *Memoirs of a Woman Doctor* was published in 1957, she was at the beginning of her literary and medical career. Since then, she has written many medical and literary books on issues of sexuality and sexual and social discrimination against women, especially in Arab countries. By the time she wrote *Memoirs from the Women's Prison* in 1981,[33] the year of her imprisonment and subsequent release, she was already a well-known figure within the Arab world and her reputation was spreading abroad. Unlike the first memoir, which publicizes the private life of a female fictional character, *Prison* is a memoir which makes public aspects of the life of a well-known public figure, the writer herself, and her prison experience. This experience is itself already a public one in the sense that the writer is not confined to solitary imprisonment but shares the same prison with hundreds of other women, both political and ordinary prisoners. One of the issues discussed here is how the private and the public are merged in *Prison* and whether the public aspect of the experience has dictated the kind of "I" the writer uses and the type of consciousness that appears in the autobiographical narrative. Has Saadawi represented a political self (well aware of its own identity and accomplishments) that has preserved a sense of uniqueness, or has her political experience allowed for some development of a collective consciousness and identification with other women?

If *Memoirs of a Woman Doctor* is a breakthrough in Arabic literature, not as a genre but in its content and feminist spirit, then *Prison* is also a leading book of its kind. Political memoirs by Arab women were rarely found before 1981. It is by no means the first prison memoir ever written by an Arab woman. In 1972 Zaynab al-Ghazali al-Jabeli, the Egyptian woman who founded the Muslim Women's Association in 1936, published her memoirs. Al-Ghazali wrote about her six years' imprisonment in a Cairo war prison, between 1965 and 1971, under Gamal Abdel Nasser for charges of collaboration with the Muslim Brethren.[34] Prison memoirs by women from outside the Arab world became available in Arabic translations. Angela Davis's memoirs, for instance, which recorded her political experience inside and outside prison, became known to the Arab public in early 1977. Although Saadawi is by no means the first Arab woman to initiate a prison memoir, she nonetheless had only a limited corpus of conventional models of political narratives to follow.

One reason why political memoirs by Arab women have been rare until recently is the limited number of women who have been involved in politics in the traditional sense of the word. It is only in the last twenty years or so that Arab regimes have gradually opened their doors to women. Due to women's education and their participation in politics, though limited, political memoirs have become more available (for example, *Diaries of a Woman from the Saudi Prisons* by Alia Makey, published in 1989; and *My Home, My Prison* by Raymonda Tawil, published in 1983).

It is not just in the Arab world that women's political memoirs have only been published recently. Hence the rarity of the theorization of women's prison narratives. That is not to say that prison writings by women, men, or both could be joined in some timeless category as if prisoners of all times and places constituted a society. Nor can prison writings be called a genre, because there are prose memoirs, poetry, songs, and other forms of writings about imprisonment. However, the experience of being imprisoned "does always have some common features, no matter what the particular historical or individual situation,"[35] which makes its theorization possible. H. Bruce Franklin attempts to theorize prison narratives in his survey of black American writings from and/or about prison experiences in *The Victim as Criminal and Artist: Literature from the American Prison*. He applies his arguments to black writings regardless of the sex of the writer, although he just briefly mentions two or three names of women who wrote about their experiences in prison, such as Bonnie Park and Edna O'Brien, both of whom published their memoirs in the mid-1930s. The following discussion only refers to what is useful and applicable to my text in his localized theory.

Another attempt at theorization is "Third World Women's Narratives of Prison" by Barbara Harlow,[36] which can be a useful guide in looking at Saadawi's *Prison*. Using examples of women from different developing countries who recorded their experiences of struggle and defiance under repressive regimes and authoritarian states, Harlow suggests that these women's prison writings, taken collectively, mark "the emergence of a new literary corpus out of contemporary conditions in the Third World."[37] She maintains that such a corpus challenges western literary, critical, and feminist theoretical developments in two simultaneous ways. First, she argues that, generically, such writings "defy traditional categories and distinctions and combine fictional forms with documentary record."[38] Second, these women's

> collective experience and the political development that they describe
> emerge out of their position within a set of social relations giving rise to
> a secular ideology, one not based on bonds of gender, race, or ethnic
> ity—which may be shared by men and may not be shared by all women.[39]

I believe that most autobiographical forms, including diaries and memoirs, whether written by westerners or otherwise, by men or women, can be said to combine the fictional and the nonfictional in one way or another. Hence, combining the fictional with the nonfictional is not an exclusive characteristic of "Third World" women's narratives, as Harlow suggests. However, Saadawi's *Prison* conforms to the twofold challenge that Harlow theorizes.

THE NARRATIVE STRUCTURE:
DOCUMENTARY, MEMORY, AND LITERARY TRANSFORMATION

First, *Prison* is a book based on diaries written while Saadawi was actually in prison. She did not have proper paper on which to write, for the prisoners were not allowed to write. When one of the cellmates asked for a pen and paper to write a letter to her mother, a senior prison administrator, referring to the power of writing, replied that it was easier to give the prisoner pistols than pens and paper (*MWP,* 49). Writing is a political issue; Saadawi and many other cellmates were imprisoned because they had written against the grain. They had committed no actual crimes in that they had not killed or robbed anyone. Their only crime was to write against the authoritarian state and express their anger against the political, social, and economic injustices practiced by Sadat's repressive regime.[40] In spite of the lack of paper, Saadawi was determined to continue writing in jail. She wrote on toilet paper and cigarette papers she bought from the prison canteen. We do not know where she got the pen. She could have hidden it when the prisoners were given pieces of paper and a pen to write down their requirements for clothes; or possibly the "shawisha" (the woman prison guard who became friendly and helpful to the political prisoners, and especially to Saadawi) gave it to her secretly; or perhaps it was an eyebrow pencil (*MWP*, 94).

When exactly did Saadawi start recording her diaries in jail? In the introduction to the Arabic version, she confirms that she wrote her first words on the day she entered prison.[41] The question of exactly when she started recording her diaries is relevant to the issue of whether the book is a pure documentary of a prison experience or whether it combines real records with fiction and imagination. Saadawi wrote to me:

> Yes, I wrote some of my prison memories on toilet paper in the cell . . . during my nights in prison . . . When I came out of prison I revised some of them, added some, which I kept in my memory. So, I can say that I did some rewriting for a part of it (not all).[42]

It is clear, then, that both diaries and memories are the storehouses from which *Prison* was written—or shall we say produced? As I have argued in the chapter on autobiography, memories can be accurate or misleading, true or false, exact or approximate, literal or figurative; and diaries (the substitute for memories and protection against forgetfulness), because they are written, can be judged according to the same criteria even when the words follow only hours after the events they describe. Reading through the 190 pages of *Prison,* one can easily feel that the dichotomy between fiction and nonfiction is false. For just as Saadawi is no doubt truthful in her documentation of her three-month prison experience, she also makes use of her literary imagination, not in creating actions or characters that did not happen or exist but in describing people and events and by making use of some fictional techniques. She does this without making her experience any less real to the reader than to herself.

The technique of *Prison* is not simple or straightforward but complex and novel-like. Events are not arranged according to their chronological order; instead many flashbacks interrupt the sequence of incidents throughout the pages because memories from the past or contemplations about the present or the future are conjured up in the mind of the narrator or because she wants to express certain feelings inspired by particular actions or scenes. For example, the book opens with a knock at the door of the flat where the narrator is sitting trying to write her novel. It takes this door seven whole pages to be opened, including four pages of flashbacks, introspection, and reflection on who is knocking and what could have happened before she actually answers the door, which has to be broken down by the impatient policeman. Between the first and the second knock, she is thinking about the novel she is writing, the one she started in 1978 when she was in Addis Ababa working for the United Nations. Between the second and the third, it is her memory of her flat in Addis Ababa, how much she missed Egypt and its poor people while abroad, and her estrangement when she returned to Egypt—losing her job because of her outspokenness and criticism of the repressive Egyptian regime and of the apparatus of the United Nations, in which "Third World women slide to the bottom of the heap" (*MWP,* 3). Between the third and fourth knock, she reflects upon how the agreement with Israel changed the attitude of the Egyptian people, who have become corrupt. The book is full of other examples of this technique.

Moreover, the language of *Prison* is the language of a literary book by a writer who has had a long experience in writing literature rather than the language of a simple chronicle of daily events. Daily memories are obviously the main source of the language; however, the descriptive details of people the narrator has met could not have come out of memory alone; they require a great deal of imagination. For example, at the police station on the day of the arrest, Saadawi is left for a while with an old guard. In her description of him she gives certain details that probably were not really remembered but rather were partly invented, such as the number of buttons he had on his jacket (*MWP,* 12).

Even if people do remember astonishing details in crucial circumstances, such as an arrest, Saadawi's inclusion of such details signifies a literary narrative. The language is also ironical and the style sometimes cynical, both of which contribute to the literariness of the narrative. For example, when the police car taking her to the station breaks down, Saadawi finds the humor to write: "Lucky for me that I was born in an underdeveloping country where police cars are ancient and liable to break down" (*MWP,* 20).

The use of myth throughout the pages of *Prison* also creates an atmosphere of fiction: for example, "Their long and sharp pointed rifles and bayonets reminded me of the needles which used to be plunged into the bodies of witches in search of the mark of the devil" (*MWP*, 23); and "On one shoulder, raised higher than the other, a black stripe perches like a black feather on the head of a mythical bird or legendary beast of ancient times" (*MWP*, 27). In fact, the whole experience of prison from the beginning—the arrest without a warrant from the chief prosecutor or investigation—to the end seems to be a nightmare for Saadawi, because at many moments she tells us that she is "still unable to believe this scene" (*MWP*, 10), as if the whole story were a myth. The use of myth is entirely illustrative and localized, however, for it does not disturb the very matter-of-fact, rational approach of the book—as is the case, for example, in Maxine Hong Kingston's *The Woman Warrior*, in which the myth takes over completely and becomes as real as the real-life story. There is nevertheless a similarity between Saadawi's and Kingston's narrative methods. In her memoirs, Kingston uses an alternative narrative pattern which deindividualizes her at the same time as it gives her a pattern in which to explain her life and struggles. As we shall see shortly, Saadawi's narrative fluctuates between a desire to identify her individual self, on the one hand, and the need to relate this self to the community of oppressed women, on the other.

PRISON SOCIETY: DIS/UNITY

Thus, we see that *Prison* combines factual and fictional aspects together with documentary and literary features. The second challenge that *Prison* offers is that—although it is a diary like any other diary or autobiographical piece of writing intended for publication, which is born out of a personal desire to share one's individual experience with the reader—it is not "intended as a display of individual genius," as Franklin argues.[43] Challenging the literary criteria dominant in the western, male, middle-class academy which celebrates what is extraordinary or unique, most recent autobiographical writing from prison "intends to show the readers that the author's individual experience is not unique or even extraordinary, but typical and representative," Franklin suggests.[44] Instead of telling the reader all about their childhood and the circumstances that led them to crime or to imprisonment, whether justly or unjustly, and about their own feelings inside prison and the way they conceive their lives, recent writers of imprisonment experiences, especially black Americans, write about the injustices of the system which led black people to crime or which unjustly led them back to jail and about other inmates and their sense of belonging with them. In Angela Davis's autobiography, for example, blackness, not gender, is the main issue. Her autobiography is an autobiography of a black woman in an American jail rather than an autobiography of a woman who happened to be black in an American jail.

In the same way, in Saadawi's memoirs gender and class differences are contained in an almost utopian solidarity among women and men of various convictions and backgrounds, all united against an oppressive regime. Defining a collective identity in prison, therefore, can be extended to non-American writers who are imprisoned under repressive governments.

Although Saadawi maintains a clear sense of achievement and self-distinction (not only in *Prison* but in most of her writings), in her record of her own imprisonment experience she manages to represent the collective experience of a group of women in prison united by social and political oppression. These women, although they have personal names, lose their specific identities at times and become representative of all Egyptian women outside prison. What happened to each of them could have happened to any other Egyptian woman. In other words, none of them, including Saadawi, is intended to represent a unique or an extraordinary case; they simply represent a sample of Egyptian women under similar conditions of social and political repression. It is interesting that Saadawi uses the title *Memoirs from the Women's Prison* — not *My Memoirs in Prison,* for example, or any other title in the singular mode — which indicates the collective nature of her book. Although her own story remains the central one, her own memoirs are interwoven with the lives of the other women she has met and admired in jail. Her own case as a political prisoner is not any more heroic or important than that of Fathiyya, for instance, who is in jail because she killed her husband for raping their own daughter.

In prison, political detainees were separated from ordinary prisoners (*MWP,* 58); however, all prisoners got together (though still separated by bars) in the afternoons for rest and exercise. Among the two sets of prisoners, a sense of ambiguous affiliation was created, producing a kind of bonding. Political detainees, most of whom were educated women and thus of middle- to upper-class background, were treated differently by the prison authorities. Their demands for better food and hygienic conditions in the cell were met (although only when the prison was under inspection by higher authorities), unlike those of the criminal offenders, most of whom were poor and dejected women. Some of the prostitutes from the second set of prisoners were ordered to clean the cell of political detainees (*MWP,* 49), a further sign of class discrimination practiced by the prison apparatus itself. When they complained of the noise coming from the ordinary prisoners and their children's cell, the authorities were very quick to build a wall separating the two cells (*MWP,* 44).

This discrimination did not deter the prisoners from both cells from communicating with each other. The ordinary prisoners sometimes acted as conduits for messages to and from the outside world. Saadawi used to give bread to Nabawiyya, a schizophrenic woman behind bars. Among the women who committed criminal offenses, it is "Fathiyya-the-murderess," a poor woman from a village who killed her husband because she found him raping their nine-year-old daughter, who poses for society "the most serious challenge to the conventional forms of social bonding and relationships."[45] If Saadawi is not putting words in her mouth, then Fathiyya also presents one of the most feminist speeches in *Prison,* considering that she is uneducated:

> I killed my husband for the sake of myself, in order to save myself from living with a man who was oppressing me. He wronged me all my life, and I served him like a slave serves a master. He never in his life said one pleasant word to me. My life with him was black from the first day to the last. Every day I'd think, "I'll kill him," until I saw him with my daughter Haniyya. A person can't kill easily, or in a single day or night. The whole time I lived with him I thought about killing him. (*MWP,* 115)

The political prisoners as well, although "of different generations, ages, and outlooks on life" (*MWP,* 35), found some kind of mutual feeling and sympathy which brought them together. These new social ties among the women prisoners challenge not only the prison apparatus, which tries to separate political from common prisoners, but also the whole social apparatus which is built on familial or biological filiation. This is Edward Said's notion of affiliative rather than filiative groupings, where individuals affiliate with a range of different groups and form their sense of identity through a set of complex allegiances.[46]

As Harlow argues, the narrative in *Prison* is

> organized on one level around the tension of conflicting personal allegiances and social ties, an ideological conflict brought out most dramatically by the physical impenetrability of the prison walls.[47]

That is to say, the wall that Saadawi is put behind does not separate her from life altogether, nor does it stop her activities as the authorities have hoped. She challenges the state, which separates her from her husband and children, by building new bonding relationships with inmates and other cellmates, some of whom are women of differing or opposing views and of different social backgrounds whom she keeps in touch with even after she is released. When she first arrived in the cell, she saw a number of veiled women (some of them old friends of hers), with whom she had discussions and disagreements about Islam and the veil. After a few days, however, a sense of love for all these women overwhelmed her and her differences from them:

> . . . all the faces around me beloved and near my heart. Even those faces hidden under the black veils . . . when the niqaabs were lifted I could see faces that were shining, clear, overflowing with love, a cooperative spirit, and humanity. (*MWP,* 39)

Like all political prisoners, Saadawi is separated from her family and not allowed to see them at all. In jail, she finds another family, though not of her own blood. Within this family of biologically unrelated women, Saadawi relives her "entire childhood" (*MWP,* 39); she lives "a communal life" (*MWP,* 39). There are moments of joy even in prison away from her husband and children and a feeling of solidarity against the common enemy, the oppressive state:

> I recaptured my happiness as a student . . . Rejoicing, growing angry and fighting, mending our differences . . . From the disagreements among us . . . one would have thought oceans separated one from another, and that each of us was an island unto herself. The dispute might yet grow more intense, but soon we would draw together, there would be harmony among us, and we would close ranks, a solid line facing the single power which had put us behind bars. (*MWP,* 40)

When the prison authorities tried to separate Nur, the Christian woman in their cell, the cellmates "stood in closed ranks, to prevent her from being taken away" (*MWP,* 40).

Unlike Shaarawi's and Tuqan's memoirs, *Prison* does not dedicate long chapters or pages to family members. Saadawi misses her husband and children, whom she mentions here and there, but we as readers do not get to know anything about them. They are absent figures in the book; we just know that they are there outside prison. She does not even mention her father much. The mother is only remembered on her deathbed. Saadawi's nine siblings are not mentioned at all. The absence of siblings might not be significant to English readers, but it is definitely so for Arab readers. The absence of family members in the book can be justified by their absence in prison. After all, Saadawi is imprisoned alone. She could have written more about them in the book, however, as absent loved ones would be remembered in circumstances like those of the prison. Instead, Saadawi focuses her memoirs on the new group of women with whom she shared the days of her imprisonment and the social, economic, and political circumstances which led each of them to be there.

Ahdaf Soueif has criticized the type of women who come to life under Saadawi's touch. He finds it curious that other women from her cell, such as Latifa al-Zayyat, Awatif Abd-el-Rahman, Shahinda Muqallad, Safinaz Kazim, and Amina Rashid, all of whom are as educated and well known as Saadawi herself, are "reduced to the role of a chorus providing backing for Saadawi's courageous outspokenness."[48] It is true that Saadawi writes more about women from the other cell, such as Dhouba, the gentle black procuress; Sabah, the mad prophetic beggar; and Fathiyya-the-Murderess, all of whom are illiterate. Soueif implies that Saadawi is not crediting the educated women by not writing about them as much as she does about the other women. Instead of seeing this as a sign of arrogance, however, it could be seen more positively as Saadawi's effort to be a spokeswoman for these illiterate women and their unjust circumstances. This is another challenge to the state, for ordinary prisoners are not allowed to communicate with the political prisoners. The other educated women are quite capable of writing whatever they want about their experiences in prison, just as Saadawi has done about hers.

The day after her release, Saadawi went back to prison, this time to take food to her cellmates who had not yet been released. Furthermore, she did not ignore the note they sent with the "shawisha" asking her to work for their transfer to a prison hospital. With her help, through some people she knew, the prisoners were first transferred and then released shortly afterward. Thus, we see that Saadawi has developed a communal consciousness which brings her together with other women. In her diary, she not only writes her own story of struggle but also rewrites the social order to include a vision of new relational possibilities that transcend ethnic, class, and familial ties.

ASSERTIVENESS

Arab male critics have always criticized and felt uneasy about Saadawi's assertive style. Her assertiveness, however, is what has made her special and differentiated her from other Arab feminists, especially those who preceded her. This assertiveness comes partially from her authoritative knowledge of medicine, which demystifies many traditional beliefs that have for centuries been responsible for a great many forms of discrimination between the sexes. Saadawi is never shy about using such knowledge to support her feminist arguments. Her literary language is also greatly influenced by her scientific knowledge. Her assertiveness is manifested not only in her authoritative use of science and medical knowledge but also in feminist terms as well. We have seen that the heroine of *Memoirs of a Woman Doctor* stands taller than many men and declares that she is cleverer than a man could be. Here again in *Prison,* Saadawi, the heroine of her own book, declares on various occasions that she is "more worthy of respect than any man, including your precious Head Director" (*MWP,* 17), as she angrily answers the guard. She does not hide her admiration for her self-image, which has features usually ascribed to the masculine, like her "tall stature and [her] strong, taut muscles" (*MWP,* 41). "Femininity is not weakness" (*MWP,* 41) for Saadawi.

Saadawi's assertiveness has sometimes been interpreted as an indication of a radical attack on men. This is a misunderstanding by her unsympathetic critics. For example, a statement such as "Behind every one of these women prisoners is a man" (*MWP,* 44), if read alone, could be used in order to label her as basically a man-hater. However, she does not make statements like this without explaining that it is not the fault of men alone as a sex but that the whole social and political apparatus is to blame. These women are pushed to crime because of "oppression by men," she explains; they are the "other face of the system," which is held responsible for both women's and men's oppression. Men are her comrades rather than enemies, especially when they themselves are oppressed by the same system—even those who hold opposite ideas to hers, those in long beards and "gallabiyyas," namely, the Muslim Brethren: "I felt that they were all my comrades—we were united by a single destiny" (*MWP,* 147), she recalls. Her recognition of economic and ideological factors in sustaining forms of oppression, including women's, is apparent in all of her writings, both literary and theoretical.

Elizabeth Winston, in her essay "The Autobiographer and Her Readers: From Apology to Affirmation," argues that British and American women who wrote autobiographies before 1920 tended to be shy about presenting themselves as successful people; instead they were apologetic in their tone and style. Women who wrote autobiographies after 1920, however, were no longer intimidated by offensive criticism and no longer apologized for their careers and success.[49] This theory can be applied to Arab women writers as well, although not with the same chronology and with a different separation date. Any person who bothers to write (even without an intention to publish) an autobiographical record must have some sense of self-achievement which she or he considers worthwhile communicating, but different people have celebrated their experiences to varying degrees. Huda Shaarawi, who wrote her memoirs before 1947, for example, was no writer; and her tone is timid and almost apologetic. This sense of timidity is manifested by dedicating longer chapters to people and circumstances she thinks she is indebted to for what she achieves later in her life. More recently, Fadwa Tuqan, whose autobiography was first serialized between 1978 and 1979, introduces her autobiography in a justifying manner, writing that she wants other people to benefit from her story of struggle. Tuqan, however, who is acknowledged even by male standards as one of the leading modern Arab poets, is not "happy about [her] life; for the tree of [her] life [has] given very few fruits."[50] It could be just humility that makes Tuqan underestimate her literary achievements, but the apologetic tone is again noticeable throughout her autobiography.

With Saadawi, whose literary career started in the late 1950s and early 1960s, apology has no place. The assertiveness or authoritativeness with which she writes—which does not necessarily make the "I" in her narratives any more individualistic than Shaarawi's or Tuqan's—does project a more confident and proud self-image. Saadawi, having been a successful medical doctor for many years, also celebrates herself as a writer. She is never on the defensive as far as her books are concerned, and chauvinist criticism does not stop her from writing: she continues to write as prolifically as ever. Saadawi openly asserts her intellectual and aesthetic gifts and her serious commitment to the literary life. Whenever she is interviewed, she insists that she is, first and second, a writer and only third or probably tenth a doctor.[51] She regards her profession as artistic, not political or social.[52] As far as Saadawi is concerned, her books "are in almost every home" in the Arab countries, and she has "left an influence" on people there.[53]

WRITING IS POWER

Saadawi is not the only person who is known for keeping a diary (from which her memoirs are constructed) on toilet paper inside prison; Ngugi wa Thiongo, from Kenya, for example, is also known for doing the same. Writing is an activity that prisoners create in order to remain sane, pass time, and feel productive; other prisoners are known to have created songs and stories. In this respect, Saadawi's memoirs are consistent with the majority of books on incarceration.[54]

For Saadawi, however, writing is the political act in her memoirs, for she was actually detained because of her writings. At the beginning of *Prison,* at the time of her arrest, she is sitting at her desk writing a novel. In fact the whole book can be seen as examining when and where writing is prohibited. Writing her diaries behind the prison wall challenges oppressive rules and regulations. But writing for Saadawi is more than just an act of disobedience. In *Prison,* she courageously writes this startling confession: "the pen is the most valuable thing in my life" and writing for her is more valuable than her life, her children, her husband, and her freedom (*MWP,* 116). She prefers jail to being free as an agent for the government and writing only what pleases the authorities. The "I" that Saadawi presents in her writings is a responsible one. It is a matter of survival that her "I" should not only be expressed but be heard as well.[55] She has a sense of her audience in mind: "I [am] not writing for angels in the sky."[56] In an interview in 1986, Saadawi stated that her writings would have no effect at all if she wrote about something her audience, the Arab people, totally rejected.[57] This means that her audience is prioritized in her writings.

Saadawi has been writing mainly for other people and not only for her own self-satisfaction. She has an ambition, though, to break through all the restrictions imposed on her by the authorities, including Arab publishers, and to "experiment with language, to experiment with ideas, to have more freedom," even though this means that her new books might not be published in the Arab world at all.[58] This does not indicate that Saadawi is becoming impatient with her audience or that she wants to be more subjective in her new writing but that she aspires for her writings to be more uncensored. She wants to write "freely about . . . religion, sex, God, authority, the State,"[59] the same subjects she has been dealing with in her writings, but in a freer mode. Thus, Saadawi's "I"—the censored and the less censored she dreams of representing—is an articulation of a self which, far from being self-centered, views its private existence as only part of a more public one.

POLITICAL ISSUES

There is no use asking why *Prison* was written at all: very few people would resist writing about a dramatic experience such as imprisonment, provided they have the linguistic skill to do so. Hundreds if not thousands of prison memoirs exist all round the world. This memoir, which on the surface seems to be an account of a prison experience, is first and foremost a book packed with political issues, which would appeal to vast numbers of Arab people with differing attitudes and interests. Throughout *Prison,* Saadawi protests against the absence of democracy and basic human rights, such as freedom of speech, under Sadat's authoritarian regime. Today most Arab countries are still ruled by one-party governments which are also autocratic, dictatorial, and oppressive to those who do not conform. She criticizes the hypocrisy and two-facedness practiced under oppressive governments. A friend of hers, for example, a "leading literary man working at a major daily Cairene news-paper" (*MWP,* 3), does not practice what he preaches; his justification is that he is afraid to lose his job, which would mean that his family would starve. It is fear which makes people submissive: "fearing servility, people become servile" (*MWP,* 3), Saadawi argues. Freedom is necessary for all men and women, especially for writers, "for when the authorities get angry with a writer, they can . . . stifle the writer's voice so that it won't reach anyone" (*MWP,* 3), a liberal view shared by most Arab intellectuals, which she raises again in *My Travels around the World.*

Prison also addresses nationalism and patriotism, motifs which run throughout the book. From the first page, Saadawi tells us that she loves her country—Egypt—and that she carries it inside her wherever she goes. How-ever, she is "estranged in [her] own country" (*MWP,* 2), a phrase with which many Arab people would sigh in agreement today. Fawqiyya, an inmate, shouts that "national duty comes before any other" (*MWP,* 115) to the veiled women who are discussing the duty of a mother in watching out for children. Saadawi does not comment on this debate in *Prison.* Although she calls her-self a socialist and a nationalist, she does not believe that socialism can get rid of women's oppression without the solidarity of women.[60] In fact, in *Prison,* the economic, intellectual, political, and social differences among women are suppressed, at times romanticized, and the whole experience of solidarity is represented as a utopian dream. The tension between wishing for or aiming at political unity (which is what Saadawi is doing in *Prison* and also again in *My Travels around the World*) and recognizing difference at the same time reflects the gap between the readership that Saadawi is trying to construct and her actual readership. In Arab countries, national and political unity is a dream; difference is reality.

In most developing countries, nationalism and socialism are intertwined. In *Prison,* Saadawi develops a constant and powerful socialist consciousness. She is clearly critical of class division in Egyptian society, mirrored in the prison apparatus. She states that she has greater love for her father's "peasant" relatives than for her mother's relatives (who were rich, upper-class people living in Cairo). They were the poor class, but they were also the people who "urinate blood" (*MWP,* 110).

As far as the religious issue is concerned, many Arab readers of Saadawi consider her books to be against religion. Saadawi's atheism is open for discussion, and one needs to read her other books before making a judgment. Yet it is evident that she does not practice any Islamic rituals. Her language in *Prison,* moreover, is free of religious connotation. She never intervenes in discussions about God, Islam, or the veil whenever these take place among the prisoners. She sarcastically mocks the idea of woman being incomplete because "she was created from the crooked rib, and only straightens up through beating" (*MWP,* 132), as Bodour, one of the veiled women, believes.

FEMINIST CONSCIOUSNESS

Although the situation of women and the issue of the veil are not discussed by Saadawi as a central topic in *Prison,* these issues do come across very strongly in the book. An interesting contrast is drawn, for example, between Saadawi's view of women and the views of women as perceived by Islamic ideologies, especially the most conservative ones. She herself is very proud of her femininity and her determined personality (*MWP,* 143). Some other women, especially the veiled ones, do not agree with Saadawi's opinions of what a woman is. For them, a woman is all shame; laughing, singing, and all pleasures are taboos; a woman's face is a blemish and must be covered. For Saadawi, "shameful blemishes are oppression, falsehood, and the eradication of the human mind, whether a woman's or a man's" (*MWP,* 29). For the conservative Muslim women, "women are not liked to be happy" (*MWP,* 38). One of the policemen thinks that, according "to Islam, women are lacking in mental power and faith" (*MWP,* 21). Yet for Saadawi, this is a matter of interpretation, for "there is more than one Islam" (*MWP,* 21). Moreover, "a woman's place is home, husband and children" for Saadawi's aunt and the Muslim women prisoners. They think that a woman is nothing without a man. For Saadawi, a woman "should be honoured for her own efforts, not because she is the wife of a man who has influence and power" (*MWP,* 78). She is critical of Sadat's wife, for example, who has done nothing to improve the conditions of Egyptian women, according to Saadawi.

One of the most crucial points expressed strongly in *Prison* is some women's denigration of their own femininity. Bodour believes that "a woman lacks intelligence and religion" (*MWP,* 132) and that is why men should not "show gentleness towards her" (*MWP,* 132). When she is asked whether she herself is not a woman, she shouts out, "No!" There are many Arab women and men who think like Bodour. This kind of audience would not read Saadawi or at least would reject her as a woman and as a writer.

Another feminist issue which recurs in most of Saadawi's writings is the problem of naming. She finds it unjustifiable that she should take the name of her grandfather—a man she never met—and not the name of her mother— the woman who gave birth to her and brought her up. She remembers that while in school she used to refuse to write her grandfather's name as her sur-name and insist on writing her mother's and father's instead, which annoyed the teacher (*MWP,* 117).

THE USES OF LITERATURE

Thus, we see that Saadawi's *Prison* could appeal to a wide audience because of the balance in the importance given to the issues raised in the book, those which can be considered purely feminist and those which emphasize the more general economic, political, and social conditions in Egypt, as only one Arab country. But at the same time there is a tension between an expression of collective identification and political and ideological differences. I would like to raise the question of whether a book like *Prison* has any practical effects on its audience. Franklin argues that prison memoirs by black Americans (characterized by the collective nature of the represented experience, where the reader does not look for what is unique, ambiguous, and original but for what is common, clear, purposeful, and useful) do more than attract admira-tion for an individual author; they impel the reader to "get up and put their message into action."[61]

This question, of course, relates to a huge debate in literary criticism and theory about the function of art in general; but it is worth considering it here in relation not only to *Prison* but to Saadawi's writings generally. The extent to which one individual writer can change her/his society is, of course, doubtful. Nevertheless, a practical way to deal with the question is to use Saadawi's testimony, which at least indicates that more people are gaining a new awareness of feminist issues. She was asked once about how she saw her role as a writer in the Arab world and whether she thought that her writings made a difference in the evolution of society and of people's attitudes.[62] She responded by recalling an incident in Tunis when she was invited to give a lec-ture; because of the great number of people who turned up, the lecture had to be moved to a place far from the place where it should have been held. Nonetheless, people took the train and traveled to listen to her. They would never have taken such trouble had her lecture, and what she is known to represent, not been very important to them. Saadawi added that the most realistic and factual of her books had the most practical effect on people. The effect of fiction "is deep, but remote. It takes a longer time. It touches life. It eliminates gradually. It moves in a different way. But facts shock you very much."[63] However, she also agreed that a novel (such as *Woman at Point Zero,* for which she is best known in the west, which is a story of a real woman who is in jail awaiting execution for murdering a man) can be more effective than purely factual books.

Finally, memoirs by women from developing countries, such as *Prison,* have had a market in the west for the last twenty or so years. This would explain why *Prison* was translated in the first place. The book is kept as precise and close to the voice of Saadawi as possible by the English translator, Marilyn Booth. There is no preface, no introduction, no glossary to explain the difficult words; there are only a few footnotes added to refer to certain historical facts which might be unfamiliar to western readers. If the language sounds formal and rather generalized to some English readers, then this is due to the standard modern Arabic in which the book is written. There is only one inaccuracy in the translated text spotted by a reviewer, who noted that:

> in the depiction of Douba delousing Nabawiyya: when the person doing the grooming finds a louse on the square, white narrow-toothed, bone comb, it is customary to crush it with the nail of her thumb, not her big toe.[64]

However, this is an insignificant mistake which does not alter the meaning; "what matters at the end is that the louse is dead," as the reviewer admits.[65]

3. From Prison to World-Stage: *My Travels around the World*

I have looked so far at two texts by Saadawi in which the self is explored in the form of fictional narrative (in *Memoirs of a Woman Doctor*) and through the medium of factual diaries of lived experiences (in *Memoirs from the Women's Prison*). In the fictional memoir, the heroine emerges as an independent character seeking to construct a unified self, in harmony with itself and with society around her. In the second memoir, the self goes through a process of unification with the other women with whom the narrator finds herself confined in a prison cell. In both memoirs, the narrator is not without some notion of self. And in both, the narrative develops two intertwined images: the emergence of an independent self from both a chosen isolation and an imposed seclusion; and the desire and the will to unify this self with the other or others.

In this section, I move from a narrative of physical immobility in a prison cell to a narrative of freedom and great motion, around the world at large. In the travel narrative *My Travels around the World*,[66] there is an even greater emergence of self from seclusion and an attempt to identify this self with an ever greater range of others in different societies of the globe. It is in the nature of most travel narratives to focus on the relationship between the subject and the object, that is, between the traveler and the landscape and people. Hence the significance of *Travels* as an ideal text for studying the development of subjectivity.

THE GENRE OF TRAVEL WRITING

There is very little, if any, theorization of Arab women's travel writings, and studies of the same genre produced by men are few and inaccessible. This is also true of such writings in the English context, although British and western women generally have been traveling and writing about their travels for much longer than Arab women. It was not until the late 1970s that scholarly inquiry into travel narratives was pursued.[67] A recent book by Sara Mills (1991) examines mid-nineteenth to early-twentieth-century travel texts by three British women and their relationship to colonialism. Within the framework of nineteenth-century British travel writings, Mills argues that there are constraints of discourse, of production, and of reception on travel writing, especially that by women. She contends that travel accounts are intertextual; that is to say, travel texts always appropriate other texts, sometimes explicitly but often by plagiarism.[68] As a result, most travel texts share similarities in the "narrative figure, narrative incidents and the description of objects."[69] Mills notes that Mary Louise Pratt divides travel writing into two types, according to the narrative figure. She calls the first the "manners and customs" figure and the second the "sentimental" figure. The first type of narrative is agentless; in it there is little account of human interaction; instead, landscapes are described as if they were empty of people. In the second type of narrative, "individual indigenous inhabitants are portrayed as taking part in a dramatic narrative."[70] Most travel narratives by women fit into the second type, which concentrates on the private sphere, whereas men's narratives conform more to the first, according to Mills.

Travel writing also shares common plots and narrative structures. Adventure in other countries, for example, is described by western writers, especially men, only to celebrate their own civilization. Western travelers describe other civilizations with an air of superiority and from a position of knowledge. Although women can be just as colonialist as men in their encounter with other cultures, Mills argues that "the choice of narratorial voice is more problematic for women writers."[71] According to conventional criticism, women travel writers are not supposed to write about certain subjects, such as sex, which men travelers can write about. Women should not be too adventurous and scientific; they are not expected "to become experts on fish . . . , discover unknown mountain ranges . . . , or provide statistical information about a country."[72] Instead, women should write "within a 'confessional' framework, revealing personal information, and not writing on serious topics."[73]

Saadawi's book does not fit easily into this range of travel books. On the contrary, her journey can indeed be seen as the opposite of the journeys made by western travelers. She is a woman from Egypt, which has been colonized by Britain. This discussion, therefore, makes use of Mills's book in this oppositional light.

According to Mills, women's travel writings have been traditionally received and read as merely autobiographical texts in an attempt to deny women "the status of creators of cultural artefacts."[74] The truthfulness of women's travel accounts has been also doubted, she argues, and labels of exaggeration and falsehood have been attached to them. Without trying to challenge Mills's argument, I read Saadawi's book as an autobiographical text, which includes such aspects of personal relations and self-revelation and representation. My objective in doing so is different from traditionalist and antifeminist criticism. I do not aim to ignore the literariness of the book. I concentrate on the autobiographical elements in *Travel* because I see it as a new mode of writing about the self, a mode not yet tried by many Arab women writers. In *Travels*, Saadawi mingles her personal experience with information relating to political, social, economic, and cultural aspects of the countries she has visited. *Travels*, therefore, serves not only to reveal information about various countries and peoples, as most travel books do, but also to uncover a culturally determined subjectivity of the traveler in her quest for an international identity. This is my concern.

PRESENTATION OF THE ARABIC AND ENGLISH EDITIONS

Saadawi has traveled extensively over thirty years in different parts of the globe. *Travels* covers the first twenty years, the 1960s and 1970s. When I wrote to Saadawi asking her why she wrote *Travels*, she replied:

To express my views about what I see in other countries, and how in this light I see the self also. It is a travel book in a different way. Both travel to the other and travel to the self. You can see both in a different light.[75]

Thus, *Travels* is both a journey to the self and a journey to the other. This purpose is also highlighted at the end of Chapter 1 of Part One of the Arabic original:

I began to realize that traveling outside the homeland is necessary, not only to know other countries and other peoples, but to know who I am and who we are. For knowing the self can only be achieved in the light of knowing the others.[76]

Over three pages, including this paragraph, are missing in the English translation, for no obvious reason. They are about Saadawi's trip to Dublin, Bangor, and London. The preceding paragraph and similar ones might very well make the Arabic reader read *Travels* in the light of discovering the self through discovering others, as the Arabic version has no introduction or preface to explain why *Travels* was written and who it was published for.

The English volume, however, is more realigned, shaped, and structured. It has an introduction by the writer herself which motivates the English readers and guides them to read the book in a special light. The cover of the book in itself can also be said to determine the kind of reading. The front cover shows a small picture of an old biplane in the right top corner, as if indicating travel in an old-fashioned way. In the middle of the cover is a picture of some pyramids, which immediately brings Egypt to mind. Saadawi's name and the title of the book are in a square at the bottom of the cover, followed by the name of the publisher, Minerva. The old biplane and the ancient pyramids indicate traveling into Egypt. This strengthens the theme of traveling into Egypt through traveling around the world. The name "Minerva," the Roman goddess of wisdom, goes very well with the picture of the pyramids, as another symbol of ancient civilization. A biplane, traveling, pyramids, ancient civilization, Minerva, wisdom, and the name of Saadawi in the middle: these could read as Saadawi probing her wisdom to discover the world through Egypt.

The Arabic volumes are presented differently. The first volume cover shows pictures of the Kremlin and Big Ben with a painted picture of young Saadawi in between. The name of the publisher, the title of the book, and the name "Dr. Nawal el-Saadawi" are at the top. This cover gives importance to Saadawi for Arabic readers, presenting her as a doctor. The pictures of the two historic buildings suggest travel to the relevant places, Russia and England. The picture of young Saadawi produces the impression of her doing the traveling; but, being a painted picture, it also creates a soft atmosphere, showing Saadawi's journey as if it were a dream. Travel was always a dream for Saadawi as a young woman. The cover of the second volume is presented more straightforwardly. Apart from the names of the publisher, the title, and the name "Doctor Nawal el-Saadawi," there are pictures of two African figures in a simple fishing boat and (what looks like) an African mask. This is misleading because it only suggests travel to Africa, whereas her trips to India and Thailand cover more than half of this volume. The mask, however, could be a Thai mask; in this case it could refer to Saadawi masquerading in men's clothing in Thailand, as we shall see later.

The purpose of knowing or learning more about the self through seeing others is stressed in the introduction to the English volume. However, the introduction also highlights a clear political extension to *Travels* and instigates a political reading of the book throughout. In addition to knowing the self, according to Saadawi:

> We see our homeland more clearly when we are away from it than when we are in it. I have seen many positives and negatives in the East and the West, which have revealed some of the positives and negatives within my own homeland. (*TAW,* viii)

The homeland, Egypt, as an Arab country is put in the context of east versus west. For the introduction goes on to give a prime political reason for travel in the sense of intellectual recognition of the position of one's own culture and the wider Arab world because of American and western imperialism. It is no accident that Saadawi has politicized the reading of her book. For when she wrote the introduction for the English version of her *Travels* in August 1990, America and its allies were preparing to attack Saddam Hussein, who had invaded Kuwait. The American interference in the Gulf and the prospect of the war, which did take place after a few months, were major events in the lives of all Arabs. Saadawi was among the many Arabs who felt that the war should be avoided by peaceful negotiation with Saddam Hussein and the whole issue should be contained within the realm of the Arab world alone. In fact, she was one of a delegation of nine women to Iraq in an attempt to reach some kind of agreement with Hussein. She also supported an International Women's Initiative for peace in the Gulf and went to New York to meet with the United Nations' secretary-general and to accompany him on a two-week tour of the United States designed to rally support not simply for an end to the war but also for a just peace in its aftermath. With her action and outspokenness, Saadawi was bound to politicize her travel book by referring to American imperialism, especially in introducing a book which covers travels to the United States and many other western countries and ex-colonies.

However, the Arabic version of *Travels,* published in 1986, was not produced without any political message at all. Like the English volume, the Arabic one is dedicated:

> To all who travel
> and who know exile
> far from the homeland.
> And to all who know exile
> in the homeland.

The message is that all Saadawi's writings are politicized in one way or another, but more so when they are produced in the west. The main reason why her writing is free to appear more political in English, for example, than in Arabic is of course the censorship that all Arabic books are subject to when published or distributed in Arab countries; as she herself writes, *Travels,* "like all my writing, has been subject to the censor's scissors or . . . publishing difficulties and restrictions" (*TAW,* viii).

Political censorship is just one pressure. There are also other discursive constraints on the production of all books: economic, social, historical, and personal forces which impinge on the process of writing itself. Sara Mills argues that textual constraints are of particular importance to travel writing, for travel texts usually appropriate other travel texts. Besides, there is "a tradition of textbooks which attempts to determine how other books are written."[77] I would add that textual constraints are also of great relevance to the reception of texts. For unless the reader is a first-time reader, he or she usually reads travel books with some notion of other travel accounts. Nevertheless, and although the book "does not contain everything I wanted to say" (*TAW,* viii), Saadawi's *Travels* (with its criticism of Arab and Egyptian politics) was published in Egypt, for Hosni Mubarak, the current Egyptian president, is less dictatorial than his predecessor Sadat as far as the media are concerned (*TAW* vii).

In reading *Travels* as a journey to the self and to the wider human world, two motifs recur throughout the book: the mirror and the border-crossing. The two motifs are connected, for Saadawi travels out of a double desire to rediscover the self through discovering the other and to cross the borders of her own country, which she calls prison, only in order to know it better.

THROUGH THE LOOKING-GLASS

Travel writing uses the other countries as mirrors in which to find one's own country and self. Saadawi travels to different countries as an Egyptian; that is, every time she is introduced to a new culture, she refers back to her Egypt and sees it in a new light. She travels in order to rediscover herself and establish new images about herself (or her selves) or she travels as a woman doctor, a feminist, a writer, and a United Nations delegate. She travels to attend medical courses, to participate in feminist conferences, to meet writers, and on United Nations missions. She travels for different reasons but always as a woman, except when she deliberately chooses to cross the borders of her gender and disguises herself in men's clothing.

Saadawi does not travel in order to escape the borders of her own country but to learn about the people of the world. Travel for her is not "flying in planes, visiting museums, sleeping and eating in luxury hotels" (*TAW,* 107); it is

> walking around the streets and dusty quarters, discovering people every-
> where, especially in those places from which tourists run or where they
> put their handkerchiefs to their noses should they happen to pass by.
> (*TAW,* 107)

Wherever she goes, Egypt and Egyptian children, women, and men are recalled to be compared and contrasted with the country she is in and its people. Initially, this might seem odd for someone who always longed to travel beyond the borders of her homeland: "My life's dream was flight and escape from prison" (*TAW,* 3). However, Saadawi's desire to escape her country is like her recurrent dream that her father was dead and, later in her youth, that her husband had died. It was the desire for freedom. Although she loved her father, it was the concept of the father as a tyrant that she wished dead. Similarly, she loved Egypt, her homeland, but wished to escape the tyranny of the regime. When she was asked once how she could bear to live in Egypt, she said she believed passionately in her country: she did not know the agony and the pain of other people as she did those of the Egyptian people.[78] While studying in Raleigh, North Carolina, she traveled to Chicago to attend a conference of the Arab students' organization at the University of Illinois. She found herself standing with seven hundred students singing an Arab patriotic song in unison (*TAW,* 38). This love-hate relationship with her country traveled with her everywhere she went. She wanted to leave the country forever; but every time she left, she went back to Egypt again: "With every trip abroad, I thought, I will not return. But I did, every time" (*TAW,* 12).

The desire to escape but also to belong explains Saadawi's position not just as a traveler but as a mother too. Although being a mother had provided her with feelings that nothing else—"no man nor work or travel" (*TAW,* 14)—could, it also meant that there were limits to how far she could go in other fields of life: "My longing for my daughter was as contradictory as my longing for the homeland, the desire to belong only equalled by the desire to escape" (*TAW,* 8).

Thus, for Saadawi, traveling beyond the borders of the homeland is not necessarily escape in the negative sense of the word. Distance, she realizes after traveling, makes the heart grow fonder. In other words, seeing other parts of the world and living outside Egypt enabled her to know Egypt better and love it more. This is also applicable to her relationship with people. Living away from her husband every now and then made her think that the marital relationship was happier if husband and wife lived apart: "distance weakens fragile marital relations but strengthens firm ones based on feelings of true love, mutual respect and understanding" (*TAW,* 113).

Saadawi saw Egypt in India. From the very moment she landed at the airport of New Delhi, she saw Egyptian faces in the faces of the poor Indian porters (*TAW,* 108). In India, she was always reminded of Egypt and of Egyptian people. She felt "as though I were not in India but in Egypt. Despite superficial differences there was a sort of strange resemblance, as though the roots were the same" (*TAW,* 111). For Saadawi, "Discovering India was like discovering Egypt" (*TAW,* 111). Distance from Egypt and living in similar conditions in India allowed her to understand the history of her own country. The poor Indian children were like the children of Egypt and like herself as a child. In Bombay, they

> looked at me with large black eyes full of hunger and surprise like the children in my far-off village on the banks of the Nile and my own eyes in the picture of me as a child standing in the first class beside my peers in primary school. (*TAW,* 146)

Not only the people but also the landscape and the climate always evoked memories of Egypt. The Algerian mountains reminded Saadawi that Egypt was flat and that the green in Egypt was not as deep (*TAW,* 17). The walk along the Seine in Paris recalled memories at al-Azbekiah in Cairo (*TAW,* 23). The hot and humid air at New York airport was like the air of Egypt (*TAW,* 33). The people of Kazakhstan with their features, Muslim customs, and characteristics were like Egyptian people, just as its weather was like Egyptian weather (*TAW,* 85). The weather in New Delhi also reminded her of spring in Egypt (*TAW,* 117).

From one chapter to another and one country to another, Saadawi is also looking at her childhood, adolescence, and adulthood, hence developing a new understanding of herself and of her life throughout. It all starts when she looks at herself in the airplane mirror on her first trip abroad. Every time she sees herself in the airplane mirror, she thinks she looks more beautiful. Is it simply crossing the borders from her homeland that makes her features look prettier or is it the good quality of the airplane mirror, she wonders (*TAW,* 27). In her review, Jill Waters calls this "childlike frankness."[79] However, Saadawi's reference to her face and the beauty she sees when she looks in airplane mirrors is more than just childish innocence in her style. It is a theme directly connected with that of self-discovery and self-worth, as if travel and meeting people from different cultures made her appreciate herself and discover her potential.

This started on one of Saadawi's first trips to Paris. When walking in the Luxembourg Gardens, she stopped a passing woman to ask her the time. After telling her what the time was, the Frenchwoman commented in French, "[Y]ou are beautiful, madame" (*TAW,* 26). From that moment onward, the words keep ringing in Saadawi's ears, and she goes back to the subject of beauty on various occasions in the book. She looks again at her face in the mirror above the washbasin on the plane and thinks that no one ever has told her that she is beautiful before. Back home, in Egypt, she does not fit the standards of beauty. She has a dark complexion and frizzy hair; people like fair skin and soft hair. She herself has always thought that she is beautiful, and now this French lady confirms it. Thinking she is beautiful has something to do with her self-confidence. Traveling to India and especially to Africa has given her this confidence.

In India, Saadawi sympathizes and identifies more with the poor Indians, who are brown-skinned like herself, than with the white and rich European travelers she sees at the airport:

> I know the movement they make, the air of superiority in their blue eyes
> when they look at brown faces such as mine or at Indian faces, grumbling
> at the sight of old suitcases and worn clothes, as though traveling by

plane were their sole right, as though the money with which they bought their expensive clothes and large suitcases were not originally the wealth of brown toiling faces, the rightful owners of the land and of the country. (*TAW*, 108)

However, it is Saadawi's journey to Africa which is her own journey of self-discovery and appreciation. The African journey is a multiple search for the roots of the Nile and for her own sources and roots. After all, her paternal grandfather used to be called Habashi (meaning Ethiopian) because he had Ethiopian blood. Being an Egyptian, she is also African, an identity which has been made "a shameful blemish" (*TAW*, 171) because of European colonization and racism. Saadawi, though, is proud to announce her Africanness. She is happy to walk in the streets of Ethiopia and Uganda without anyone noticing that she is a foreigner and to be with African people in Dar es Salaam:

> I felt relaxed with them and at ease with myself, with my brown skin. The real parts of myself had emerged, filling me with confidence and pride, a feeling I had not had on my trips to Europe and America and Asia, feelings which after I experienced them, made me regret that my journey to Africa came so late. (*TAW*, 172)

Saadawi is also honest about the fact that she has not always been happy about her brown skin, a feeling which stems from childhood. For she had constantly been teased about her dark complexion by her maternal grandmother, who was fair-skinned, calling her "Slavegirl warwar" (*TAW*, 172). Being dark and being a girl have been determining factors which have oppressed her for a long time, as she herself admits. It took her some time before she finally decided to stop wearing white makeup and face the world as she really is, a dark-skinned woman:

> The one true love of my life is the love of my real self. In spite of that, I only gave up make-up completely after I understood the worth of my mind, and then had the courage to face the world with a clean and washed face. (*TAW*, 172)

The frequent use of the mirror in *Travels* is, therefore, not accidental; it signifies similarity between people and cultures in spite of their differences. Although Saadawi travels to different and differing countries, she manages to stress similarity—not only on the personal level (that is, between herself and other people) but also between cultures—more than difference, thus emphasizing internationalism and sisterhood through her humanist outlook, which we have seen in the previous works as well. On the very first trip abroad, aboard the plane to Algeria, she—the dark-skinned Egyptian doctor—meets a blonde and fair-skinned Italian prostitute. Her immediate shock is soon, after chatting with the prostitute, turned into familiarity and later into some kind of understanding and sisterhood. Even in America, where difference could be highlighted more than anywhere else, she makes one of her best friendships with fair, green-eyed Marion. Among other American women, Saadawi has a special relationship with Marion: "I did not feel strange with her, but as though we'd been born in the same country and had spent our childhood together" (*TAW,* 43).

Saadawi's hatred for U.S. imperialism does not blind her to the good things in America. At New York University, where she has been doing her research, she admiringly describes the academic atmosphere: "Professors admitted to mistakes and knew each student well. A kind of humanity and spirit of fellowship pervaded the university" (*TAW,* 53). This might, of course, make more sense to an Arabic reader, for it serves as a contrast to the academic atmosphere in Arabic universities. On campus, she even feels at home: "My feet sped across the ground with light and easy steps as though I'd been born here, would die here, and knew no other place" (*TAW,* 53). She feels unity with the students demonstrating against American intervention in Vietnam:

> The faces were like those of my family, white, black, brown, all of them alike, forming one human body. And I was part of this body, their breathing mine, their fervour mine, the final dissolution of the last drop of alienation and loneliness in my blood. (*TAW,* 53–54)

In Helsinki, Saadawi also feels unity with the women she meets for the women's conference. On the train to Leningrad, they all sing together, and feelings of oneness bring them nearer to each other:

> . . . voices and songs in different languages and accents rang through the air, Arab tunes mixed with Russian, Afghani, with American, with Spanish, with English, with French, with Vietnamese. I found myself singing a song, the words and language of which I did not know. We became one group, from one country, and the artificial differences that separate people from each other disappeared. (*TAW,* 77–78)

With the men and women writers in Kazakhstan, Saadawi drank to friendship between the people of Asia and Africa:

The laughter and chatter grew louder as the formality between Indian, Egyptian, Algerian, Sudanese, Russian and African writers disappeared and we all became people of the same country, the country of art and literature. (*TAW,* 83)

In that united atmosphere, she even ate horse meat and drank mare's milk, which she had never done before: "I hid my surprise. Hands holding glasses of mare's milk were raised in toast to art and friendship, so I raised mine too and drank" (*TAW,* 84).

BORDER-CROSSINGS

In her book *Border Traffic: Strategies of Contemporary Women Writers,* Maggie Humm argues that women writers, particularly those from developing countries, challenge political and cultural barriers of racism and sexism in their writings. According to her, women writers from different races, cultures, and nationalities often choose alternative routes to the traditional borders of discipline, hence crossing the borders of genre, of history, of sexual preference, of bodies, and of politics.[80] Saadawi's writings in general can be described as border writings. In her *Travels,* however, the border-crossing is at its most evident.

The motif of border-crossing is manifested in three ways. First, Saadawi physically crosses international borders in the sense of traveling to various countries. Second, in the course of her life, she crosses borders that are socially established: those of femininity and womanhood. Third, in the narrative of *Travels,* she crosses borders of genre.

Saadawi's first border-crossing immediately fills her with feelings of self-worth. The childhood image of the homeland is shattered once she looks out of the plane window from above. The homeland looks so small from the plane, and she herself feels much bigger:

I had believed that my homeland was the whole world, just as when I was a child I believed that our street was the whole homeland. As I grew up so the street grew smaller. But when my being reached beyond the homeland, the earth shrank and new feelings, that I was larger than before, filled me. (*TAW,* 8–9)

When Saadawi first crosses the borders of her own country, she does this with delight, joy, and excitement. She cannot believe that at last she is actually crossing the customs line at Cairo airport, having waited a long time for an exit visa or the government's permission to leave the country. After all the years, she can never forget the first border-crossing she ever made. Saadawi relates the incident with the details of the conversation with the policeman. She can still remember "the movement of his hand as he raised it and brought down the black stamp like an iron hammer on my passport and let me pass" (*TAW,* 7). Her first border-crossing is a challenge in feminist terms. She not only travels alone but (as a Muslim woman) travels without permission from any man, for she has divorced her husband. She would not pass without correcting the passport man who read the word "Mutallika," which means "has divorced her husband," as "Mutallaka," meaning "has been divorced."[81]

From a feminist point of view, Saadawi also presents more challenges when she travels to America pregnant and leaving behind a young daughter and a husband, a triple challenge that hardly any Arab woman had met before her. She travels to pursue postgraduate studies in the United States, putting her academic ambitions ahead of her motherly and wifely duties, hence challenging the traditional concepts of motherhood and marriage. She does not even go home to have her baby there; instead she has her baby in the United States on her own, away from all of her family.

Saadawi seizes all the opportunities available to her in order to enjoy her travels by doing the things she has dreamt of doing but could not do back home in Egypt. In Paris, she crosses social borders, sitting on the pavement of a cafe enjoying the sun and looking at people passing by. In Egypt, cafes "are for men" (*TAW,* 25). For the sake of being an integral part of a group in Kazakhstan, she crosses dietary borders, as we have seen, drinking mare's milk and eating horse meat. In Thailand, she goes so far as to cross gender borders physically. Out of curiosity, she disguises herself in men's clothing in order to visit one of Bangkok's "massage parlours," where women, "except those who work there, were forbidden to enter: their role was solely to provide a service whereas consumption was the sole right of men" (*TAW,* 163).

In her life, Saadawi has crossed many socially established borders. Discarding her makeup box, given to her by her maternal aunt to cover her dark skin (*TAW,* 27), and straightening the stoop that her paternal aunt advised her to walk with to hide her height (*TAW,* 27), Saadawi grew to build an identity through transgressing many prescribed roles and rules of what a woman should be and could do. In the Department of Medicine at Cairo University, she was one of the very few female students. Having rebelled against an early marriage, she also divorced two husbands and married for the third time. Divorced women in her country hardly ever marry again. For a few years of her career, as a married woman with children, Saadawi worked for the United

Nations, traveling from one country to another. She criticized the establishment of the United Nations and left a post that many people would want to
keep for its financial value. As a medical doctor, she chose to specialize in psychiatry, a field that not many Egyptian doctors, even men, would choose. As
a writer, her main concern was the social, political, and economic conditions
of the oppressed, both men and women. Her outspokenness led her to prison
for a few months, but she would not end her mission of fighting for her
causes in a society and a world that are still behind as far as the rights of the
oppressed are concerned. For that was what she learned from her extensive
travel—the oppressed, albeit of different forms and shapes, were in every
country she went to.

TEMPORAL CRISS-CROSSING

The original *Travels* was produced in two volumes published one month
apart in 1986. Volume 1 consists of seven parts. Volume 2 is introduced by the
publisher and has four parts. The part on India is divided between the two
volumes. The English translation is produced in one volume, which joins the
parts on India into one and removes a small part which covers the trip to
Thailand, making it an independent part. This makes eleven parts with an introduction by Saadawi herself. The structure of *Travels* as a whole is simple;
it is arranged according to the chronological sequence of the trips Saadawi
has made over about twenty years. The introduction was written in August
1990 for the publication of the English translation, as mentioned before. The
rest of the book is based on diaries which Saadawi has written over the years
about her trips to the different countries while she was traveling or just after
every trip.[82] The diaries were revised later before the publication of the book.
An example of the revision process is found in the passage in which she writes
about her encounter with the university administrator in Raleigh and the ap-
plication form she is completing: "At the box for previous convictions and
crimes, I had written nothing for I had not yet been in prison" (*TAW*, 37).
Saadawi's trip to America was in 1965, and she was imprisoned in 1982.

The structure within each separate part, however, is not as simple as the
structure of the book as a whole. It is multidimensional in nature and anything but chronological. Travel usually refers to movement in space; in Saadawi's *Travels,* there is also movement in time. On the one hand, there is a
chronological movement in time, for the narrative takes a span of about
twenty years from beginning to end. On the other hand, there are irregular
movements in time inside each part. The narrative structure of every part,

then, opposes linear time, for the movement in time alternates between heading forward at some times and retreating backward at other times.

PRIVATE SELF AND PUBLIC PERSONA

If one examines *Travels* as a whole, one notices a change in Saadawi's narrative and language from beginning to end. As she gradually develops into some kind of celebrity, her narrative moves from being highly personal to becoming more generalized. The parts that cover her trips over the 1960s and 1970s, during which Saadawi had not yet become known outside Egypt, are more concerned with the self and its creation. As such, these parts are structured in a sophisticated way around a multiplicity of themes, such as life and death, flight and prison, fatherhood, motherhood, wifehood—all woven in a canvas of dreams and fantasies. The other parts, which cover Saadawi's trips during the 1980s, when she became a more or less international figure, are less introspective. The self-mobilization, self-creation, and self-questioning which characterize the first six parts are less dominant in the parts that follow. The self becomes less fluid and more of a fixed persona. Saadawi becomes more self-confident; her tone is assured, at times didactic, occasionally even self-congratulatory. This following passage, for example, shows little respect for the people worshipping in an Indian temple and presumes her knowledge of what is inside the worshippers' minds:

> The very few who are educated are always in a hurry. They pray quickly and their movements do not show contrition or humiliation but rather a desire to finish praying as quickly as possible and go on to other more important things. Whilst praying they do not close their eyes completely but keep them half open. They do not give anything to the poor around the temple, neither do they offer gifts except those that are obligatory religious duties. They do not ask God to heal the sick because they use doctors and medicine, but they ask God for other things, depending on their demands in life and their ability or inability to meet these demands. (*TAW,* 136)

Another shift of emphasis is from a predominance of literary analysis in the first six parts to more political analysis in the following parts. The journey into the self becomes a journey into countries. The second half of the book, in other words, is more like an ordinary travel book. There are more touristic descriptions than in the first half of the book, and the narrative becomes rather journalistic. The style becomes flatter and less subtle, and there are generalizations. For example, she notices that in India "in general women . . .

still want to please men. In most families it is the man who dominates; the male children get more care, better food and more education than female children" (*TAW,* 123). Such a statement, even if it has an element of truth, sounds odd from the pen of an analyst and social scientist like Saadawi, who should be aware of the dangers of generalizing from particular cases in such a huge and varied society as India. Some of the details and descriptions are rather banal and obvious, especially to western readers, who are more well-traveled than Arab readers. Although I find this public persona which emerges in the last sections of the volume less intriguing than the earlier more fluid and complex self, the goodwill is still there, as well as the compassionate concern for others.

CONCLUSION

The move in tone in the narrative from being personal, self-reflective, and analytical to becoming more didactically political, self-assured, and descriptive can be said to mark Saadawi's transformation into a public figure. The self that she tries to discover and build in the first half of the book seems to be lost behind the public persona in the second half. Paradoxically, she becomes at once more self-assertive yet less concerned with self-exploration and is more turned outward toward concern for other people and for the surroundings.

    Travels presents a contribution to the question of identity. Is identity rooted in the mother culture or does it grow out of borders into a more expanded sisterhood? This is what the book is about. The narrative reflects the tension between personal and public identities. Identity does not have to be resolved, and indeed it is not in Saadawi's narrative. The journey continues in *Travels;* Saadawi is a constant traveler. She does not allow one monolithic voice to dominate her narrative. The Arab or Egyptian identity that she carries with her everywhere does not take over other images that Saadawi seems to be willing to embrace. In this sense she is a multicultural person and a multicultural writer.

    Saadawi is a passionate writer, which is probably why she often falls prey to sweeping generalization. I have noted before that her best-known nonfiction book among westerners, *The Hidden Face of Eve,* which is actually a book on Egyptian women, is introduced as a book on *Women in the Arab World.* The practice of female circumcision is alien to many Arab people, especially in Syria, yet Saadawi writes about it as if it were the norm in all Arab regions. She no doubt has opened the way for many women to follow her path and continue the struggle. Saadawi is still very active within the ASWA, the Arab Women Solidarity Association she founded in 1982, and she is still writing too.[83] She will probably continue to affect male Arab readers in that mysterious way that Hisham Sharabi talks about: "it is difficult to explain to the non-Arab reader the effect . . . [Saadawi's prose] can have on the Arab Muslim male."[84]

In the same year that Saadawi's *Travels* was published in English (1991), another book with an attractive title appeared both in London and in New York: *Veiled Half-Truths: Western Travellers' Perceptions of Middle Eastern Women* by Judy Mabro. One wonders about the rationale behind publishing such a book, which collects and republishes travel accounts by westerners in the nineteenth- and early-twentieth-century Middle East. Is it because, as Mabro argues, the prejudice presented in such writings "can be found in [western] books and films today"?[85] Mabro makes her motive quite clear, however. She is hoping to show "the fact and fiction concerning the position of women in European societies . . . the ideas which travelers took with them about women's place in society," reflected in the travelers' representation of Middle Eastern women.[86] Her introduction goes on to criticize those travel accounts that she has selected. One can still wonder why so many of these prejudiced accounts should be published in the 1990s. Mabro could have written a book in which she made her criticism very clear without actually publishing the accounts or at least so many of them. One can read the travel accounts without having to read Mabro's brief comments. In this case, the book looks as Orientalist as the travel accounts are. In her *Discourses of Difference: An Analysis of Women's Travel Writing and Colonialism* (also published in 1991), Mills, as I have argued earlier, was able to deliver the same message as Mabro, without having to publish so many examples of travel accounts. Mills's book is more sophisticated and can only be read as a critique of such travel writings.

In spite of Mabro's good intention, her book, when read selectively, can perpetuate Orientalist and colonial discourse. Saadawi's travel book, being part of the counter-discourse or writing-back discourse, could be an alternative to Mabro's book. Westerners can read in *Travels* how a woman from the Middle East travels in other countries and how she represents other people, both men and women. Saadawi's book, I hope, is just one example of a new genre. Instead of republishing old accounts, publishers might now be able to publish new travel accounts by women from different countries.

The Literary and the Political

I have stressed the issue of change in Chapters 1 and 2 of this book. Change in the Arab world regarding women has been accelerating over the last decade. One could write books on women in modern Arab countries in the 1990s alone. I can only refer here to evidence of such change in what I see on the shelves of bookstores. In the 1980s the number of books by Arab women was very limited—not anymore. Both the number of Arabic bookshops around the world and the number of books by Arab women have increased.

Syrian, Lebanese, and Egyptian women have been known as writers for decades. But women writers from the Gulf countries were rarely found. Now there are books by women from many countries, including Saadia Mifreh from Kuwait, Nojoum al-Ghanim from the Emirates, Faozia al-Sanadi from Bahrain, Samira al-Mani from Iraq, and Sultana Abdul Aziz al-Sidiri and Huda al-Rasheed from Saudi Arabia. Beside the name of the well-known Syrian writer Zainat Nassar, who has been publishing since at least the early 1980s, there are also new names such as Lina Tibi and Laila al-Atrash from Syria; and May Muzafar, Huda Barakat, Nour Suleiman, Laila Ouseiran, and Salwa al-Said from Lebanon. Hanan al-Shaikh from Lebanon and Samira Azzam and Sahar Khalifa from Palestine have been publishing since the 1980s.

The other encouraging issue is the number of new Arab publishers. Apart from the known publishers in Beirut, Damascus, and Cairo, there are now many new publishers in Bahrain, Kuwait, the Emirates, and even Riyadh. I say even Riyadh, because Saudi Arabia has been known to be the most conservative of all Arab countries, especially when it comes to women and the media. However, the increased access to education for women in the Gulf in the last thirty years is very encouraging. Moreover, the booming economy in these countries has played a role in the increase of publishing businesses there. One of the women, Maysoon Saqar al-Qasimi, a poet and a painter from the Emirates, publishes her books at her own expense. She has published three volumes of poetry, *Al-Bait* (The House, 1992), *Jarayan fi Madat al-Jasad* (Flowing in the Tissues of the Body, 1992), and *Makan Akhar* (Another Place [poetry for children], 1994), all of which are illustrated by her own paintings.

The well-known Ghada al-Samman from Syria also owns her own publishing company, which she started back in the early 1970s. She has published a book that many consider the brave beginning of a new genre in Arabic literature: literary letters. The book is called *Ghassan Kanafani's Letters to Ghada al-Samman* (Beirut: Dar al-Taliya, 1992; reprinted in 1993). Kanafani was one of the leading Palestinian writers, who was killed by the Israelis in 1972. He had a love relationship with al-Samman, a leading Syrian and Arab writer in her own right. The book is meant as a tribute to a writer, a friend, and a fighter who loved his country and fought for its freedom. The new thing is that this is a book by a female writer acknowledging a male writer. It is more usual for a man to be acknowledging a woman, as we have seen in Chapter 7: al-Qasim acknowledging Tuqan. If a woman's verdict on a man can be published in this manner, then this must be a feminist triumph.

There are also many new biographical titles. Hayat Sharara has edited a book called *Pages from the Life of Nazik el-Malaeka* (London: Riad el-Rayyes, 1994). Nazik el-Malaeka, an Iraqi poet, is considered at least among Arab poets themselves to be one of the pioneers of modern Arab poetry. *Daughter of Damascus* is an autobiography by Siham Tergeman, translated into English and published in Texas. Other recent books include Fatima Mernissi's *Dreams of Trespass: Tales of Harem Girlhood* (1994), Samar Attar's *Lina: A Portrait of a Damascene Girl* (1994), Leila Ahmed's *A Border Passage: From Cairo to America: A Woman's Journey* (1999), Fay Afaf Kanafani's *Nadia, Captive of Hope: Memoir of an Arab Woman* (1999), and many others. Fadwa Tuqan has published an autobiography which looks like a continuation of the first one (discussed in Chapter 7), called *The Most Difficult Journey* (Amman: Dar el-Shorouq, 1993). The book that seemed to attract more attention than others because of its title was *The Princess: The Real Story behind the Veil*. Already in its third edition, this book has been translated from English by Dar Oukaz, a new Arab publisher, probably an oppositional Saudi institution based in London. The original book, *Princess,* was written in English by Jean P. Sasson on behalf of a Saudi princess. Part 1, which was published in 1992, is not available; but Part 2, *Princess: Sultana's Daughter,* was published in 1994 in America by Bantam Books. The Arab publishers introduce the book as one which has greatly upset the Saudi royal family.

The mid-1990s also witnessed the birth of a first-of-its-kind monthly cultural review, *Al-Katiba* (The Female Writer), which is in itself a very promising and pioneering feminist adventure.[1] *Al-Katiba*'s second title is "Woman's Adventure in Writing/The Adventure of Writing in Woman," and it advertises itself as "A New Voice in Arabic Culture." It was started in December 1993 in London by a large group of writers, both men and women, from different Arab countries. In this review, one reads various articles on feminist topics that have not been dealt with before.

Two leading articles are striking, especially for an Arab reader. The first is "Man's Femininity." Eleven male writers and poets are asked to talk about the feminine in them. All of them were astounded to be confronted with a question like this, but they went ahead and answered it.[2] The second is an article called "Challenges of a Free Woman: Celebrating a Belly-Dancer, Tahia Karioka," by Edward Said.[3] The translator claims that this article was published in English in 1990, but he does not state where and by whom. Tahia Karioka has been one of the leading Egyptian belly-dancers since the early 1940s at least, and Said knows her personally. (She is not a dancer anymore but a "Hajja," meaning she has been to Mecca for pilgrimage.) In his usual way, Said looks at Karioka's career from a political point of view. According to him, Karioka is the most refined belly-dancer. She is also a symbol of a national culture. What is unusual to read is Said's description of Karioka's attractive body and erotic dance. It has not been known in Arabic writing for a belly-dancer to be made a symbol of national culture. In this sense, Said's article offers a new dimension to the existing streams of Arab feminism.

There is an urgent need for flexible theoretical frameworks in the light of which these new forms of writings can be analyzed. My study can be seen as an attempt to initiate theory that can include both the similarities and the differences in Arab women's autobiographical writings. I call for a theory or theories that describe the conditions of both production and reception of a text without making rigid judgments about its literariness, as male critics have been doing with such texts.

Indeed, I hold the view that aesthetic issues should only be seen as directly related to political ones and that such a relationship is different from one reader to another. Divorcing the aesthetic from the political leads to reductivity, selectivity, and the creation of hierarchies.

To conclude, I should like to make the following points. Aesthetics and politics are inseparable, especially when it comes to reading texts such as those I have dealt with in this book. These should be read in a special way for two main reasons. First, the texts are translated from another language or languages; they have been written or recited or dictated in Arabic (or in the case of the interviews with the Moroccan women, possibly in Berber or French) and then translated into English. Translation from one language to another necessarily affects the aesthetic value of a text. Second, the texts that I have read have a feminist, hence a political, message. This message is also double: the texts are published in order to make the women's voices heard and also in order to change certain western views about the women concerned in these texts. These two facts about the texts are of prime importance. Besides, one should remember that women's literary production is still on the margin of established canons, which are predominantly male, whether in Arabic or western traditions.

The aesthetic is both a personal and a relative issue: aesthetic valuation of a text should not be done according to whether it is better or worse than another but according to its own de/merits or what it has to offer to the reader. Many factors determine the de/merits of a text. I believe that basically it is the reader who gives meaning to a text. Hence, the reader's culture (nationality, class, gender), level of education, and knowledge about the subject have a considerable effect on how the text is read. The time and place in which a text is written are important, for values change from one period to another and from one place to another. For example, if one reads Shaarawi's memoirs by current standards, one might find her achievements very ordinary; if one reads her according to the standards of her own time, however, one might consider her revolutionary.

In a word, as a text is produced under a set of conditions, as explained by Michele Barrett and Janet Wolff,[4] it is also read under a similar set of conditions. As the writer of a text is conditioned ideologically, socially, economically, technologically, and politically, the reader is similarly conditioned in her/his reading of a text. Hence, the conditions of both production and reception of a text are equally significant. Considering modes of production and modes of reception in my reading of the texts that I have chosen should be more illuminating than merely detecting what is so aesthetically moving in images or figures of speech.

In the end, there is a lot to say about Shahrazad of the 1990s. She has different images and takes various shapes. Above all, she may at least have control over her life. She is no longer the poor girl who had to tell interesting stories to save her life, but a woman who makes her life by telling, or writing, on a wider, more multicultural platform than that offered to her in the original story.

Translation of the Introduction to the Arabic Edition of *Memoirs from the Women's Prison* by Nawal el-Saadawi

Introduction

Because I was born in a strange time, when a human being is driven to prison because one has got a brain that thinks; because one has a heart that palpitates to truth and justice; because one writes poetry or fiction; because one has published scientific or literary research, or an article which shouts out for freedom; or because one has philosophical inclinations.

Because I was born in such a time, it was not strange that I was taken to prison. For I have committed all the crimes altogether . . . I have written stories, novels, and poetry; and published scientific and literary research, and articles that call for freedom. And I have philosophical inclinations.

But the greatest crime is that I am a free woman at a time when they want nothing but woman servants and slaves; and I was born with a thoughtful brain when they are trying to deform minds.

My father was free, and so was my mother. Since childhood freedom circulated in my veins together with my blood. I saw my mother rebelling and rejecting the military authority of her father; I saw her flying into a rage when her husband shouted at her. I also saw my father angrily rising against the government and against the British. My poor, peasant grandmother I heard singing against brutality, poverty, and unhappiness.

My brother was older than me. When he raised his hand to slap me, I raised mine higher and slapped his face. He did not try again. When my first husband wanted to deny my existence, I canceled him out of my life. When my second husband shouted: "Me or your writings!" I said: "My writings!"; and we separated. When the minister of health trembled, shouting: "Obedience or sacking!" I answered: "Sacking!"; and I lost my job.

And when Sadat said: "Freedom is stirring and so are justice, prosperity, and peace"; I said: "Where is freedom when people are chained, and censorship is like a sword on thoughts and minds? Where is justice or prosperity when the poor are getting poorer and the rich richer while piling up the millions? Where is peace when trade in weapons is increasing and the war in Lebanon is getting more brutal?"

I have never played the game of politics or parties or the media, ever in my life. Nor election, nor women's societies under the presidency of rulers' wives. Even my medical profession I have renounced. I saw doctors buying villas and erecting buildings with the blood of the sick and the poor. People are getting ill because of poverty, starvation, and oppression; and in the world of medicine, there are no pills to cure such diseases.

I have no weapon left but the pen to defend myself, my freedom, and the freedom of the human being everywhere. I have nothing but the pen to express the tragedies of the poor, women, and slaves; and to tell people that I hate tyranny but love justice, and that I respect the human being and do not participate in referendums, nor listen to the radio or to superstitions, and I close my door to the servants of the court. I do not offer sacrifices of thanksgiving. I obey nothing but my own mind. I do not write anything except my own opinions. I do not walk in processions. I do not belong to a band. I do not attend social parties. I do not wear makeup like women of the harem and do not use American shampoo. I do not drink Israeli beer. And it sickens me if I read newspapers.

Perhaps for this reason, they broke down my door by armed force and drove me to prison. I was not shocked, for truth, in the time of lying, cannot be left free. I was not frightened but angry, and I refused to open my door for them quietly. I refused to hide in the dark without a noise, or in the silence without a voice, or to be driven to prison or to death without a rage of anger!

I was not ashamed, but proud, why not be proud? A whole police state fears me, an unarmed woman, whose fingers touched nothing but the pen. To this extent they fear my words on paper!

I will keep writing, then. I will write even if they bury me alive. I will write, if they take the pen and the papers away, I will write on the wall, the ground, on the face of the sun and on the moon.

Nothing is called impossible in my life . . .

And when the prison policeman shouted: "Had I found a gun with you, it would have been easier for you than if I had found a pen and paper," I decided to get hold of a pen and a paper before the end of the day.

How . . . I do not know!

But I badly wanted the pen and the paper; I never wanted anything so badly without getting it . . .

And before the prison warden closed the door of the cell at 4 o'clock that afternoon, I had the pen and the paper. It was toilet paper, but my letters were clear and I could read what I wrote . . .

When the warden and the officer disappeared and the night crept on, I got up and sat under the yellow electric lamp, on the turned-over can, and I leaned my back to the wall, and wrote my first words in prison:

Because democracy here is a lie, the human being who writes poetry or a love story may enter prison.

A true love story can be in its strength more dangerous than an explosive box or time bombs. For it discovers the roots of decay and iniquity in society. Those who tell lies in bedrooms are the same who deceive in the parliaments and on the seats of governments and on the pages of newspapers. For a person cannot have a lying body and a true mind. But those who both lie and tell the truth are those with deformed faces and deformed minds.

The great historical tragedy is that those deformed are those who inherit the seats of power, and in their hands the treasures accumulate. And the richer they become, the greedier they grow; just like a sick stomach: water can make it only thirsty.

This is why wars never stop, and the number of the deformed increases more and more, and you see them interested in nothing but warfare and political affairs.

I hated politics when I was a little girl; and I hated it when I became an adult; I hated the war. Political affairs never troubled me; and I was never thrilled by the headlines of the front page in any newspaper.

I was busily involved in arts and literature; but I discovered that arts and literature do not exist without truth, and the truth cannot exist without freedom, but freedom cannot be achieved without revolution.

For the sake of freedom, the artist finds him/herself in the political field. For the sake of freedom, arts cannot be separated from politics. Freedom is the revolution. The freedom of all the members of a society, men and women.

If women are deprived of freedom, then there will not be a revolution; how can a revolution be fulfilled if half of the society is chained?

Our way to freedom is still very long. For politics is hypocrisy and deceit, and men of politics have striped colors, like men of the press. The most dangerous men of politics and of the press live in all ages. They sit on the thrones of the press, politics, arts, literature, and medicine, as firm as the sun in its center. Only their skin changes; they never essentially change.

I am a woman. Yes. And my life is all hard, from when I was born till I entered prison. In spite of its difficulty, my heart never changes. I cannot distrust a human being; the human being, for me, is innocent; the gods are guilty. Man was neither born evil nor is his nature evil. The prison warden, who had my cell's keys, I trusted from the first moment. I had a frightening intuition since childhood. It grew with me; and it is still growing. And I fear that it may grow more to the extent that I would see more than the society can forgive. After prison, what is left for them to do to me?

But still, I am not contented with my writings. For I do not write freely enough, or as freely as I would like to. I have lived in a world that prefers deceit in everything, in politics, in sociology, in morality, in arts, and in science. Some people have books that they do not read. Those who do read do not think with their own minds, but with other people's minds. Each of them rejoices when he says he is a friend of the ruler, or if the ruler says so to him. I have never seen any of them belonging to himself. They practice in the dark what they do not dare to do openly; and they write what they do not live.

I feel estranged when I see or hear them. I write what I live . . . I am a woman who decided what she wanted and lived what she wanted. My self is mine and the people as well. I also own part of the sky because I can dream.

In prison, I did not lose the ability to dream, to hope, and to rebel, even, when I want to. One day I threatened to set the whole prison and the cells on fire with a match.

Hope, in me, sometimes sinks down toward the bottom and enters into the cavity of the earth, then it pulls itself up out of the abdomen of the whale and heads toward the branches . . . and flies in the sky like a bird . . . How can hope be so strong, in me? How can a human being hope and live with it? I cannot sleep while I realize that a bomb will definitely explode nearby. I cannot sleep and dream that I am happy for twenty-four hours without the dream being interrupted by the sound of a shot.

Conflicts are inside and outside, and are inside me too, clash and make me say things. I live vigorously. I say them now and they appear to me to be little, meaningless words. In spite of all that, I sleep and wake up and dream of the revolution. The gun is shooting bullets; and words on paper, what do they shoot?

Prison is a stagnant place. But a human being inside it is not stagnant.

In prison, one discovers the color of things and recognizes the prettiest hues and prettiest people, and ugliest people too. But one thing sweeps all colors: the hope of breaking the doors, the bars, the locks, and the hope of being free again like a bird singing in the sky.

Hope is revolution, it is the singing of the free bird.

But I am still not contented with myself, I still do not have my freedom. I have not written the book I dream of, nor the novel that lives in me. I have not lived the life I was born for. I was not born in the right time. There are so many men and women in our countries who still believe that the face of the woman is an "aura."[1] Other people believe that revolution is like the face of a woman: it needs a veil. And there are those who talk about the revolution everyday. We are told that many revolutions have happened in our countries: one revolution after another, one revolution correcting another. Because of the many revolutions we have heard of, we began to dream of a life without a revolution. For the word has lost its meaning. To be safe is to be in prison. Revolution means nonrevolution or aborting the revolution. Food safety means food poisoning. I said to myself, I will stop writing until I find new words, words that have not been devalued yet.

Can the revolution mean more poverty, submission, and humility? Can it mean that the human being who is native to a country enjoys less honor and dignity than a foreigner?

Can the revolution mean putting singing birds in cages, and setting free crows, hawks, vultures, and all those with sharp claws, capable of hunting and abducting?

Introduction

1. Amal Amireh and Lisa Suhair Majaj (eds.), *Going Global: The Transnational Reception of Third World Women Writers,* investigates the process of reading and writing about third-world women and their narratives.

2. Janet Wolff, *The Social Production of Art,* p. 1.

Chapter One. Why Colonial Discourse?

1. For examples of some of the reviews of Said's *Orientalism* and other articles inspired by his book, see Sadik Jalal al-Azm, "Orientalism and Orientalism in Reverse," *Khamsin* 8 (1981); James Clifford, "Orientalism," *History and Theory* 19 (1980); James Clifford, "On Orientalism," in *The Predicament of Culture;* Lata Mani and Ruth Frankenberg, "The Challenge of Orientalism," *Economy and Society* 14, no. 2 (May 1985); Ernest J. Wilson III, "Orientalism: A Black Perspective," *Journal of Palestinian Studies* 10, no. 2 (1981); Emmanuel Sivan, "Edward Said and His Arab Reviewers," in *Interpretations of Islam Past and Present;* Robert Young, "Disorienting Orientalism," in *White Mythologies: Writing History and the West;* Xiaomei Chen, "Occidentalism as Counterdiscourse: 'He Shang' in Post-Mao China," *Critical Inquiry* 18, no. 4 (Summer 1992); and Paul A. Bove, "Hope and Reconciliation: A Review of Edward Said," *Boundary 2* 20, no. 2 (Summer 1993). See also "An Interview with Edward Said," *Boundary 2* 20, no. 1 (Spring 1993); and Benita Parry's excellent critique in "Problems in Current Theories of Colonial Discourse," *Oxford Literary Review* 9, nos. 1–2 (1987).

2. Anouar Abdel-Malek, "Orientalism in Crisis," *Diogenes* 44 (1963).

3. See Masao Miyoshi, "A Borderless World?: From Colonialism to Transnationalism and the Decline of the Nation-State," *Critical Inquiry* 19, no. 4 (Summer 1993); and Clifford, "Orientalism."

4. Gayatri Chakravorty Spivak, "Three Women's Texts and a Critique of Imperialism," *Critical Inquiry* 12, no. 1 (Autumn 1985): 243.

5. Miyoshi, "A Borderless World?" p. 728.

6. For a critique of feminism and colonial discourse, see Chandra Mohanty, "Under Western Eyes: Feminist Scholarship and Colonial Discourses," *Feminist Review* 30 (1988); also in *Boundary 2* 12, no. 3, and 13, no. 1 (1984). See also Spivak, "Three Wom-

en's Texts and a Critique of Imperialism"; Gayatri Chakravorty Spivak, "French Feminism in an International Frame," in *In Other Worlds: Essays in Cultural Politics;* and *Inscriptions: Feminism and the Critique of Colonial Discourse* 3–4 (1988). Sara Mills studies western women's relationship to colonial discourse in her "Alternative Voices to Orientalism," *Journal of Literature Teaching Politics* 5 (1986). Rana Kabbani, a Syrian settled in London, wrote *Europe's Myths of Orient: Devise and Rule;* however, her book follows Said's method of analysis and does not stress the connection between feminism and Orientalism.

7. Quoted by John McBratney, "Images of Indian Women in Rudyard Kipling: A Case of Doubling Discourse," *Inscriptions: Feminism and the Critique of Colonial Discourse* 3–4 (1988): 47.

8. By Spivak, see *The Post-Colonial Critic: Interviews, Strategies, Dialogues,* ed. Sarah Harasym; *In Other Worlds: Essays in Cultural Politics;* and "Acting Bits/Identity Talk," *Critical Inquiry* 18, no. 4 (Summer 1992): 770–803. By Mohanty, see "Under Western Eyes." By Homi Bhabha, see "Interrogating Identity," in Lisa Appignanesi (ed.), *Identity: The Real Me;* "Signs Taken for Wonders: Questions of Ambivalence and Authority under a Tree outside Delhi, May, 1817," *Critical Inquiry* 12, no. 1 (Autumn 1985); "Sly Civility," *October* 34 (1985); "Of Mimicry and Man: The Ambivalence of Colonial Discourse," *October* 28 (1985); "Representation and the Colonial Text: A Critical Exploration of Some Forms of Mimeticism," in Frank Gloversmith (ed.), *The Theory of Reading;* and "The Commitment to Theory," *New Formations* 5 (1988). See also Sara Danius and Stefan Jonsson's interview with Spivak in *Boundary 2* 20, no. 2 (Summer 1993): 24–50; and Miyoshi, "A Borderless World?"

9. See, for example, bell hooks, *Feminist Theory: From Margin to Center;* Cherríe Moraga and Gloria Anzaldúa (eds.), *This Bridge Called My Back: Writings by Radical Women of Color;* and Maria Lugones and Victoria Spelman, "Have We Got a Theory for You?: Feminist Theory, Cultural Imperialism, and the Demand for the Woman's Voice," *Women's Studies: International Forum* 6, no. 6 (1983).

10. Spivak, "Three Women's Texts," p. 243.

11. See Elizabeth Fox-Genovese, "Placing Women's History in History," *New Left Review* 133 (May–June 1982).

12. Mohanty, "Under Western Eyes," p. 61.

13. Ibid., p. 66.

14. Marnia Lazreg, "Feminism and Difference: The Perils of Writing as a Woman on Women in Algeria," *Feminist Studies* 14, no. 1 (Spring 1988): 87.

15. Ibid., p. 88.

16. Charles Hirschkind and Saba Mahmood, "Feminism, the Taliban, and Politics of Counter-Insurgency," *Anthropological Quarterly* 75, no. 2 (Spring 2002): 339.

17. Ibid., p. 340.

18. Ibid., p. 345.

19. Ibid., p. 341.

20. Edward Said, *Orientalism*, pp. 325–326.

21. For a detailed study of the term "culture," see Raymond Williams, *Key Words: A Vocabulary of Culture and Society*.

22. For the origin and meaning of the term "Arabs," see Peter Mansfield's "Who Are the Arabs?" in his book *The Arabs*. For the history and development of the Arab world, see Joel Carmichael, *The Shaping of the Arabs;* Yousef M. Choueiri, *Arab History and the Nation-State: A Study in Modern Arab Historiography 1820–1980;* Giacomo Luciani (ed.), *The Arab State;* Albert Hourani, *A History of the Arab Peoples;* and Albert Hourani, Philip S. Khoury, and Mary C. Wilson (eds.), *The Modern Middle East: A Reader*. On modern Arab politics, see also Fouad Ajami, *The Arab Predicament: Arab Political Thought and Practice since 1967;* and Issa J. Boullata, *Trends and Issues in Contemporary Arab Thought*.

23. Carmichael, *The Shaping of the Arabs,* p. 2.

24. Fatima Mernissi, *Beyond the Veil: Male-Female Dynamics in Muslim Society,* p. 16.

25. Nawal el-Saadawi, *The Hidden Face of Eve: Women in the Arab World*.

26. It has been suggested that Sati al-Husri was perhaps the first to offer a sustained discussion of the term "Arab world," in *Opinions and Discussions on Nationalism and Internationalism* and *Lectures on the Emergence of Nationalism*.

27. Carmichael, *The Shaping of the Arabs,* p. 2.

28. See Choueiri, "The Pharaohs or the Arabs," in *Arab History and the Nation-State,* pp. 104–108.

29. See Carmichael, *The Shaping of the Arabs*.

30. Ibid., p. 211.

31. Ibid., p. 212.

32. Ibid., p. 214.

33. Ibid., p. 215.

34. Quoted on the cover of *Diaspora* 1, no. 1 (Spring 1991).

35. Roger Kimball, "Tenured Radicals: A Postscript," *New Criterion* (January 1991).

36. Henry Louis Gates Jr., "Pluralism and Its Discontents," *Contentions* 2, no. 1 (Fall 1992).

37. Rosalind Brunt, "The Politics of Identity," in Stuart Hall and Martin Jacques (eds.), *New Times: The Changing Face of Politics in the 1990's,* pp. 150–159.

38. Chicago Cultural Studies Group, "Critical Multiculturalism," *Critical Inquiry* 18, no. 3 (Spring 1992): 531.

39. Ibid.

40. Kimball, "Tenured Radicals," p. 5.

41. McBratney, "Images of Indian Women," p. 56.

42. Ibid., pp. 56–57.

43. See Peter Stallybrass and Allon White, *The Politics and Poetics of Transgression*.

44. Chandra Mohanty, "Us and Them: On the Philosophical Bias of Political Criticism," *Yale Journal of Criticism* 2, no. 2 (1989).

45. Lazreg, "Feminism and Difference," p. 98.

46. Ibid.

47. Ibid.

48. Ibid.

49. Spivak, *In Other Worlds*, p. 205.

50. Trinh T. Minh-ha is known for films such as *Reassemblage* (1983) and *Surname Viet Given Name Nam* (1989). See also *Woman, Native, Other: Writing, Postcoloniality and Feminism* and *When the Moon Waxes Red: Representation, Gender, and Cultural Politics*.

51. Trinh T. Minh-ha, "Not You/Like You: Post-Colonial Women and the Interlocking Questions of Identity and Difference," *Inscriptions* 3/-4 (1988): 71.

52. Ibid.

53. Ibid., p. 72.

54. Ibid., p. 77.

55. Ibid., p. 73.

56. On the postcolonial, see Kwame Anthony Appiah, "Is the Post- in Postmodernism the Post- in Postcolonial?" *Critical Inquiry* 17 (Winter 1991); Sara Suleri, "Woman Skin Deep: Feminism and the Postcolonial Condition," *Critical Inquiry* 18, no. 4 (Summer 1992); Helen Tiffin, "Post-Colonialism, Post-Modernism and the Rehabilitation of Post-Colonial History," *Journal of Commonwealth Literature* (1987); and Simon During, "Postmodernism or Postcolonialism?" *Landfall* 39 (September 1985).

57. The inadequacy of the term "patriarchy" is discussed in the next chapter.

Chapter Two. Feminism, Nationalism, and Colonialism in the Arab World

1. See Lazreg, "Feminism and Difference," p. 89: "the exercise of freedom of expression often has a dizzying effect and sometimes leads to personal confession in the guise of social criticism." Lazreg argues that when western-educated women write about women from their societies, the question of to "what extent they do violence to the women they claim authority to write and speak about" has to be raised.

2. On the subject of women and change in the Middle East, see Magida Salman, Hamida Kazi, Nira Yuval-Davis, Laila al-Hamdani, Salma Botman, and Debbie Lerman, *Women in the Middle East,* edited by the Khamsin Collective; see also Susan C. Bourque and Donna Robinson Divine (eds.), *Women Living Change.*

3. Of course, change also affected nineteenth-century Egyptian women. Gabriel Baer's view that "evidently the traditional structure of the family and the status of women did not undergo any change at all" (*Studies in the Social History of Modern*

Egypt, p. 210) is an obvious colonialist and Orientalist kind of analysis. Many others have described the radical changes that have affected Arab women's lives since the eighteenth century. The issue of change is discussed later in this chapter.

4. Most research on Arab feminism touches on the interconnection between feminism and nationalism in the Arab world. See, for example, Kumari Jaywardena, *Feminism and Nationalism in the Third World in the C19th and C20th: History of the Women's Movement;* Margot Badran and Miriam Cooke (eds.), *Opening the Gates: A Century of Arab Feminist Writing;* Elizabeth Warnock Fernea and Basima Qattan Bezirgan (eds.), *Middle Eastern Muslim Women Speak;* Margot Badran, "Dual Liberation: Feminism and Nationalism in Egypt, 1870s–1925," *Feminist Issues* (Spring 1988); and Jeffrey Louis Decker, "Terrorism (Un)Veiled: Frantz Fanon and the Women of Algiers," *Cultural Critique* 17 (Winter 1990–1991). Decker argues that the Algerian nationalist struggle during the late fifties was also accompanied by a "struggle over sexism—in relationship to the French occupier as well as the indigenous Muslim male population" (p. 183).

5. On the ascendancy of conservative religious trends, see Nahid Toubia (ed.), *Women of the Arab World: The Coming Challenge.* Over the last twenty years or so, there has been a movement to republish old books on women and Islam by religious authorities, claiming that such books save Muslim society from the danger represented by change. See, for example: Ibn al-Jawzi (who died in the year 589 of the Hijra), *Kitab Ahkam al-Nisa'* (Statutory Provisions concerning Women); Ibn Taymiyya (who died in the year 728 of the Hijra), *Fatwa al-Nisa'* (Fatwas concerning Women) (fatwas are judgments by religious authorities); and Muhammad Siddiq Hasan Khan al-Qannuji (who died around the turn of the twentieth century), *Husn al-Uswa Bima Tabata Minha Allahi fi al-Niswa* (roughly, Good Manners for Women)—all cited in Fatima Mernissi, *Women and Islam: An Historical and Theological Enquiry.*

6. Jaywardena, *Feminism and Nationalism,* p. 1.

7. Jaywardena extends this argument to include most Asian and African women's movements, as in Turkey, Iran, India, China, Indonesia, Sri Lanka, Vietnam, Afghanistan, and Japan.

8. Elly Bulkin, "Semite vs. Semite/Feminist vs. Feminist," in Elly Bulkin, Minnie Bruce Pratt, and Barbara Smith (eds.), *Yours in Struggle: Three Feminist Perspectives on Anti-Semitism and Racism,* pp. 167–168.

9. Freda Hussain, *Muslim Women,* p. 71.

10. There are many publications on the subject of Islam and women; for example, see Mernissi, *Women and Islam,* and *Beyond the Veil;* Mernissi also published, under the pseudonym Fatna A. Sabbah, *Woman in the Muslim Unconscious;* Aziza al-Hibri (ed.), *Women and Islam;* Madelain Farah, *Marriage and Sexuality in Islam;* and Naila Minai, *Women in Islam: Tradition and Transition in the Middle East.*

11. Lazreg, "Feminism and Difference," p. 95.

12. Laila Ahmed, "Western Ethnocentrism and Perceptions of the Harem," *Feminist Studies* 8 (Fall 1982): 529, 531.

13. Emily Apter, "Female Trouble in the Colonial Harem," *Difference: A Journal of Feminist Cultural Studies* 4 (Spring 1992): 211–212.

14. Ibid., p. 209.

15. Peter A. Lienhardt expresses this dilemma in his article "Some Social Aspects of the Trucial States," in Derek Hopwood (ed.), *Postmodernism: A Reader* (p. 220):

> And though the segregation of women from men not closely related to them is one of the things that must at once meet the eye of any visitor to the towns and villages of the Trucial Coast, this segregation makes it difficult for a visitor to gain any precise knowledge of the women's position. Apart from its being difficult for a man to talk to women there, it is not even proper for him to ask very much about them, particularly to ask in any detail about specific cases . . . one can easily be misled, particularly in assessing the extent of male dominance.

16. Ahmed, "Western Ethnocentrism," p. 525.

17. Delarue-Mardus cited in Apter, "Female Trouble," p. 211.

18. Mernissi, *Women and Islam,* p. 95.

19. For the development of the veil, see ibid., especially Chapter 5, pp. 85–101, and Chapter 10, pp. 180–188.

20. Mervat Hatem, "The Politics of Sexuality and Gender in Segregated Patriarchal Systems: The Case of Eighteenth- and Nineteenth-Century Egypt," *Feminist Studies* 12, pt. 2 (1986).

21. One interesting example cited in al-Hibri, *Women and Islam,* p. viii, shows that differing interpretations of the same Quranic verse are possible but also suggests that one interpretation is more probable in order to suit one's argument:

> The Qur'anic phrase "khalaqa lakom min anfusikom azwaja" can be divided into two shorter parts, each of which can be interpreted in at least two ways. First, "khalaqa lakom min anfusikom" can mean either "we created from amongst yourselves," or as Saadawi suggested "we created out of you." The first reading is closer to the letter of the original and less ambiguous than the second reading. Second, "azwaja" often means "mates" in the Qur'an. However, it is also possible to interpret it as "couples," as Saadawi chose to do. Thus, the most damaging interpretation of this passage is not Saadawi's, but rather the following: "we created out of you mates." Patriarchy can now use the passage to reassert the inferiority of women on a Qur'anic basis. However, before Patriarchy can succeed in its attempt, it has to do two things. First, it has to show that the passage is addressed to men (or else the claim that Adam was created out

of Eve would be equally good), and second, that its interpretation is better than others. On the first point, there is no evidence that the passage is addressed solely to men (el-Saadawi's claim to the contrary notwithstanding). Second, the interpretation "we created from amongst yourselves mates" is superior in its adherence to the letter of the phrase, and fits better the meaning and spirit of the rest of the ayah. It is most probably this latter interpretation that Smith and Haddad worked out.

22. Ibid., p. 202.

23. For an account of women's role in the Iranian Revolution, see Guity Nashat (ed.), *Women and Revolution in Iran.*

24. Gerda Lerner, *The Creation of Patriarchy.*

25. Laila Ahmed, *Women and Gender in Islam: Historical Roots of a Modern Debate,* p. 104. Even in classical Greece, Ahmed argues, Alexander the Great, having conquered Persia, tried to compete with Persian kings and kept harems as large as theirs (p. 28).

26. Examples of ethnographic writings on the Middle East include Talal Asad, *The Kababish Arabs: Power, Authority and Consent in a Nomadic Tribe;* Donald Cole, "Social and Economic Structures of the Murrah: A Saudi Arabian Bedouin Tribe"; Ian Cunnison, *The Baggara Arabs: Power and Lineage in a Sudanese Nomad Tribe;* and Emmanuel Marx, *Bedouin of the Negev.*

27. Cynthia Nelson, "Public and Private Politics: Women in the Middle Eastern World," *American Ethnologist* 1, no. 3 (1974): 561.

28. Ibid., pp. 558–559.

29. Sayigh does not specify any studies. However, one can assume that she means works done by Nawal el-Saadawi, Fatima Mernissi, and others.

30. Rosemary Sayigh, "Roles and Functions of Arab Women: A Reappraisal," *Arab Studies Quarterly* 3, pt. 3 (1981); see especially pp. 257–68.

31. E. L. Peters, "The Bedouin Sheikhs: Aspects of Power among Cyrenaican Pastoralists." "Wasta" is an Arabic term meaning mediation through influential people.

32. Sayigh, "Roles and Functions of Arab Women," p. 270.

33. See Frantz Fanon, *Studies in a Dying Colonialism,* especially Chapter 1 ("Algeria Unveiled") and Chapter 3 ("The Algerian Family"); C. Fluerh-Lobban, "The Political Mobilization of Women in the Arab World," in J. Smith (ed.), *Women in Contemporary Muslim Societies;* C. Fluerh-Lobban, "Agitation for Change in the Sudan," in A. Schlegel (ed.), *Sexual Stratification: A Cross-Cultural View;* M. Molyneux, "Women and Revolution in the People's Democratic Republic of Yemen," *Feminist Review* 1 (1977); Yvonne Haddad, "Palestinian Women: Patterns of Legitimation and Domination," in Khalil Nakhleh and Elia Zureik (eds.), *Sociology of the Palestinians;* and B. Rahbek, "Oppressive and Liberating Elements in the Situation of Palestinian Women."

34. Mernissi, *Women and Islam,* pp. 192–195.

35. Ahmed, "Western Ethnocentrism," p. 527.

36. Ibid., p. 529.

37. Ibid. See also a study by Clara Makhlouf-Obermeyer, *Changing Veils: A Study of Women in South Arabia.*

38. Ahmed, "Western Ethnocentrism," pp. 528–529.

39. Lama Abu Odeh, "Post-Colonial Feminism and the Veil: Thinking the Difference," *Feminist Review* 43 (Spring 1993).

40. Ibid., p. 27. See the example of killing women in the name of family honor.

41. Ibid., p. 29.

42. Ibid., p. 30.

43. Ibid., p. 37.

44. Deniz Kandiyoti, "Identity and Its Discontents: Women and the Nation," in Patrick Williams and Laura Chrisman (eds.), *Colonial Discourse and Post-Colonial Theory: A Reader,* p. 380.

45. See Badran and Cooke, *Opening the Gates,* p. xx.

46. The following passage, ibid., pp. xxiv–xxv, is a brief illustration of the twentieth-century political map of Arab countries:

> The Arab East, or the Mashriq excluding Egypt, remained under direct Ottoman rule until after the First World War. In the 1920s, the territory was broken up into the states of Lebanon, Syria, Palestine and Transjordan under French and British mandates. In the late nineteenth century, Sudan fell under Anglo-Egyptian control. In the Maghrib or Arab West, Algeria in 1830 and Tunisia in 1881 fell under French colonial rule, while Morocco and Libya were occupied early in the twentieth century by the French and Italians respectively. In the Arabian Peninsula, the Ottoman pressures and controls on the cities and caravan routes in the nineteenth century were eliminated in the early twentieth century. Although the Arabian Peninsula was never colonised, much of the western littoral of the Indian Ocean became Trucial States under British control, and South Yemen (Aden) became a strategic outpost. By the 1960s, most Arab lands had thrown off colonial rule and the final vestiges of foreign occupation. Palestine was the exception. In 1948, it was taken over by the new state of Israel.

47. This argument has been drawn from Albert Hourani, *A History of the Arab Peoples,* especially Part III.

48. For the argument on the class system in nineteenth-century Egypt, I am indebted to Juan Ricardo Cole's "Feminism, Class, and Islam in Turn-of-the-Century Egypt," *International Journal of Middle East Studies* 13 (1981); and also Judith Tucker's

"Decline of the Family Economy in Mid–Nineteenth Century Egypt," *Arab Quarterly* 1, pt. 3 (Summer 1979): 245–271.

49. The theory of the backwardness and decline of Islam is also taken up by Orientalists such as H. A. R. Gibb and Harold Bowen; see Roger Owen, "The Middle East in the Eighteenth Century: An 'Islamic Society' in Decline?" *Review of Middle East Studies* 1 (1975). David Waines goes so far as to claim that "the birth of Islam is also the genesis of its decline"; quoted in Bryan S. Turner, *Weber and Islam: A Critical Study*, p. 6.

50. S. Zubaida, "Islam, Cultural Nationalism and the Left," *Review of Middle East Studies* 4 (1988): 7.

51. Jaywardena, *Feminism and Nationalism*, pp. 21–22.

52. Ibid., p. 23.

53. Thomas Philipp, "Feminism and Nationalism in Egypt," in L. Beck and Nikki Keddie (eds.), *Women in the Muslim World*, p. 279.

54. Badran and Cooke, *Opening the Gates*, p. xix.

55. Kandiyoti, "Identity and Its Discontents," p. 379.

56. Ibid., p. 379.

57. See Miriam Cooke, "Telling Their Lives: A Hundred Years of Arab Women's Writings," *World Literature Today: A Literary Quarterly of the University of Oklahoma* 60, pt. 2 (Spring 1986).

58. Cited in Eileen Philipps, "Casting Off the Veil," *Marxism Today* (August 1986).

59. This passage, from Badran and Cooke, *Opening the Gates*, pp. xxvii–xxviii, summarizes the political participation of women in other countries:

In the late 1930s, during the Arab Revolt in Palestine, women from the Mashriq, who had earlier channelled their energy mainly into philanthropic and literary societies, became active as nationalist and feminist militants. In 1938 and 1944, at pan-Arab conferences in Cairo, they joined forces in cementing Arab feminist consciousness. In 1944, they formed the Arab Feminist Union. Among Palestinian women during the mandate period and after the creation of the state of Israel, women's nationalism took priority with the impending and actual loss of their country. In Sudan, women participated in the national independence struggle in the mid-1950s and continued as an organised feminist movement. During the Algerian Revolution, 1954–1962, most of the women who participated were young and only much later did some become feminists. In the late seventies and eighties, Palestinian women increasingly asserted themselves as feminists and nationalists simultaneously. Meanwhile women in the Arabian Peninsula took advantage of new educational opportunities, and state policies to reduce large foreign work forces opened new possibilities for work. In Kuwait, where women have more opportunities to organise and are freer to express controversial views, feminism has the most visible face, while in Saudi Arabia, where greater constraints are imposed upon women and candid expression, it is the least visible.

60. Ahmed, *Women and Gender in Islam*, p. 175.

61. Mineke Schipper (ed.), *Unheard Words: Women and Literature in Africa, the Arab World, Asia, the Caribbean and Latin America*, p. 10.

62. On the subject of the state as an expression of men's interest, see C. MacKinnon, "Feminism, Marxism, Method and the State: An Agenda for Theory," *Signs* 7, no. 3 (1989); D. Burstyn, "Masculine Dominance and the State," *Socialist Register* (1983): 45–89; and M. Mies, *Patriarchy and Accumulation on a World Scale*. For a critique of these works, see R. W. Connell, "The State, Gender and Sexual Politics: Theory and Appraisal," *Theory and Society* 19, no. 5 (1990): 507–544; and N. Yuval-Davis and F. Anthias (eds.), *Woman-Nation-State*.

63. For more discussion on the terminology, see Badran and Cooke, *Opening the Gates*, p. xviii.

64. Jaywardena, *Feminism and Nationalism*, pp. v–vi.

Chapter Three. Huda Shaarawi's *Harem Years*:
The Memoirs of an Egyptian Feminist

1. Huda Shaarawi, *Harem Years: The Memoirs of an Egyptian Feminist*, ed. and trans. Margot Badran. Page references are included in the text with the letters *HY*.

2. As I have argued before, there is a Eurocentric view that the movement for women's liberation is not indigenous to developing countries or Asian, African, and Latin American countries but has been either imported or imposed by western colonialism. My position is similar to that of Kumari Jaywardena, who argues in *Feminism and Nationalism* that feminism

was *not* imposed on the Third World by the West, but rather that historical circumstances have produced important material and ideological changes which affected women; for example, there were debates on women's rights and education in eighteenth-century China, movements for women's social emancipation in early nineteenth-century India, while feminist struggles originated between sixty and eighty years ago in many countries of the Third World. The fact that such movements for emancipation and feminism flourished in several non-European countries during this period has been, in a sense, "hidden from history." It is only recently, with the rise of feminist movements all over the world, that some attention has been directed to early feminism in the Third World and to the women who took part in these struggles. (pp. 1–2)

3. See Joseph Tufeek Zeidan, "Women Novelists in Modern Arabic Literature," pp. 176 – 188.

4. See Cooke, "Telling Their Lives"; and Zeidan, "Women Novelists in Modern Arabic Literature."

5. Fernea and Bezirgan, *Middle Eastern Muslim Women Speak,* p. 196.

6. I would like to draw an analogy between Shaarawi's memoirs and Winnie Mandela's *Part of My Soul,* which is more a chronicle of Nelson Mandela's life and character than of Winnie's.

7. The significance of such a distinction is explained later in this chapter.

8. Seeking refuge in nature is a common theme, at least for Shaarawi and Saadawi; I would like to explore the possibility of expanding it. Nature was always celebrated in Arabic literature. But there is at least one main difference between the way it was deployed in classical Arabic poetry and in modern Arabic prose and poetry. In the past, it was wild nature that was being described or taken refuge in: the hot sand or desert, the shining sun or the guiding moonlight, the overwhelming darkness, the faraway sounds of the beasts, the horse, the lion, or the wolf. The poets used to put themselves in harsh natural surroundings to prove their patience or strength or express a lonely mood. Under the influence of romanticism, which was brought into Arabic literature by late-nineteenth-century poets in exile, nature becomes greener and timider, full of trees, flowers, and fresh air. It is mainly used as a refuge for solitude and escape from modern technological life. In Shaarawi's memoirs, it is an artificial type of nature that she escapes to: a garden.

9. For more details on the brother-sister relationship in Arab societies, see Hasan el-Shamy, "The Brother-Sister Syndrome in Arab Family Life, Socio-Cultural Factors in Arab Psychiatry: A Critical Review," in *International Journal of Sociology of the Family* 11 (1981).

10. Julia Kristeva, *About Chinese Women,* p. 28.

11. Sidonie Smith, *A Poetics of Women's Autobiography: Marginality and the Fictions of Self-Representation,* p. 53.

12. See Minai, *Women in Islam,* especially "Motherhood, Polygamy, and Divorce."

13. My mother, for example, and the rest of her siblings were all brought up by a stepmother, since their own mother died prematurely. They always talk about their stepmother as if they were talking about their own biological mother, not even calling her a stepmother. According to them, she was as good as a biological mother could have been.

14. See Pierre Macherey, *A Theory of Literary Production;* and Terry Eagleton, *Criticism and Ideology: A Study in Marxist Literary Theory.*

15. Eagleton, *Criticism and Ideology,* p. 43.

16. Macherey, *A Theory of Literary Production,* p. 85.

17. Laila Ahmed also raises this point in her essay "Between Two Worlds: The Formation of a Turn-of-the-Century Egyptian Feminist," in Bella Brodzki and Celeste Schenck (eds.), *Life/Lines: Theorizing Women's Autobiography.*

18. Fernea and Bezirgan, *Middle Eastern Muslim Women Speak,* p. 200.

19. Ibid., p. 196.

20. Ibid., p. 195.

21. Ibid., p. 194.

22. Ibid., pp. 199–200.

23. Ahmed, "Western Ethnocentrism."

Chapter Four. Autobiography and Sexual Difference

1. Philip Dodd, "Criticism and the Autobiographical Tradition," *Prose Studies* 8, no. 2 (September 1985): 11.

2. Brodzki and Schenck, *Life/Lines,* p. 285.

3. Elizabeth Bruss, *Autobiographical Acts,* p. 8.

4. Edward W. Said, "Opponents, Audience, Constituencies," *Critical Inquiry* 9, no. 1 (September 1982).

5. Paul John Eakin, "Malcolm X and the Limits of Autobiography," in James Olney (ed.), *Autobiography: Essays Theoretical and Critical.*

6. Miller cited in ibid., p. 181.

7. Nancy Miller, "Writing Fiction: Women's Autobiography in France," in Brodzki and Schenck, *Life/Lines,* p. 47.

8. Quoted by Miller in ibid., p. 47.

9. Smith, *A Poetics of Women's Autobiography,* p. 6.

10. See Miller, "Writing Fiction," pp. 60–61.

11. Smith, *A Poetics of Women's Autobiography,* p. 6.

12. Georges Gusdorf, "Condition and Limits of Autobiography," in Olney, *Autobiography,* p. 28.

13. Ibid., p. 38.

14. Olney, *Autobiography,* p. 240.

15. Ibid., p. 22.

16. Paul de Man, "Autobiography as Defacement," *Modern Languages Notes* 94, no. 1 (January 1979): 920.

17. Doris Sommer, "Not Just a Personal Story: Women's *Testimonios* and the Plural Self," in Brodzki and Schenck, *Life/Lines,* p. 119.

18. Olney, *Autobiography,* p. 324.

19. Ibid., p. 325.

20. Smith, *A Poetics of Women's Autobiography,* p. 47.

21. Françoise Lionnet, "*Métissage,* Emancipation, and Female Textuality in Two Francophone Writers," in Brodzki and Schenck, *Life/Lines,* p. 261.

22. Linda Anderson, "At the Threshold of the Self: Women and Autobiography," in Moira Monteith (ed.), *Women's Writing: A Challenge to Theory,* p. 59.

23. Ibid., p. 59.

24. Ibid., p. 65.

25. Smith, *A Poetics of Women's Autobiography,* p. 46.

26. Ibid.

27. Ibid., p. 45.

28. Sommer, "Not Just a Personal Story," p. 120.

29. Ibid.

30. Ibid.

31. Lionnet, *"Métissage,* Emancipation, and Female Textuality," p. 260.

32. David Murray, "Authenticity and Text in American Indian, Hispanic and Asian Autobiography," in A. Robert Lee (ed.), *First Person Singular: Studies in American Autobiography,* p. 178.

33. Gusdorf, "Condition and Limits of Autobiography," p. 29.

34. Ibid.

35. Ibid., p. 33.

36. Lee, *First Person Singular,* p. 57.

37. Gusdorf, "Condition and Limits of Autobiography," p. 34.

38. Ibid.

39. Mary Beard, *The Majority Finds Its Past,* p. xxii.

40. Susan Stanford Friedman, "Women's Autobiographical Selves: Theory and Practice," in Shari Benstock (ed.), *The Private Self: Theory and Practice of Women's Autobiographical Writings,* p. 36.

41. Olney, *Autobiography,* p. 239.

42. Patricia Meyer Spacks, "Selves in Hiding," in Estelle C. Jelinek (ed.), *Women's Autobiography: Essays in Criticism,* p. 112.

43. Friedman, "Women's Autobiographical Selves," p. 36.

44. Ibid., p. 37.

45. Stephen Spender, "Confessions and Autobiography," in Olney, *Autobiography,* pp. 115–122.

46. Roland Barthes, *Roland Barthes par Roland Barthes,* p. 56.

47. Carolyn G. Heilbrun, "Non-Autobiographies of 'Privileged' Women: England and America," in Brodzki and Schenck, *Life/Lines,* p. 66.

48. Jelinek, *Women's Autobiography,* p. xi.

49. Spacks, "Selves in Hiding," in ibid., p. 127.

50. Ibid., p. 130.

51. Ibid., pp. 113–114.

52. Ibid., pp. 115–116.

53. Jelinek, *Women's Autobiography,* p. xii.

54. "Introduction," in Brodzki and Schenck, *Life/Lines*, p. 12.

55. Cynthia S. Pomerleau, "The Emergence of Women's Autobiography in England," in Jelinek, *Women's Autobiography*, pp. 21–38.

56. Carol Edkins, "Quest for Community: Spiritual Autobiographies of Eighteenth-Century Quaker and Puritan Women in America," in Jelinek, *Women's Autobiography*, p. 57.

57. Helen Carr, "In Other Words: Native American Women's Autobiography," in Brodzki and Schenck, *Life/Lines*, p. 153 (Carr was kind enough to send me a copy of her article before publication).

58. Ibid., p. xi.

59. Domna C. Stanton (ed.), *The Female Autograph: Theory and Practice of Autobiography from the Tenth to the Twentieth Century*, p. vii.

60. Ibid., p. xi.

61. Germaine Bree, "Foreword," in Brodzki and Schenck, *Life/Lines*, p. ix.

62. Smith, *A Poetics of Women's Autobiography*, p. 51.

63. Benstock, *The Private Self*, p. 1.

64. Biddy Martin, "Lesbian Identity and Autobiographical Difference[s]," in Brodzki and Schenck, *Life/Lines*, p. 103.

65. Benstock, *The Private Self*, p. 4.

66. Sheila Rowbotham, *Woman's Consciousness, Man's World*, p. 31.

67. Ibid., p. 28.

68. As cited in Mary Jean Green, "Structures of Liberation: Female Experience and Autobiographical Form in Quebec," in Brodzki and Schenck, *Life/Lines*, p. 189.

69. Benstock, *The Private Self*, p. 39.

70. Sommer, "Not Just a Personal Story," p. 108.

71. Ibid., p. 111.

72. Elizabeth Fox-Genovese, "Afro-American and Third World Literature," in Benstock, *The Private Self*, p. 67.

73. Ibid.

74. Ibid.

75. Ibid.

76. Maggie Humm, *Feminist Criticism: Women as Contemporary Critics*, p. 13.

77. Ellman cited in Toril Moi, *Sexual/Textual Politics: Feminist Literary Theory*, p. 31.

Chapter Five. Arab Autobiography: A Historical Survey

1. I have used three Arabic references in this chapter: Ihsan Abbas, *Fannul Sira* (The Art of Autobiography); Yahyia Abdul Dayem, *Attarjama Azzatiya fi al-Adab al-Arabi al-Hadith* (Autobiography in Modern Arabic Literature); and Muhammad Abdul Ghani Hassan, *Attarajum wal Siar* (Biographies and Autobiographies).

2. See Ferial Jabouri Ghazoul, *The Arabian Nights: A Structural Analysis*. Ghazoul

argues that the stylistic feature of *Ayyam al-Arab* (The Days of the Arabs) "is that it is made of episodes loosely linked within a framework that is at times not chronological. They are adorned with poetical quotations and are particularly impressive in the description of battles rather than in giving an organic study of their connections" (p. 72). She adds that the "Pahlavi epics, with which the Arabs were familiar, were something of biographies and concentrated on relating the lives and deeds of kings or dynasties" (p. 73).

3. Hassan defines autobiography: "To write one's autobiography is to write one's history, registering events and happenings, recording works and achievements, and remembering childhood, youth, and old age and all the important and less significant experiences that one has undergone in one's lifetime. Autobiography has a tendency toward exaggeration and overemphasis, and can be sometimes a means for boasting about oneself. However, when it is moderate, it is the truest story that can be written of a man and the best reflection of his life, because autobiography is not suppositional or conjectural but can be verified and proven" (*Attarajum wal Siar,* p. 23).

4. Abbas, *Fannul Sira,* p. 37.

5. This was also typical of tribal Greece. We find the tradition in Homer's *Iliad:* when someone asks Telemachus who he is, he replies: "I am Telemachus, the son of Odysseus, the son of Laertes, the son of Autolycus" (Karl J. Weintraub, "Autobiography and Historical Consciousness," *Critical Inquiry* 1 [June 1975]: 835).

6. See Hassan, *Attarajum wal Siar,* p. 23.

7. This is also argued by Ghazoul, *The Arabian Nights.*

8. The analogy between autobiography and *sira* is inspired by Ghazoul's study, *The Arabian Nights.*

9. David Murray, "Authenticity and Text in American Indian, Hispanic and Asian Autobiography," in Lee, *First Person Singular,* p. 178.

Chapter Six. Anthologies

1. Nayra Atiya, *Khul-Khaal: Five Egyptian Women Tell Their Stories.* Page references are included in the text with the letters *KK.*

2. Fatima Mernissi, *Doing Daily Battle: Interviews with Moroccan Women,* trans. Mary Jo Lakeland. Page references are included in the text with the letters *DDB.*

3. Bouthaina Shaaban, *Both Right and Left Handed: Arab Women Talk about Their Lives.* Page references are included in the text with the letters *BRLH.*

4. Quoted in James Clifford, *The Predicament of Culture: Twentieth-Century Ethnography, Literature and Art,* p. 39.

5. Ibid.

6. Ibid.

7. Ibid., p. 38.

8. Carr, "In Other Words," p. 2.

9. Examples of such autobiographies include Donald Jackson (ed.), *The Life of Black Hawk: An Autobiography;* S. M. Barrett (ed.), *Geronimo: His Own Story* (1906), newly edited by Frederick W. Turner III; and Nancy O. Lurie (ed.), *Mountain Wolf Woman: Sister of Crashing Thunder.*

10. Vincent Crapanzano, *Tuhami: Portrait of a Moroccan.*

11. Ibid., p. 8.

12. Ibid., p. 138.

13. Om Gad reminds me of my own mother, who is also illiterate; although she has never worked outside the home, she has looked after her husband's and children's welfare with amazingly successful management using the limited income of my (educated) father.

14. In *Harem Years,* Shaarawi also talks about how she publicly took the veil off at the Cairo train station in 1923.

15. But, of course, the bad working conditions of the uneducated women force many of them—like Malika, who weaves carpets—to accept a husband who can promise a more comfortable life for them, according to Mernissi.

16. The subject of female circumcision has recently been said to have caused political rows between Egypt and America after the Cable News Network (CNN, which is one of the most widespread satellite television networks worldwide) broadcast three times in one week a circumcision operation on a ten-year-old Egyptian girl. The CNN researcher was arrested in Cairo and charged with "distorting the image of Egypt." The Egyptian reaction is interesting, to say the least. The CNN report has upset the Egyptian government, although it is said to be campaigning against the practice of female circumcision. The documentary is "disgusting," according to the Egyptian newspaper *al-Akhbar,* and CNN should not have shown it—especially after the "unlimited hospitality shown by the Ministry of Tourism to actress Jane Fonda, wife of CNN owner Ted Turner." Should hospitality and friendship be a pretext for concealing facts? See the *Independent,* September 13, 1994.

17. Ghada al-Samman is a very prolific writer; unfortunately she has not been translated into English. Hanan al-Shaikh has had one of her books translated as *Women of Sand and Myrrh.* Huda Barakat wrote *Hajar Addahek* (The Stone of Laughter). Sahar Khalifa wrote *The Cactus, We Are No More Slaves to You, The Gate of the Yard,* and *Memoirs of an Unrealistic Woman,* all in Arabic.

18. I myself experienced inhibition when I used to spend some of my holidays in our village with my cousins. In the city where we lived, I used to have my own room, so I never had to undress, let alone bathe, in the presence of anybody else. In the village, however, nine brothers and sisters had to share bedrooms. Females also used the bathroom together, two or three at a time. Unlike me, my cousins felt no inhibition or embarrassment in doing so. But sexuality was still an issue for them, though in a different way.

19. Friedrich Engels, *The Origin of the Family: Private Property and the State,* p. 108.

20. Ibid., p. 109.

21. Claude Lévi-Strauss, *The Elementary Structures of Kinship,* ed. Rodney Needham, p. 496.

22. Ibid., pp. 478–479.

23. Engels, *The Origin of the Family,* p. 108.

24. Ibid., p. 108.

25. Ibid.

Chapter Seven. Fadwa Tuqan's *Mountainous Journey, Difficult Journey*

1. *Addouha* (Kuwait, February 1984): 20.

2. See the Arabic original of Tuqan's autobiography: *Rihla Jabalyia, Rihla Saaba: Sira Zatyia* (Mountainous Journey, Difficult Journey: An Autobiography).

3. Fadwa Tuqan, "Mountainous Journey—Difficult Journey: The Memoirs of Fadwa Tuqan," trans. Donna Robinson Divine, in Stanton, *The Female Autograph,* pp. 187–204. The same translation is reprinted in Badran and Cooke, *Opening the Gates.*

4. Stanton, *The Female Autograph,* p. vii.

5. See also Fedwa Malti-Douglas, *Woman's Body, Woman's Word: Gender and Discourse in Arabo-Islamic Writing,* p. 161 (footnote).

6. Tuqan, "Mountainous Journey—Difficult Journey," trans. Divine, p. 187.

7. My translation of the Arabic original of Tuqan's autobiography, *Rihla Jabalyia, Rihla Saaba,* p. 39. I have translated several passages for this chapter and remain responsible for my translations. However, the reader may also wish to consult the complete translation that came to my attention after I had finished the manuscript of this book (I would have offered a more comprehensive study had I known earlier about this translation): Fadwa Tuqan, *A Mountainous Journey: An Autobiography,* trans. Olive Kenny and Naomi Shihab Nye.

8. Tuqan, "Mountainous Journey—Difficult Journey," trans. Divine, pp. 199–200.

9. See the Arabic text, *Rihla Jabalyia, Rihla Saaba,* pp. 33–34.

10. Tuqan, "Mountainous Journey—Difficult Journey," trans. Divine, p. 200.

11. Ibid., p. 202; see also the Arabic text, *Rihla Jabalyia, Rihla Saaba,* p. 37.

12. Donna Robinson Divine, "Palestinian Arab Women and Their Reveries of Emancipation," in Bourque and Divine, *Women Living Change,* p. 69.

13. Ibid.

14. Ibid., p. 74.

15. My translation of the Arabic text, *Rihla Jabalyia, Rihla Saaba,* p. 12.

16. Ibid., p. 9.

17. Ibid., p. 10.

18. Ibid., p. 103.

19. Ibid., p. 85.

20. My translation of the dedication in ibid.

21. My translation of Tuqan's prologue in ibid., pp. 9–10.

22. Ibid., pp. 10–11.

23. Ibid., p. 10.

24. Ibid., pp. 134–135.

25. Ibid., p. 108.

26. Ibid., p. 90.

27. Ibid., p. 154.

28. Ibid., p. 12.

29. Ibid.

30. Malti-Douglas, *Woman's Body, Woman's Word*, p. 165.

31. My translation of the Arabic text, *Rihla Jabalyia, Rihla Saaba*, p. 12.

32. Ibid.

33. Ibid., p. 135.

34. Ibid., p. 24.

35. Ibid.

36. Ibid., p. 26.

37. Ibid., p. 56.

38. Ibid., pp. 96–97.

39. Ibid., p. 81.

40. Ibid., p. 133.

41. Ibid., pp. 132–133; and Tuqan, "Mountainous Journey—Difficult Journey," trans. Divine, p. 192.

42. See the Arabic text, *Rihla Jabalyia, Rihla Saaba*, p. 27.

43. Ibid., p. 57.

44. My translation of ibid., p. 54.

45. Ibid.

46. Ibid., p. 100.

47. See, for example, the following passage: "How proud and exhilarated I felt when I read Dr. Omar Farroukh's introduction to one of my poems in his *Al-Amali*, the Lebanese journal: 'These lines are for a young poet. At a time when many of our male poets are writing effeminate and sensitive poetry, this young girl is reviving in our imagination the memories of Abu Tammam and al-Mutanabbi'" (the pillars of Arabic poetry), ibid., p. 89.

Chapter Eight. Nawal el-Saadawi

1. Saadawi's autobiography was translated into parts: *A Daughter of Isis* and *Walking through Fire,* trans. Sherif Hatata.

2. My translation of an interview with Saadawi on Syrian Television in Cairo, 1989.

3. Ibid.

4. Nawal el-Saadawi, *The Hidden Face of Eve: Women in the Arab World*, p. 8.

5. Badran and Cooke, *Opening the Gates*, p. 386.

6. Interview with Saadawi on Syrian Television in Cairo, 1989.

7. Badran and Cooke, *Opening the Gates*, p. 397.

8. Ibid.

9. Saadawi expressed this in one of her letters to me. She has kindly allowed me to quote from her letters.

10. Badran and Cook, *Opening the Gates*, p. 400.

11. Ibid.

12. This is mentioned in one of Saadawi's letters to me.

13. Nawal el-Saadawi, *Memoirs of a Woman Doctor*, trans. Catherine Cobham. Page references are included in the text with the letters *MWD*.

14. "Nawal el-Saadawi's Reply," in George Tarabishi, *Woman against Her Sex: A Critique of Nawal el-Saadawi*, p. 190.

15. Ibid., pp. 190–191.

16. Ibid., p. 192.

17. See the Arabic text of Tuqan's autobiography, *Rihla Jabalyia, Rihla Saaba*, p. 69.

18. Ibid., p. 37.

19. Mary Barnes and Joseph Berke, *Mary Barnes*, pp. 11–12.

20. Simone de Beauvoir, *The Second Sex*, p. 60.

21. Tarabishi, *Woman against Her Sex*, p. 38.

22. Ibid., pp. 217–218.

23. John Stuart Mill, *The Subjection of Women*, p. vi.

24. See Nancy Huston, "The Matrix of War: Mothers and Heroes," in Susan Rubin Suleiman (ed.), *The Female Body in Western Culture: Contemporary Perspectives*.

25. Annis Pratt, *Archetypal Patterns in Women's Fiction*, p. 21 (chapter written with Barbara White).

26. Tarabishi, *Woman against Her Sex*, p. 69.

27. Saadawi in ibid., p. 209.

28. Badran and Cooke, *Opening the Gates*, p. 399.

29. See Barrett J. Mandel, "Full of Life Now," in Olney, *Autobiography*, p. 55.

30. From one of Saadawi's letters to me.

31. Catherine Cobham kindly wrote this in her letter to me dated June 23, 1989.

32. Interview with Saadawi on Syrian Television in Cairo, 1989.

33. Nawal el-Saadawi, *Memoirs from the Women's Prison*, trans. Marilyn Booth. Page references are included in the text with the letters *MWP*.

34. See Miriam Cooke, "Prisons: Egyptian Women's Writing on Islam," *Religion and Literature* 20, pt. 1 (Spring 1988).

35. H. Bruce Franklin, *The Victim as Criminal and Artist: Literature from the American Prison*, pp. 235–236.

36. Barbara Harlow, "Third World Women's Narratives of Prison," *Feminist Studies* 12, pt. 3 (Fall 1986).

37. Ibid., p. 506.

38. Ibid., p. 503.

39. Ibid.

40. See the Appendix, my translation of Saadawi's introduction to the Arabic edition.

41. See ibid.

42. From one of Saadawi's letters to me.

43. Franklin, *The Victim as Criminal and Artist*, p. 250.

44. Ibid.

45. Harlow, "Third World Women's Narratives of Prison," p. 513.

46. Edward W. Said, *The World, the Text, the Critic*, p. 24.

47. Harlow, "Third World Women's Narratives of Prison," p. 513.

48. Ahdaf Soueif, "In the Beggars' Cell," *New Society* 15 (August 1986): 23.

49. Elizabeth Winston, "The Autobiographer and Her Readers: From Apology to Affirmation," in Jelinek, *Women's Autobiography*, p. 93.

50. See Chapter 7 (Tuqan, *Rihla Jabalyia, Rihla Saaba*, p. 9).

51. Interview with Saadawi on Syrian Television in Cairo, 1989.

52. Badran and Cooke, *Opening the Gates*, p. 401.

53. Ibid., p. 404.

54. Michelle Aarouns, "The Toilet Paper Diary of a Prisoner," *Weekly Mail*, September 19–September 24, 1985, p. 15.

55. Saadawi expressed this in one of her letters to me.

56. Saadawi cited in Badran and Cooke, *Opening the Gates*, p. 404.

57. Ibid.

58. Ibid.

59. Ibid., p. 403.

60. Saadawi expressed this in one of her letters to me; see also *Marxism Today* (August 1986): 40.

61. Franklin, *The Victim as Criminal and Artist*, p. 251.

62. Badran and Cooke, *Opening the Gates*, pp. 400–402.

63. Saadawi cited in ibid., p. 402.

64. Soueif, "In the Beggars' Cell," p. 24.

65. Ibid.

66. Nawal el-Saadawi, *My Travels around the World*, trans. Shirley Eber. Page references are included in the text with the letters *TAW.*

67. See Sara Mills, *Discourses of Difference: An Analysis of Women's Travel Writing and Colonialism*, p. 2. See also Linda Kraus Worley, "Through Others' Eyes: Narratives of German Women Travelling in Nineteenth-Century America," *Yearbook of German and American Studies* 21 (1986): 39.

68. Mills, *Discourses of Difference*, pp. 73–74.

69. Ibid., p. 74.

70. Pratt cited in ibid., pp. 75–76.

71. Ibid., p. 77.

72. Ibid., p. 81.

73. Ibid.

74. Ibid., p. 12.

75. From one of Saadawi's letters to me.

76. This is my translation; see the Arabic edition, *Rihlati Hawlal Alam*, p. 56.

77. Mills, *Discourses of Difference*, p. 74.

78. Jill Waters, "Banned and Threatened and Striding Ahead," *Independent*, July 13, 1991.

79. Ibid.

80. See Maggie Humm, *Border Traffic: Strategies of Contemporary Women Writers.*

81. According to Islamic law, a married woman can only travel with her husband's permission (i.e., a husband can stop his wife from traveling). This is why the immigration man at the airport had to ask Saadawi whether she was married or not.

82. As Saadawi wrote in one of her letters to me.

83. See Nawal el-Saadawi, *The Innocence of the Devil*. She has also written *The Well of Life, She Has No Place in Paradise*, and most recently *Al-Hub fi Zaman al-Naft* (Love in the Age of Oil [Cairo: Maktabat Madbuli, 1993]), three novels, and *Twelve Women in One Cell*, a play.

84. Hisham Sharabi, *Neopatriarchy: A Theory of Distorted Change in Arab Society*, p. 33.

85. Judy Mabro, *Veiled Half-Truths: Western Travellers' Perceptions of Middle Eastern Women*, p. ix. Rana Kabbani demonstrates, in her book *Letter to Christendom*, that prejudice against Islam and Muslims still characterizes western culture. Kabbani's book can be seen as a travel text; however, the journey is taking place in her mind.

86. Mabro, *Veiled Half-Truths*, p. ix.

Conclusion. The Literary and the Political

1. *Al-Katiba* (London, December 1993). Unfortunately, *Al-Katiba* stopped publication in 1995; but it was to be launched on-line in August 2002, according to the editor, Nourie al-Jarrah.

2. See *Al-Katiba* 5 (April 1994): 48–61.

3. See *Al-Katiba* 8 (July 1994): 4–9.

4. See Michele Barrett, *Women's Oppression Today: Problems in Marxist Feminist Analysis,* p. 99; and Wolff, *The Social Production of Art.* For Wolff, any human act is "multiply determined—by social factors, psychological factors, neurological and chemical factors" (p. 20). In literature, as in other artistic forms, many people are involved in producing and finishing a text. Moreover, a text is only important when it is read; hence the reader is as essential as the writer. Institutional factors are also intrinsic to the production of texts. Wolff gives a good analysis of how technology, social institutions, and economic factors play roles in "artistic" productions. Factors from the availability of ink and paper, to the printing and publishing facilities, to the way society always conditions who is to become a writer (recruitment and training of artists), to direct and indirect "patronage" systems or censorship or the role of the academy, to the role of critics ("mediators"), to economic determinants interact jointly in literary and artistic productions, according to Wolff, and should not be overlooked in any analysis. This is why she rightly believes that "ideological analysis is insufficient if it is not supplemented by an understanding of groups, pressures, hierarchies and power relations within organizations involved in the general process of the production of culture" (pp. 30–31).

Appendix. Translation of the Introduction to the Arabic Edition of *Memoirs from the Women's Prison* by Nawal el-Saadawi

1. "Aura," as explained in an Arabic-English dictionary, refers to defectiveness, faultiness, weakness, deficiency, imperfection, the pudendum, and genitals. However, it is generally used with a sexual connotation.

Main Texts

Atiya, Nayra. *Khul-Khaal: Five Egyptian Women Tell Their Stories*. London: Virago, 1988.

Mernissi, Fatima. *Doing Daily Battle: Interviews with Moroccan Women*. Trans. Mary Jo Lakeland. London: Women's Press, 1988.

el-Saadawi, Nawal. *Memoirs from the Women's Prison*. Trans. Marilyn Booth. London: Women's Press, 1986.

———. *Memoirs of a Woman Doctor*. Trans. Catherine Cobham. London: al-Saqi Books, 1988.

———. *My Travels around the World*. Trans. Shirley Eber. London: Methuen, 1991.

———. *Rihlati Hawlal Alam* (My Travels around the World). Cairo: Dar al-Hilal, 1986.

Shaaban, Bouthaina. *Both Right and Left Handed: Arab Women Talk about Their Lives*. London: Women's Press, 1988.

Shaarawi, Huda. *Harem Years: The Memoirs of an Egyptian Feminist*. Ed. and trans. Margot Badran. London: Virago, 1986.

Tuqan, Fadwa. *A Mountainous Journey: An Autobiography*. Trans. Olive Kenny and Naomi Shihab Nye. St. Paul, Minn.: Graywolf Press/London: Women's Press, 1990.

———. "Mountainous Journey—Difficult Journey." Trans. Donna Robinson Divine. In Domna C. Stanton (ed.), *The Female Autograph: Theory and Practice of Autobiography from the Tenth to the Twentieth Century*, pp. 187–204. Chicago and London: University of Chicago Press, 1984). Also in Margot Badran and Miriam Cooke (eds.), *Opening the Gates: A Century of Arab Feminist Writing*, pp. 27–39. London: Virago Press, 1990.

———. *Rihla Jabalyia, Rihla Saaba: Sira Zatyia* (Mountainous Journey, Difficult Journey: An Autobiography). 3rd ed. Amman: Dar Ashrouq, 1988.

References and Other Texts

Aarouns, Michelle. "The Toilet Paper Diary of a Prisoner." *Weekly Mail*, September 19–September 25, 1985, p. 15.

Abbas, Ihsan. *Fannul Sira* (The Art of Autobiography). Beirut: Darul Thaqafa, 1956.

Abdel-Malek, Anouar. "Orientalism in Crisis." *Diogenes* 44 (1963): 103–140.

Abdul Dayem, Yahyia. *Attarjama Azzatiya fi al-Adab al-Arabi al-Hadith* (Autobiography in Modern Arabic Literature). Beirut: Dar Annahda al-Arabia, 1975.

Abel, Elizabeth (ed.). *Writing and Sexual Difference*. Brighton: Harvester Press, 1982.

Abu Odeh, Lama. "Post-Colonial Feminism and the Veil: Thinking the Difference." *Feminist Review* 43 (Spring 1993): 26–37.

"Acting Bits/Identity Talk." *Critical Inquiry* 18, no. 4 (Summer 1992): 770–803.

Addouha (Kuwait). February 1984.

Ahmed, Laila. "Between Two Worlds: The Formation of a Turn-of-the-Century Egyptian Feminist." In Bella Brodzki and Celeste Schenck (eds.), *Life/Lines: Theorizing Women's Autobiography,* pp. 154–174. Ithaca and London: Cornell University Press, 1988.

———. "Western Ethnocentrism and Perceptions of the Harem." *Feminist Studies* 8 (Fall 1982): 521–534.

———. *Women and Gender in Islam: Historical Roots of a Modern Debate*. New Haven and London: Yale University Press, 1992.

Ajamy, Fouad. *The Arab Predicament: Arab Political Thought and Practice since 1967.* Cambridge and New York: Cambridge University Press, 1981.

Althusser, Louis. *Essays on Ideology*. London: Verso, 1971.

Amireh, Amal, and Lisa Suhair Majaj (eds.). *Going Global: The Transnational Reception of Third World Women Writers*. New York and London: Garland Publishing, 2000.

Anderson, Linda. "At the Threshold of the Self: Women and Autobiography." In Moira Monteith (ed.), *Women's Writing: A Challenge to Theory*. Brighton: Harvester Press, 1986.

Appiah, Kwame Anthony. "Is the Post- in Postmodernism the Post- in Postcolonial?" *Critical Inquiry* 17 (Winter 1991): 336–357.

Apter, Emily. "Female Trouble in the Colonial Harem." *Difference: A Journal of Feminist Cultural Studies* 4 (Spring 1992): 205–221.

Arkin, Marian, and Barbara Shollar (eds.). *An Anthology of World Literature by Women*. London and New York: Longman, 1989.

Asad, Talal. *The Kababish Arabs: Power, Authority and Consent in a Nomadic Tribe*. London: C. Hurst, 1970.

Asante, Molefi Kete. *The Afrocentric Idea*. Philadelphia: Temple University Press, 1986.

al-Azm, Sadik Jalal. "Orientalism and Orientalism in Reverse." *Khamsin* 8 1981: 5–26.

Badran, Margot. "Dual Liberation: Feminism and Nationalism in Egypt, 1870s–1925." *Feminist Issues* (Spring 1988): 15–34.

Badran, Margot, and Miriam Cooke (eds.). *Opening the Gates: A Century of Arab Feminist Writing*. London: Virago Press, 1990.

Baer, Gabriel. *Studies in the Social History of Modern Egypt*. Chicago: University of Chicago Press, 1969.

Barnes, Mary, and Joseph Berke. *Mary Barnes*. Harmondsworth: Penguin Books, 1973.

Baron, B. "Women's Nationalist Rhetoric and Activities in Early Twentieth-Century Egypt." In L. Anderson (ed.), *The Origins of Arab Nationalism*. New York: Columbia University Press, 1991.

Barrett, Michele. *Women's Oppression Today: Problems in Marxist Feminist Analysis*. London: Verso, 1980.

Barrett, S. M. (ed.). *Geronimo: His Own Story* (1906). Newly edited by Frederick W Turner III. London: Abacus, 1974.

Barthes, Roland. *Roland Barthes par Roland Barthes*. New York: Hill and Wang, 1977.

Beard, Mary. *The Majority Finds Its Past*. New York: Oxford University Press, 1981.

Beauvoir, Simone de. *The Second Sex* (1949). London: Picador, 1988.

Belsey, Catherine. *Critical Practice*. London and New York: Methuen, 1980.

Bennett, Tony. *Formalism and Marxism*. London and New York: Methuen, 1979.

Benstock, Shari (ed.). *The Private Self: Theory and Practice of Women's Autobiographical Writings*. Chapel Hill and London: University of North Carolina Press, 1988.

Bhabha, Homi. "The Commitment to Theory." *New Formations* 5 (1988): 5–23.

———. "Interrogating Identity." In Lisa Appignanesi (ed.), *Identity: The Real Me*, pp. 5–46. ICA Documents 6. London: Institute of Contemporary Arts, 1987.

———. "Of Mimicry and Man: The Ambivalence of Colonial Discourse." *October* 28 (1985) 125–133.

———. "Representation and the Colonial Text: A Critical Exploration of Some Forms of Mimeticism." In Frank Gloversmith (ed.), *The Theory of Reading*, pp. 93–122. Brighton: Harvester Press, 1984.

———. "Signs Taken for Wonders: Questions of Ambivalence and Authority under a Tree outside Delhi, May, 1817." *Critical Inquiry* 12, no. 1 (Autumn 1985): 144–165.

———. "Sly Civility." *October* 34 (1985): 71–80.

Bhavani, Kum-Kum. "Towards a Multicultural Europe?: 'Race,' Nation and Identity in 1992 and Beyond." *Feminist Review* 45 (Autumn 1993): 30–45.

Boullata, Issa J. *Trends and Issues in Contemporary Arab Thought*. Albany: State University of New York Press, 1990.

Bourque, Susan C., and Donna Robinson Divine (eds.). *Women Living Change*. Philadelphia: Temple University Press, 1985.

Bove, Paul A. "Hope and Reconciliation: A Review of Edward Said." *Boundary 2* 20, no. 2 (Summer 1993): 266–282.

Brodzki, Bella, and Celeste Schenck (eds.). *Life/Lines: Theorizing Women's Autobiography.* Ithaca and London: Cornell University Press, 1988.

Brunt, Rosalind. "The Politics of Identity." In Stuart Hall and Martin Jacques (eds.), *New Times: The Changing Face of Politics in the 1990's,* pp. 150–159. London: Lawrence and Wishart, in association with *Marxism Today,* 1990.

Brunt, R., and C. Rowan (eds.). *Feminism, Culture and Politics.* London: Lawrence and Wishart, 1982.

Bruss, Elizabeth. *Autobiographical Acts.* Baltimore and London: Johns Hopkins University Press, 1976.

Bulkin, Elly. "Semite vs. Semite/Feminist vs. Feminist." In Elly Bulkin, Minnie Bruce Pratt, and Barbara Smith (eds.), *Yours in Struggle: Three Feminist Perspectives on Anti-Semitism and Racism.* Brooklyn: Long Haul Press, 1984.

Burstyn, D. "Masculine Dominance and the State." *Socialist Register* (1983): 45–89.

Butor, Michel. "Travel and Writing." *Mosaic* 8, no. 1 (Fall 1974): 1–16.

Carmichael, Joel. *The Shaping of the Arabs.* London: George Allen and Unwin, 1967.

Carr, Helen. "In Other Words: Native American Women's Autobiography." In Bella Brodzki and Celeste Schenck (eds.), *Life/Lines: Theorizing Women's Autobiographies,* pp. 131–153. Ithaca and London: Cornell University Press, 1988.

Chen, Xiaomei. "Occidentalism as Counterdiscourse: 'He Shang' in Post-Mao China." *Critical Inquiry* 18, no. 4 (Summer 1992): 686–712.

Chernin, Kim. *In My Mother's House: A Daughter's Story.* New York: Harper, 1984.

Chicago Cultural Studies Group. "Critical Multiculturalism." *Critical Inquiry* 18, no. 3 (Spring 1992): 530–555.

Chodorow, Nancy. *The Reproduction of Mothering: Psychoanalysis and the Sociology of Gender.* Berkeley: University of California Press, 1978.

Choueiri, Yousef M. *Arab History and the Nation-State: A Study in Modern Arab Historiography 1820–1980.* London and New York: Routledge, 1989.

Clifford, James. "On Orientalism." In *The Predicament of Culture: Twentieth-Century Ethnography, Literature and Art,* pp. 255–276. Cambridge, Mass.: Harvard University Press, 1988.

———. "Orientalism." *History and Theory* 19 (1980): 726–751.

———. *The Predicament of Culture: Twentieth-Century Ethnography, Literature and Art.* Cambridge, Mass.: Harvard University Press, 1988.

Cole, Donald. "Social and Economic Structures of the Murrah: A Saudi Arabian Bedouin Tribe." Ph.D. dissertation, University of California, Berkeley, 1971.

Cole, Juan Ricardo. "Feminism, Class, and Islam in Turn-of-the-Century Egypt." *International Journal of Middle East Studies* 13 (1981): 387–407.

Connell, R. W. "The State, Gender and Sexual Politics: Theory and Appraisal." *Theory and Society* 19, no. 5 (1990): 507–544.

Cooke, Miriam. "Prisons: Egyptian Women's Writing on Islam." *Religion and Literature* 20, pt. 1 (Spring 1988): 139–153.

———. "Telling Their Lives: A Hundred Years of Arab Women's Writings." *World Literature Today: A Literary Quarterly of the University of Oklahoma* 60, pt. 2 (Spring 1986): 212–216.

Crapanzano, Vincent. *Tuhami: Portrait of a Moroccan.* Chicago and London: University of Chicago Press, 1980.

Cunnison, Ian. *The Baggara Arabs: Power and Lineage in a Sudanese Nomad Tribe.* Oxford: Clarendon Press, 1966.

Danius, Sara, and Stefan Jonsson. Interview with Gayatri Chakravorty Spivak. *Boundary 2* 20, no. 2 (Summer 1993): 24–50.

Davies, Miranda (comp.). *Third World: Second Sex, Women's Struggle and National Liberation—Third World Women Speak Out.* London: Zed Books, 1983.

Decker, Jeffrey Louis. "Terrorism Unveiled: Frantz Fanon and the Women of Algiers." *Cultural Critique* 17 (Winter 1990–1991): 177–195.

de Man, Paul. "Autobiography as Defacement." *Modern Languages Notes* 94, no. 1 (January 1979): 919–930.

Diaspora 1, no. 1 (Spring 1991).

Dinesen, Isak. *Out of Africa.* New York: Vintage Books, 1965.

Dodd, Philip. "Criticism and the Autobiographical Tradition." *Prose Studies* 8, no. 2 (September 1985): 1–13.

During, Simon. "Postmodernism or Postcolonialism?" *Landfall* 39 (September 1985): 366–380.

Eagleton, Terry. *Criticism and Ideology: A Study in Marxist Literary Theory.* London and New York: Verso, 1975.

———. *Literary Theory: An Introduction.* Oxford: Basil Blackwell, 1983.

———. *Marxism and Literary Criticism.* London: Methuen, 1976.

Eakin, Paul John. "Malcolm X and the Limits of Autobiography." In James Olney (ed.), *Autobiography: Essays Theoretical and Critical,* pp. 181–193. Princeton: Princeton University Press, 1980.

Ecker, Gisela. *Feminist Aesthetics.* London: Women's Press, 1985.

Engels, Friedrich. *The Origin of the Family: Private Property and the State.* Harmondsworth: Penguin Books, 1985.

Fanon, Frantz. *Studies in a Dying Colonialism.* New York: Monthly Review Press, 1965.

Farah, Madelain. *Marriage and Sexuality in Islam.* Salt Lake City: University of Utah Press, 1984.

Farraj, Afif. *Freedom in Women's Literature.* Beirut: Institution of Arabic Research, 1985.

Fernea, Elizabeth Warnock, and Basima Qattan Bezirgan (eds.). *Middle Eastern Muslim Women Speak.* Austin and London: University of Texas Press, 1977.

Fluerh-Lobban, C. "Agitation for Change in the Sudan." In A. Schlegel (ed.), *Sexual Stratification: A Cross-Cultural View.* New York: Columbia University Press, 1977.

———. "The Political Mobilization of Women in the Arab World." In J. Smith (ed.), *Women in Contemporary Muslim Societies.* Lewisburg: Bucknell University Press, 1980.

Foster, Stephen William. "The Dilemma of Polyculturalism for a Moroccan Woman." In Susan C. Bourque and Donna Robinson Divine (eds.), *Women Living Change,* pp. 147–182. Philadelphia: Temple University Press, 1985.

Foucault, Michel. *Discipline and Punish: The Birth of the Prison.* Trans. Alan Sheridan. New York: Vintage Books, 1977.

Fox-Genovese, Elizabeth. "Placing Women's History in History." *New Left Review* 133 (May–June 1982): 5–29.

Franklin, H. Bruce. *The Victim as Criminal and Artist: Literature from the American Prison.* New York: Oxford University Press, 1978.

Friedman, Susan Stanford. "Women's Autobiographical Selves: Theory and Practice." In Shari Benstock (ed.), *The Private Self: Theory and Practice of Women's Autobiographical Writings.* Chapel Hill and London: University of North Carolina Press, 1988.

Gates, Henry Louis Jr. "Pluralism and Its Discontents." *Contentions* 2, no. 1 (Fall 1992): 69–77.

Ghazoul, Ferial Jabouri. *The Arabian Nights: A Structural Analysis.* Cairo: Cairo Associated Institution for the Study and Presentation of Arab Cultural Values, 1980.

Gilroy, Paul. "It Ain't Where You're From, It's Where You're At . . . The Dialectics of Diasporic Identification." *Third Text* 13 (Winter 1990–1991): 3–16.

Giroux, Henry A. "Post-Colonial Ruptures and Democratic Possibilities: Multiculturalism as Anti-Racist Pedagogy." *Cultural Critique* 21 (Spring 1992): 5–39.

Grant, Linda. "A Heavy Load of Cultural Baggage." *Independent,* July 21, 1991.

Green, Gayle, and Coppelia Kahn (eds.). *Making a Difference: Feminist Literary Criticism.* London and New York: Methuen, 1980.

Haddad, Yvonne. "Palestinian Women: Patterns of Legitimation and Domination." In Khalil Nakhleh and Elia Zureik (eds.), *Sociology of the Palestinians,* pp. 147–175. London: Croom Helm, 1980.

Hafez, Sabry. "Intentions and Realisation in the Narratives of NAWAL EL-SAADAWI." *Third World Quarterly* (July 1989): 1–11.

Harlow, Barbara. "Third World Women's Narratives of Prison." *Feminist Studies* 12, pt. 3 (Fall 1986): 501–524.

Hassan, Ihab. "Pluralism in Postmodern Perspective." *Cultural Inquiry* 12. no. 3 (Spring 1985): 503–520.

Hassan, Muhammad Abdul Ghani. *Attarajum wal Siar* (Biographies and Autobiographies). Cairo: Darul Maarifa, 1980.

Hatem, Mervat. "The Politics of Sexuality and Gender in Segregated Patriarchal Systems: The Case of Eighteenth- and Nineteenth-Century Egypt." *Feminist Studies* 12, pt. 2 (1986): 253–254.

al-Hibri, Aziza (ed.). *Women and Islam*. Oxford and New York: Pergamon Press, 1982.

Hirschkind, Charles, and Saba Mahmood. "Feminism, the Taliban, and Politics of Counter-Insurgency." *Anthropological Quarterly* 75, no. 2 (Spring 2002): 339–354.

hooks, bell. *Feminist Theory: From Margin to Center*. Boston: South End Press, 1984.

Hourani, Albert. *A History of the Arab Peoples*. London: Faber and Faber, 1991.

Hourani, Albert, Philip S. Khoury, and Mary C. Wilson (eds.). *The Modern Middle East: A Reader*. London and New York: I. B. Tauris and Co., 1993.

Humm, Maggie. *Border Traffic: Strategies of Contemporary Women Writers*. Manchester: Manchester University Press, 1991.

———. *Feminist Criticism: Women as Contemporary Critics*. Brighton: Harvester Press, 1986.

al-Husri, Sati. *Lectures on the Emergence of Nationalism*. Beirut: n.p., 1956.

———. *Opinions and Discussions on Nationalism and Internationalism*. Cairo: n.p., 1944.

Hussain, Freda. *Muslim Women*. New York: St. Martin's Press, 1984.

Huston, Nancy. "The Matrix of War: Mothers and Heroes." In Susan Rubin Suleiman (ed.), *The Female Body in Western Culture: Contemporary Perspectives*, pp. 119–136. Cambridge, Mass.: Harvard University Press, 1986.

Ibn Taymiyya. *Fatwa al-Nisa'* (Fatwas concerning Women). Cairo: Maktabat al-'Irfan, 1983.

"An Interview with Edward Said." *Boundary 2* 20, no. 1 (Spring 1993): 1–25.

Jackson, Donald (ed.). *The Life of Black Hawk: An Autobiography*. Urbana: University of Illinois, 1933.

al-Jawzi, Ibn. *Kitab Ahkam al-Nisa'* (Statutory Provisions concerning Women). Cairo: Maktabat al-'Irfan, 1983.

Jaywardena, Kumari. *Feminism and Nationalism in the Third World in the C19th and C20th: History of the Women's Movement*. Lecture Series. The Hague: Institute of Social Studies, 1982.

Jefferson, Ann, and David Roby (eds.). *Modern Literary Theory: A Comparative Introduction*. London: B. T. Batsford, 1982.

Jelinek, Estelle C. (ed.). *Women's Autobiography: Essays in Criticism.* Bloomington and London: Indiana University Press, 1980.

Kabbani, Rana. *Europe's Myths of Orient: Devise and Rule.* London: Pandora Press, 1986.

———. *Letter to Christendom.* London: Virago, 1989.

Kandiyoti, Deniz. "Identity and Its Discontents: Women and the Nation." In Patrick Williams and Laura Chrisman (eds.), *Colonial Discourse and Post-Colonial Theory: A Reader.* New York and London: Harvester Wheatsheaf, 1993.

al-Katiba 5 and 8 (1994).

Kimball, Roger. "Tenured Radicals: A Postscript." *New Criterion* (January 1991): 4–13.

Kingston, Maxine Hong. *The Woman Warrior: Memoirs of a Girlhood among Ghosts.* London: Picador, 1977.

Kristeva, Julia. *About Chinese Women.* London and New York: Marion Boyars, 1977.

Lazreg, Marnia. "Feminism and Difference: The Perils of Writing as a Woman on Women in Algeria." *Feminist Studies* 14, no. 1 (Spring 1988): 81–107.

Lee, A. Robert (ed.). *First Person Singular: Studies in American Autobiography.* London: Vision Press/New York: St. Martin's Press, 1988.

Lemu, B. Aisha, and Fatima Heeren. *Women in Islam.* London: Islamic Council of Europe, 1979.

Lerner, Gerda. *The Creation of Patriarchy.* New York: Oxford University Press, 1986.

Lévi-Strauss, Claude. *The Elementary Structures of Kinship.* Ed. Rodney Needham. London: Eyre and Spottiswood, 1969.

Lienhardt, Peter A. "Some Social Aspects of the Trucial States." In Derek Hopwood (ed.), *The Arabian Peninsula: Society and Politics,* pp. 219–229. London: Allen and Unwin, 1972.

Lovibond, Sabina. "Feminism and Postmodernism." In Thomas Docherty (ed.), *Postmodernism: A Reader,* pp. 390–414. New York and London: Harvester Wheatsheaf, 1993.

Lowe, Lisa. "Heterogeneity, Hybridity, Multiplicity: Marking Asian American Differences." *Diaspora* 1, no. 1 (Spring 1991): 24–44.

Luciani, Giacomo (ed.). *The Arab State.* Berkeley: University of California Press, 1990.

Lugones, Maria, and Victoria Spelman. "Have We Got a Theory for You?: Feminist Theory, Cultural Imperialism, and the Demand for the Woman's Voice." *Women's Studies: International Forum* 6, no. 6 (1983): 573–589.

Lurie, Nancy O. (ed.). *Mountain Wolf Woman: Sister of Crashing Thunder.* Ann Arbor: Michigan University Press, 1961.

Mabro, Judy. *Veiled Half-Truths: Western Travellers' Perceptions of Middle Eastern Women.* London and New York: I. B. Tauris and Co., 1991.

Macherey, Pierre. *A Theory of Literary Production.* London and New York: Routledge and Kegan Paul, 1978.

MacKinnon, C. "Feminism, Marxism, Method and the State: An Agenda for Theory." *Signs* 7, no. 3 (1989): 515–544.

Makey, Alia. *Diaries of a Woman from the Saudi Prisons.* London: Al-Safa, 1989.

Makhlouf-Obermeyer, Clara. *Changing Veils: A Study of Women in South Arabia.* Austin: University of Texas Press, 1979.

Malti-Douglas, Fedwa. *Woman's Body, Woman's Word: Gender and Discourse in Arabo-Islamic Writing.* Princeton: Princeton University Press, 1991.

Mandel, Barrett J. "Full of Life Now." In James Olney (ed.), *Autobiography: Essays Theoretical and Critical,* pp. 49–72. Princeton, N.J.: Princeton University Press, 1980.

Mandela, Winnie. *Part of My Soul.* Harmondsworth: Penguin Books, 1985.

Mani, Lata, and Ruth Frankenberg. "The Challenge of Orientalism." *Economy and Society* 14, no. 2 (May 1985): 174–192.

Mansfield, Peter. "Who Are the Arabs?" In *The Arabs,* pp. 13–34. Harmondsworth: Penguin Books, 1978.

Marx, Emmanuel. *Bedouin of the Negev.* New York: Praeger, 1967.

Mason-John, Valerie. "A Woman of Substance." *Voice,* week ending June 28, 1986.

McBratney, John. "Images of Indian Women in Rudyard Kipling: A Case of Doubling Discourse." *Inscriptions: Feminism and the Critique of Colonial Discourse* 3–4 (1988): 47–57.

McRobbie, Angela. "Feminism, Postmodernism and the Real Me." *Theory, Culture and Society: Explorations in Critical Social Science* (London, Newbury Park, and New Delhi) 10, no. 4 (November 1993): 127–142.

Mernissi, Fatima. *Beyond the Veil: Male-Female Dynamics in Muslim Society.* London: al-Saqi Books, 1985.

———. *Islam and Democracy: Fear of the Modern World.* London: Virago, 1993.

———. *Women and Islam: An Historical and Theological Enquiry.* Oxford: Basil Blackwell, 1991.

Mies, M. *Patriarchy and Accumulation on a World Scale.* London: Zed Press, 1986.

Mill, John Stuart. *The Subjection of Women.* Cambridge, Mass., and London: MIT Press, 1970.

Miller, Nancy. "Writing Fiction: Women's Autobiography in France." In Bella Brodzki and Celeste Schenck (eds.), *Life/Lines: Theorizing Women's Autobiography.* Ithaca and London: Cornell University Press, 1988.

Mills, Sara. "Alternative Voices to Orientalism." *Journal of Literature Teaching Politics* 5 (1986): 78–91.

———. *Discourses of Difference: An Analysis of Women's Travel Writing and Colonialism.* London and New York: Routledge, 1991.

Minai, Naila. *Women in Islam: Tradition and Transition in the Middle East.* New York: Seaview Books, 1981.

Minh-ha, Trinh T. "Not You/Like You: Post-Colonial Women and the Interlocking Questions of Identity and Difference." *Inscriptions* 3/4 (1988): 71–77.

———. *When the Moon Waxes Red: Representation, Gender, and Cultural Politics.* London and New York: Routledge, 1991.

———. *Woman, Native, Other: Writing, Postcoloniality and Feminism.* Bloomington: Indiana University Press, 1989.

Miyoshi, Masao. "A Borderless World?: From Colonialism to Transnationalism and the Decline of the Nation-State." *Critical Inquiry* 19, no. 4 (Summer 1993): 726–751.

Mohanty, Chandra. "Under Western Eyes: Feminist Scholarship and Colonial Discourses." *Feminist Review* 30 (1988): 61–88.

———. "Us and Them: On the Philosophical Bias of Political Criticism." *Yale Journal of Criticism* 2, no. 2 (1989): 1–13.

Moi, Toril. *Sexual/Textual Politics: Feminist Literary Theory.* London and New York: Methuen, 1985.

Molyneux, M. "Women and Revolution in the People's Democratic Republic of Yemen." *Feminist Review* 1 (1977).

Monteith, Moira (ed.). *Women's Writing: A Challenge to Theory.* Brighton: Harvester Press, 1986.

Moraga, Cherríe, and Gloria Anzaldúa (eds.). *This Bridge Called My Back: Writings by Radical Women of Color.* New York: Kitchen Table, Women of Color Press, 1983.

Murray, David. "Authenticity and Text in American Indian, Hispanic and Asian Autobiography." In A. Robert Lee (ed.), *First Person Singular: Studies in American Autobiography,* pp. 177–197. London: Vision Press, 1988.

Nashat, Guity (ed.). *Women and Revolution in Iran.* Boulder, Colo.: Westview, 1983.

Nelson, Cynthia. "Public and Private Politics: Women in the Middle Eastern World." *American Ethnologist* 1, no. 3 (1974): 551–563.

Nusbaum, Martha. "Human Functioning and Social Justice: In Defense of Aristotelian Essentialism." *Political Theory* 20, no. 2 (May 1992): 202–243.

Olney, James (ed.). *Autobiography: Essays Theoretical and Critical.* Princeton: Princeton University Press, 1980.

Owen, Roger. "The Middle East in the Eighteenth Century: An 'Islamic Society' in Decline?" *Review of Middle East Studies* 1 (1975): 101–112.

Parry, Benita. "Problems in Current Theories of Colonial Discourse." *Oxford Literary Review* 9, nos. 1–2 (1987): 27–58.

Peters, E. L. "The Bedouin Sheikhs: Aspects of Power among Cyrenaican Pastoralists." Paper presented at a seminar on Leadership and Development in the Arab World, American University of Beirut, November 1979.

Philipp, Thomas. "Feminism and Nationalism in Egypt." In L. Beck and Nikki Keddie (eds.), *Women in the Muslim World.* Cambridge, Mass.: Harvard University Press, 1978.

Philipps, Eileen. "Casting Off the Veil." *Marxism Today* (August 1986): 288–289.

Pratt, Annis. *Archetypal Patterns in Women's Fiction.* Bloomington: Indiana University Press, 1981.

al-Qannuji, Muhammad Siddiq Hasan Khan. *Husn al-Uswa Bima Tabata Minha Allahi fi al-Niswa* (Good Manners for Women). Beirut: Mu'assasa al-Rislal, 1981.

Rahbek, B. "Oppressive and Liberating Elements in the Situation of Palestinian Women." Mimeo, 1980.

Ravitch, Diane. "Multi-culturalism." *American Scholar* 59, no. 3 (Summer 1990): 337–354.

Rowbotham, Sheila. *Woman's Consciousness, Man's World.* London: Pelican Books, 1973.

el-Saadawi, Nawal. *A Daughter of Isis.* Trans Sherif Hatata. London: Zed Books, 1999.

———. *The Fall of the Imam.* London: Minerva, 1988.

———. *The Hidden Face of Eve: Women in the Arab World.* London: Zed Books, 1980.

———. *The Innocence of the Devil.* London: Methuen, 1994.

———. *Two Women in One.* London: Al-Saqi Books, 1985.

———. *Walking through Fire.* Trans Sherif Hatata. London: Zed Books, 2002.

———. *Woman at Point Zero.* London: Zed Books, 1983.

Sabbah, Fatna A. *Woman in the Muslim Unconscious.* New York and Oxford: Pergamon Press, 1984.

Said, Edward W. *Culture and Imperialism.* New York: Alfred A. Knopf, 1993.

———. "Opponents, Audience, Constituencies." *Critical Inquiry* 9, no. 1 (September 1982).

———. *Orientalism.* London: Penguin Books, 1978.

———. "Orientalism Reconsidered." *Race and Class* 27, no. 2 (1985): 1–15.

———. *The World, the Text, the Critic.* Cambridge, Mass.: Harvard University Press, 1983.

Salman, Magida, Hamida Kazi, Nira Yuval-Davis, Laila al-Hamdani, Selma Botman, and Debbie Lerman. *Women in the Middle East.* Edited by the Khamsin Collective. London: Zed Books, 1987.

Sasson, Jean P. *Princess: Sultana's Daughter.* London and New York: Bantam Books, 1994.

Sayigh, Rosemary. "Roles and Functions of Arab Women: A Reappraisal." *Arab Studies Quarterly* 3, pt. 3 (1981): 258–274.

Schipper, Mineke (ed.). *Unheard Words: Women and Literature in Africa, the Arab World, Asia, the Caribbean and Latin America.* London and New York: Allison Busby, 1984.

Selden, Raman. *A Reader's Guide to Contemporary Literary Theory*. Brighton: Harvester Press, 1985.

el-Shamy, Hasan. "The Brother-Sister Syndrome in Arab Family Life, Socio-Cultural Factors in Arab Psychiatry: A Critical Review." *International Journal of Sociology of the Family* 11 (1981): 313–323.

Sharabi, Hisham. *Neopatriarchy: A Theory of Distorted Change in Arab Society*. New York: Oxford University Press, 1988.

al-Shaykh, Hanan. *The Story of Zahra*. London, Pan Books, 1987.

———. *Women of Sand and Myrrh*. London and New York: Quartet Books, 1989.

Showalter, Elaine (ed.). *The New Feminist Criticism: Essays on Women, Literature and Theory*. London: Virago, 1985.

Sivan, Emmanuel. "Edward Said and His Arab Reviewers." In *Interpretations of Islam Past and Present*, pp. 133–154. Princeton: Darwin Press, 1985.

Smith, Sidonie. *A Poetics of Women's Autobiography: Marginality and the Fictions of Self-Representation*. Bloomington and Indianapolis: Indiana University Press, 1987.

Soueif, Ahdaf. "In the Beggars' Cell." *New Society* 15 (August 1986): 23–24.

Spivak, Gayatri Chakravorty. *In Other Worlds: Essays in Cultural Politics*. London and New York: Methuen, 1987.

———. *The Post-Colonial Critic: Interviews, Strategies, Dialogues*. Ed. Sarah Harasym. London and New York: Routledge, 1990.

———. "Three Women's Texts and a Critique of Imperialism." *Critical Inquiry* 12, no. 1 (Autumn, 1985): 243–261.

Stallybrass, Peter, and Allon White. *The Politics and Poetics of Transgression*. Ithaca and New York: Cornell University Press/Philadelphia: Temple University Press, 1986.

Stanton, Domna C. (ed.). *The Female Autograph: Theory and Practice of Autobiography from the Tenth to the Twentieth Century*. Chicago and London: University of Chicago Press, 1984.

Suleri, Sara. "Woman Skin Deep: Feminism and the Postcolonial Condition." *Critical Inquiry* 18, no. 4 (Summer 1992): 756–769.

Tarabishi, George. *Woman against Her Sex: A Critique of Nawal el-Saadawi*. London: Al-Saqi Books, 1988.

Tawil, Raymonda. *My Home, My Prison*. London: Zed Press, 1983.

Tergeman, Siham. *Daughter of Damascus*. Austin: University of Texas, Center for Middle Eastern Studies, 1994.

Tiffin, Helen. "Post-Colonialism, Post-Modernism and the Rehabilitation of Post-Colonial History." *Journal of Commonwealth Literature* (1987) 169–181.

Toubia, Nahid (ed.). *Women of the Arab World: The Coming Challenge*. London: Zed Books, 1988.

Tucker, Judith. "Decline of the Family Economy in Mid–Nineteenth Century Egypt." *Arab Quarterly* 1, pt. 3 (Summer 1979): 245–271.

Turner, Bryan S. *Weber and Islam: A Critical Study.* London: Routledge and Kegan Paul, 1974.

Waters, Jill. "Banned and Threatened and Striding Ahead." *Independent,* July 13, 1991.

Wilder, Laura Ingalls. *The Little House.* New York: Harper and Row, 1971.

Williams, Raymond. *Key Words: A Vocabulary of Culture and Society.* London: Flamingo, 1983.

———. *Marxism and Literature.* Oxford and New York: Oxford University Press, 1977.

Wilson, Ernest J., III. "Orientalism: A Black Perspective." *Journal of Palestinian Studies* 10, no. 2 (1981): 59–69.

Wolff, Janet. *The Social Production of Art.* London: Macmillan Education, 1981.

Woodward, Bob. *Veil: The Secret Wars of the CIA 1981–1987.* New York: Simon and Schuster, 1987.

Woolf, Virginia. "A Sketch of the Past." In Jeanne Schulkind (ed.), *Moments of Being,* pp. 61–138. London: Hogarth Press, 1978.

Worley, Linda Kraus. "Through Others' Eyes: Narratives of German Women Travelling in Nineteenth-Century America." *Yearbook of German and American Studies* 21 (1986): 39–50.

Young, Robert. *White Mythologies: Writing History and the West.* London and New York: Routledge, 1990.

Yuval-Davis, N., and F. Anthias (eds.). *Woman-Nation-State.* London: Macmillan, 1989.

Zeidan, Joseph Tufeek. "Women Novelists in Modern Arabic Literature." Ph.D. dissertation, University of California at Berkeley, 1982.

Zubaida, S. "Islam, Cultural Nationalism and the Left." *Review of Middle East Studies* 4 (1988).